Michael Walzer
on
War and Justice

Michael Walzer
on
War and Justice

Brian Orend

McGill-Queen's University Press
Montreal & Kingston & London & Ithaca

#45190594

© Brian Orend, 2000

ISBN 0–7735–2223–9 (cloth)
ISBN 0–7735–2224–7 (paper)

McGill-Queen's University Press acknowledges the financial support of the Government of Canada through the Book Publishing Industry Development Program (BPIDP) for its activities.

Canadian Cataloguing in Publication Data

Orend, Brian, 1971–
    Michael Walzer on war and justice

Includes bibliographical references and index.
ISBN 0–7735–2223–9 (bound) – ISBN 0–7735–2224–7 (pbk.)

    1. Walzer, Michael--Contributions in just war doctrine.
2. Walzer, Michael--Contributions in distributive justice.
3. Just war doctrine.   4. Distributive justice.   I. Title.

U22.O72 2000   172   C00–901398–9

Typeset by Action Publishing Technology Ltd, Gloucester
Printed in Great Britain by Dinefwr Press, Llandybïe

Contents

FOR JANE

Acknowledgements

Without Howard Williams, this book would never have happened. Thanks so much, Howard, for the idea and for the opportunity to be part of this exciting series. Thanks to everyone at the University of Wales Press, especially Susan Jenkins, Duncan Campbell, Ceinwen Jones, Richard Houdmont and Liz Powell. Thanks, too, to Peter Nicholson, Terry Nardin and Frances Kelly.

Continued thanks to all my colleagues at the University of Waterloo for providing such a supportive work environment. Continued thanks are also due to two talented philosophers, my former professors at Columbia: Thomas Pogge and Bonnie Kent.

Thanks, as always, to my family and friends for all their encouragement: my mother Mary Lou and her partner Barry; my sister Krista; my grandparents Al and Leo; and to Jane's family – Marie, Vic and Paul. Thanks especially to my wife, Jane, for helping make this year 2000 a marvellously memorable millennium.

Brian Orend

Introduction

Michael Walzer's renown as a contemporary political philosopher rests most heavily on his accomplishments in two fields: his earlier theory of justice in war and his later theory of distributive justice. He has written about bullets, bombs and blood, on the one hand, and the distribution of money, power and health care on the other. The stark differences between these two topics have meant that each has generated its own critical discourse. Very few scholars broach the question of how these two projects might be linked in a broader account of justice in general.

This study of Walzer's work will consider precisely this question of whether he offers us an overarching theory of justice, one which can unite these two topics and put them in their proper perspective. Picking up on some of Walzer's most recent works,[1] it will be argued that the link between the two topics is at least twofold: formal, since Walzer's treatment of them demands we take a conventionalist and interpretative approach to political philosophy; and material, since Walzer's substantive principles in both topics are quite similar, focusing on the rights of both persons and communities to enjoy a protected space within which they are free to make choices in accord with their own conception of the good life.

Following this discussion about Walzer's account of justice in general, focus will shift to this book's primary concern, war. Why spend more time on Walzer's just war theory than on his account of distributive justice? There are several reasons. First, Walzer's account of distributive justice has been extensively analysed and debated, in both academic journals and university seminars. The theory has even been the subject of several books. It has, in my judgement, already received plenty of searching attention. It should be stressed, however, that even though this book's main focus is on war, there is still a serious examination of Walzer's distributive theory. It can be found in chapter 2, and the subject is revisited in chapter 7. So his theory of distributive justice is present, but more fully accounted for elsewhere.[2] Our concern with the distributive theory here is mostly for the sake of coming to a fuller understanding of Walzer's overall theory of justice in general, including especially the additional information it gives us about the central role that community plays in Walzer's political thought.

The second reason for this work's focus on war is that there is no comparable book-length study dissecting Walzer's theory of wartime justice, though of course there have been journal articles.[3] These articles, however, were mostly published in the early 1980s, and so fail to consider the relevance of Walzer's war theory to the contemporary, post-Cold War context of international affairs. This study seeks to contribute to that important task. Finally, it is my view that Walzer's war theory leads him into fuller, and more profound, consideration of the fundamental issues of applied political philosophy than does his work on distribution. The war theory is not only more dramatic but also deeper than the distributive theory, wrestling as it does with the core relationship between the self and the state, with what is worth protecting (at times with force), with what we owe to humanity versus what we owe to our community, and with our hopes for a better and more peaceful future.

It is unfortunate, but true, that war's grim spectre haunts us still. In spite of the optimism sparked by the end of the Cold War in 1989–90, the promise of a more peaceful world order seems mainly unfulfilled.[4] Even a selective listing of recent wars is distressingly large: the Persian Gulf War (1991); the Bosnian civil war (1992–5); the Somalian intervention (1993); the Rwandan civil war (1994–5); wars throughout central Africa (1996–present); Russia's Chechnya campaigns (1994–6 and 1999–2000); and the conflict over the Kosovo region in Serbia (1998–9).

Some thinkers, appalled by these recent wars, have almost expressed a kind of nostalgia for the days when the superpower rivalry between the USA and the old USSR kept war cold and relatively contained. Better that strategic struggle over socio-economic ideology, they reason, than the more uncontrollable kind of white-hot hatred fuelling some recent wars, especially in the Balkans and central Africa. So gruesome has warfare been in those regions that we now have the first international war crimes tribunals since the Second World War ended in 1945. In fact, at Rome in June 1998 the community of states authorized the construction of a permanent international court for trying war crimes and other crimes against humanity. War has become so brutal that it has persuaded nation-states, jealous of their own prerogatives, to set up a world court to police it and judge it after the fact.[5]

The rising red tide of armed conflict has revived great interest in the ethics of war and peace, and international justice more generally. Increasingly, politicians, lawyers and intellectuals are posing searching questions about these issues. Can a thing as dark and dangerous as warfare ever be justified? Can the violence war unleashes ever be effectively contained? Why do we put people on trial for war crimes? Is war itself a crime? Might we change the very structure of international relations, so that the incidence and destructiveness of war become reduced, if not eliminated?

Walzer's work offers some plausible answers to these difficult questions. His 1977 masterwork, *Just and Unjust Wars*, remains the definitive modern discourse on the ethics of war and peace. Here Walzer contends that war can be morally justified, provided that it is begun for the right reasons and that it is fought with strict adherence to rules of right conduct. These commitments imply, as Walzer himself emphasizes, that he is a kind of just war theorist.[6]

This book will explain and evaluate Walzer's just war theory, and consider its contribution not only to current debates over international justice but also to the most searching issues of political philosophy. This study will situate Walzer's work on war within his broader account of social justice, according to which we determine what we ought to do by best interpreting our deepest shared commitments. Walzer's conventionalism, often bitterly denounced by critics, is itself a substantial contribution to contemporary political philosophy.

The first two chapters will discuss Walzer's conventionalist methodology, how he sees interpretation as a more plausible philosophical path than those of discovery and invention, and how his account of justice splits into two domains: the first being thick, robust, complex and particular, concerned with distributive justice within national boundaries; the second being thin, intense, straightforward and universal, concerned with the foremost rights and duties of justice, including those operative during times of war.

The core, and controversial, proposition of Walzer's just war theory is that, sometimes, states can have moral justification for resorting to armed force in the international system. This just war declaration distinguishes it from its main rivals, realism and pacifism. Realism, the most influential understanding of international relations, sports a profound scepticism about the application of moral concepts, such as justice, to the key problems of foreign policy. Power and national security, realists claim, motivate states during wartime, and thus moral appeals are strictly wishful thinking. Pacifism, by contrast, does not share realism's moral scepticism. For the pacifist, moral concepts can indeed be applied meaningfully to international affairs. But the result of such application, in the case of war, is always that war should not be resorted to. Where just war theory is sometimes permissive with regard to war, pacifism is always prohibitive.

No just war theorist can ignore these two formidable challenges to the very idea of a just war in our time. Walzer is no exception, and so we must consider why he sets these rival doctrines aside and whether he is successful in doing so. Walzer's rejection of realism, for instance, is acclaimed and often reprinted, whereas his clash with pacifism, by his own admission, is less thorough, more tentative. These concepts will be analysed in the third chapter, as will Walzer's related contention that wartime justice must be anti-utilitarian in nature. Walzer argues, rather vehemently, that the most plausible account of wartime ethics – the best interpretation of the war convention we all share – is a rights-based account that foregoes the unpredictable cost–benefit calculations of utilitarianism in favour of firm rules and regulations, grounded in respect for the life and liberty of the human person. The dialectic between rights and utility is omnipresent in Walzer's just war work. It is one of the most problematic and interesting relations he identifies.

Just war theory can be divided into three parts, which in the literature are referred to, for the sake of convenience, in Latin. These parts are: (1) *jus ad bellum*, which concerns the justice of resorting to war in the first place; (2) *jus in bello*, which concerns the justice of conduct within war, once it has begun; and (3) *jus post bellum*, which concerns the justice of peace agreements and the termination phase of war. It seems sensible to divide this study along these lines, and to explain and examine Walzer's views on the most pressing and topical issues within each of them.

Jus ad bellum concerns the rules by which states decide whether they have moral justification in resorting to war. Walzer discusses the six traditional rules: just cause, right intention, public declaration by a legitimate authority, last resort, probability of success and proportionality. While he endorses most of them in some fashion, he leaves out public declaration and is unclear about the scope and strength of right intention and proportionality. He is most clear and passionate about what constitutes a just cause for resorting to warfare. For Walzer this just cause is in response to aggression, defined as the violation of state rights to political sovereignty and territorial integrity. Walzer is very much concerned with questions of sovereignty, membership and the link between territory and community. He has a refreshingly keen interest in concrete social arrangements, in the vitality and meaning of national associations. He has come under withering fire for this, with critics lambasting his so-called 'romance of the nation-state'.[7] It is important to consider these issues in detail, especially in light of all the recent pressures on the extent and force of state authority in the era of globalization. How serviceable today is a theory of international justice in general, and of just war in particular, which is centred around the institution of the nation-state? Does such a theory exude a communitarianism which is indefensible in our more cosmopolitan era? Does it needlessly privilege the state and its narrow prerogatives over the human rights of individual persons? Does it put shared customs and social meanings on a higher plane than personal protections and freedom of choice?

Exploring Walzer's *jus ad bellum* account is rewarding not only for the answers it can provide to these pressing questions, but also because it is by no means limited to traditional forms of state-to-state combat, like the Persian Gulf War. Walzer applies *jus ad bellum* concepts to such cutting-edge issues as civil war, anticipatory attack, and armed intervention in a country which has not committed aggression against another country, yet within which massive human rights violations are occurring.

Jus in bello deals with what rules of conduct states should obey during the course of fighting a war. It is thought that, even if a state has justice in resorting to war, it does not follow that it may prosecute that war in any way it wants. Walzer enumerates three rules in accordance with which states should conduct themselves: (1) innocent, non-combatant civilians should not be directly targeted with armed force; (2) proportionality of benefits to costs must also be considered in planning specific attacks; and (3) no weapons or methods may be employed which 'shock the moral conscience of mankind'.[8] Walzer mentions rape campaigns and nuclear weapons as examples of such intrinsically corrupt means.

Many issues of great political, and philosophical, interest will be discussed in connection with Walzer's account of *jus in bello*. These include: why he says soldiers have an equal right to kill each other, regardless of the justice of their cause in fighting; the meaning of 'innocence' in wartime; his controversial employment of the 'doctrine of double effect' to permit military measures which will result in civilian casualties; and, above all, his construction of a 'supreme emergency' escape clause from the rules of war.

Walzer's doctrine of supreme emergency has attracted much attention and criticism, yet without much resolution. His general idea is this: states are, in the ordinary course of war, to obey the three moral rules of *jus in bello* mentioned above. Sometimes, however, states can be faced with a genuine supreme emergency, in which their very survival as independent political communities is at grave risk. At such a moment, states may disregard the rules of *jus in bello* and do what they see fit to survive the extreme crisis. Great controversy has surrounded this claim. In particular, commentators have wondered about the nature of this escape clause: can it be moral for states to set aside the rules of morality during these crises? If so, can Walzer really be so far from the utilitarianism he denounces? Indeed, can he even be logically consistent? Or is the claim rather that morality no longer applies in such fearsome conditions, and thus only the harsh requirements of survival can be appealed to? In the era of weapons of mass destruction, we want a clearer answer to these questions.

Jus post bellum concerns questions of justice when wars end. Walzer devotes one chapter to this crucial third category, and so does not ignore it, as far too many just war theorists do. At the same time, we will see that the theory of war termination he presents is quite deficient, being too general, vague and patchy. Content and detail desperately need to be added here. This demand is clearest when we note that many of the thorniest problems in recent conflicts, especially the Persian Gulf War, Bosnia and Kosovo, have focused on the terms of the peace. After considering Walzer's contribution, proposals consistent with his general principles will be made to advance the state of the art. Issues relevant for discussion include: war crimes trials; punishing aggression and, in doing so, distinguishing between the innocent and the guilty; compensation and apologies for aggression; demilitarization and disarmament; political restructuring and 'rehabilitation' in the aggressor regime; and restoring the status of the former belligerents back to full participating members in the international community.

This book's final chapter will deal with international justice in general. A number of theorists have suggested that concern with just war theory is misplaced, since it ignores the 'deepest' questions about international justice, like whether the world should be carved up into nation-states at all. Such scholars as Brian Barry, Charles Beitz and Thomas Pogge have asked: ought something to be done about refashioning the international landscape itself – through new global institutions, for example – to dampen both the incidence and destructiveness of warfare? Walzer has been accused of ignoring these questions, owing to his conventionalism, and thus of acquiescing in a gravely deficient status quo. He has recently, however, commented on this issue in a way which provides an interesting starting-point for discussion. Still committed to the nation-state and its 'community of character', Walzer nevertheless calls for international reform of a kind. He suggests that our international efforts should not be aimed at anything like world government but rather something like 'the completion, and then complication' of the state system as we know it. The goal should not be to replace the state system with new global institutions but rather to balance the state system and civilize it, so that we can keep our deepest commitments to universal human rights on the one hand and to communal difference on the other. Rights protection, alongside cultural pluralism, is Walzer's recipe for a more just world ordering.[9]

It is always appropriate, before beginning a book that deals mostly with war and justice, to stress the difficulty and complexity of the issues, even when one is guided by an authority like Walzer. For no less a genius than Immanuel Kant once said: 'The greatest difficulty in the right of nations has to do precisely with right during a war; it is difficult even to form a concept of this or to think of law in this lawless state without contradicting oneself.' While this kind of humbling acknowledgement is required, so too is a conviction regarding the importance and relevance of the topic. War is an issue which very much demands our attention and inquiry, and ultimately our remedial action. Kant recognized this, stating that in spite of this 'greatest difficulty' surrounding wartime ethics, the goal of a peaceful world order is still 'the entire ultimate purpose of the theory of right', truly, 'the highest political good'.[10]

I have found that working on Walzer affords considerable pleasure. One reason is that the research is so appealing, Walzer being one of the most gifted writers in contemporary political theory. But, as with reading Richard Rorty, one needs to be careful not to let the pleasant prose seduce one into quick agreement with the arguments being presented. I resist that temptation here, in spite of my admiration for Walzer's skills and his historical awareness. While I offer a sympathetic reconstruction, I do not defend what I believe indefensible. Sometimes I come to his defence, at other times I reject his claims utterly. Though many of Walzer's commentators have erred on the side of criticism, and have failed to acknowledge fully the important contributions he has made to political philosophy, deep questions remain concerning his views. Even when they do, however, such questions are usually among the most fruitful and provocative on the contemporary philosophical scene.

1 • Interpretation: The Method of Walzer's General Theory of Justice

Perhaps the most problematic feature of my exposition is the use of the plural pronouns: we, our, ourselves, us. That . . . [we all] share a common morality is the critical assumption . . .

Walzer[1]

Any theory of just war depends upon a broader theory of justice, and Michael Walzer's is no exception. Since the broader theory is logically prior to the just war theory, we must examine Walzer's thoughts about justice in general before delving into his provocative perspective on the relationship between justice and armed force. The difficulty with this is that Walzer's general theory of justice is neither simple nor, at first glance, clear. Walzer has resisted the temptation to write a single, all-encompassing tome which elucidates his general theory. This makes for harder, but perhaps more interesting, labour on the part of any Walzer scholar. Works on such diverse topics as war, equality, social criticism and toleration must be pored over for clues as to the form and content of Walzer's general theory.

The task is made no easier by the fact that Walzer's thoughts about justice in general actually seem conflictual. There appears to be a pervasive tension between the kind of universality presented in earlier works, like *Just and Unjust Wars*, and the particularity of later works, like *Spheres of Justice*. How to render a consistent general theory out of such conflictual comments as 'the moral reality of war . . . is fixed . . . by the opinions of mankind' and '(j)ustice is a human construction, and it is doubtful that it can be made in only one way'? Consider the substance of these two acclaimed works, for which Walzer is most widely known. The first offers a unitary theory of international justice, designed to help us cut through 'the fog of war' and see clearly which wars are just and which not. The second is a work of distributive justice devoted not merely to acknowledging different interpretations of the meaning of social goods, like money, but to advocating that such goods ought to be distributed, in their own separate 'spheres', in strict accordance with the meaning of that good within the particular national culture. For instance, he says that the meaning of health care in the United States entails that it ought to be distributed there on the basis of medical need rather than on ability to pay.[2]

Walzer's universalism is disclosed when he says:

> There is a particular arrangement, a particular view of the moral world, that seems to me to be the best one. I want to suggest that the arguments we make about war are most fully understood . . . as efforts to recognize and respect the rights of individual and associated men and women. The morality I shall expound is in its philosophical form a doctrine of human rights.

He continues: 'At every point, the judgments we make . . . are best accounted for if we regard life and liberty as something like absolute values.' Elsewhere, Walzer refers approvingly to 'universal prohibitions . . . of murder, deception, betrayal, gross cruelty . . . [which] have been accepted in virtually every human society'.[3]

Yet rarely is a human rights theorist also a cultural relativist. How can someone who endorses 'absolute values' and 'universal prohibitions' also claim that '[t]here is no single set of primary or basic goods conceivable across all moral and material worlds' and that all goods ought to be distributed, in any given community, according only to the meaning of those goods within that community?[4] How can someone claim that human rights form part of the 'best particular view of the moral world' and yet insist that '[a] philosopher who reports to us on the existence of . . . natural rights or any set of objective moral truths . . . has walked the path of discovery'. But 'the whole elaborate apparatus of . . . objectivity . . . is . . . to guarantee correctness. The truth [,however,] is that there is no guarantee, any more than there is a guarantor.'[5]

In summary, how can Walzer in the earlier part of his career have devoted himself to a universal theory of wartime justice, applicable to all nations and heavily reliant on human rights, and later on have devoted himself to a theory of distributive justice which is emphatically, even defiantly, relative to the social meanings present in a particular nation, and in which human rights play next to no role? Will future scholars debate the differences between 'The Early Walzer' and 'The Late Walzer', much as past scholars have done for Marx, or for the pre- and post-Critical Kant? The answer, I think, is no. For Walzer himself has recently done work on integrating these apparently disparate projects into a more or less unified general theory of justice. The most relevant works here are *Interpretation and Social Criticism* and *Thick and Thin*.

The following two chapters will be devoted to developing more fully Walzer's general theory, his broad and distinct approach to the deepest questions of political philosophy. The present chapter will focus on the form, or method, of Walzer's general theory, which can be described variously as interpretative, hermeneutic or conventionalist. The following chapter will discern what content Walzer uses to fill in his theory's general form, so as to bring it to completion. This content, we'll see, features both 'thin' and universal, as well as 'thick' and particularist, norms to guide both personal conduct and the shaping of social institutions. The most important aim of the next two chapters, then, is to show that Walzer does in fact have a single general theory of justice, consistent both in its method and in its substantive conclusions. Having constructed it, we can then proceed to examine Walzer's just war theory, which is the main focus of this work.

The three paths

Walzer describes his philosophical approach as interpretative. Although there are a large number of unique methods in moral and political theory, he suggests we focus our attention on the three most common, important and enduring 'paths': discovery, invention and interpretation.

Discovery and invention

The path of discovery is arguably the most ancient. The image here, as Walzer sees it, is of the philosopher divesting himself of all his attachments and prejudices, scaling the mountain of contemplation, discovering the really real, and returning with the moral truth which will set us free. Religious ethics, with its commitment to divine law, is a clear example. So too is a secular defence of natural law. Discoverers seek The Truth of morality and justice, through either reason or revelation. We do not ourselves invent or construct moral and political principles; rather, we discover them either through arduous intellectual enquiry or through some kind of divine dispensation. Such principles, in turn, provide us with the objective, authoritative standards by which we ought to shape our lives, both personally and politically. Walzer likens this path of political theory to the executive branch of a modern Western government: the theorist here, like Moses in the Old Testament or Plato's philosopherking, discovers the truth and then strives to proclaim and enforce it throughout his domain.[6]

Though noting discovery's distinguished pedigree, Walzer does not find it the most compelling method in contemporary normative theory. His foremost objection centres on discovery's pretence of objectivity. While Walzer concedes that there is such a thing as 'stepping back' from one's own particular commitments and interests, he does not believe that such divestiture can ever achieve the kind of completeness and certainty demanded by discoverers. In contrast to Thomas Nagel's recent definition of the objective stance as looking at the world from nowhere in particular, Walzer insists that we can only grasp the world from somewhere. We can never escape from our situatedness. We cannot see everything, once and for all, as it 'really' is. We are always perceiving *from a point of view*, straining to interpret what we perceive, and then coming to terms with our emotional and cognitive responses to it. Our inescapable situatedness, our firm rootedness in perspective, means that we can never be sure that we have indeed stumbled across the unadorned truth, which holds across all the perspectives and endures as the timeless standard of ethical conduct. And that leaves unsaid the potent scepticism which can be raised regarding the very existence of this supposedly objective and timeless standard, subsisting somewhere and somehow externally to us, just awaiting our discovery.[7]

The path of invention, Walzer says, is a twentieth-century construction built over the romantic yet ruined foundations of the path of discovery. Invention seeks to provide what discovery, either by appealing to God or nature, could not: 'a universal corrective for all the different social moralities'.[8] The path of invention, unlike the path of discovery, is not committed to the idea that The Truth exists, waiting only to be unearthed. Invention acknowledges that we have no choice but to construct our own principles for living together, for deciding how we should treat each other. Waiting for the discovery of the truth is, inventors would say, like waiting for Godot, that is, for someone or something destined never to arrive. Since we must decide on how to act, and how to shape our common institutions, we cannot afford the luxury of waiting for the truth to make its presence felt: we have to get down to the business of proposing, and then negotiating, the principles of social co-operation. Invention is analogous to the legislative branch of government, constructing for us the general guidelines which we find most accommodating. The most formidable expression of the path of invention, Walzer believes, is John Rawls's famous theory of justice.[9]

Rawls's renowned method invites us to consider ourselves as self-interested rational agents, coming together to negotiate the terms of social co-operation in the original position behind the veil of ignorance. The original position refers to the pre-political situation when all agents come together to bargain, as prudent and self-interested parties, on the rules which will shape basic social institutions, in particular government. All such agents are, by stipulation, behind a veil of ignorance, which deprives them of information which Rawls believes would poison the bargaining session, and generate slanted, unfair results. The agents are to negotiate on principles of justice not knowing what their social standing, gender, race, intelligence, natural endowments, religion, income, partisan political attachments, etc., will be once the veil is lifted and they find themselves in society. Rawls believes that such agents would agree on two core principles of justice, according to which social institutions should be shaped: the liberty principle, allowing for the maximum amount of freedom for each which is compatible with the same degree of liberty for all; and the difference principle, allowing only those social inequalities which benefit all, including especially the least advantaged member of society, and which occur in a context of equality of opportunity.[10]

Walzer's response to Rawls's influential invention begins by claiming that

> [m]en and women behind the veil of ignorance ... will, perhaps, find a *modus vivendi* – not a way of life but a way of living. But even if this is the only possible *modus vivendi* for these people in these conditions, it does not follow that it is a universally valuable arrangement.

In other words, Walzer objects to what some have called Rawls's excessive abstraction, insisting that Rawls's principles lack the complexity and richness of a full-blown moral culture. Walzer asks

rhetorically: 'Why should newly invented principles govern the lives
of people who already share a moral culture and speak a natural
language?'[11]

Walzer suggests that Rawls's invention invites us to see ourselves
much like refugees, each from different countries, newly arrived in an
unknown land and stuck in temporary lodgings, like a decrepit hotel
by the airport, as we await processing through immigration. We do
not know where we stand or what will happen to us next; indeed, we
do not even know exactly who our fellow refugees are, what
language they speak, what values they have, and so on. All of us, in
the hotel, need to come up with some very basic principles of social
co-operation, comprehensible to all, that will serve everyone's fundamental interests. At the very least, we all want to survive until our
refugee claims are processed by the local authorities. Walzer argues
that Rawls's core principles of justice may well serve people caught
in such circumstances, but is sceptical of any broader application for
them. For the first and foremost goal of the refugees in the hotel,
Walzer points out, is to make it out of there and become functioning
members of their new society. Once there, they will require moral
and political principles infinitely more complex and subtle than those
on offer by Rawls.[12]

Walzer's objection may be rooted in what some have called 'the
problem of defection' for Rawls: granted that Rawlsian agents in the
original position may well settle on his two principles of justice, what
is to prevent them from defecting from these principles once the veil
is lifted and they find out about their full-blown commitments and
interests? Walzer's point boils down to the claim that we simply are
not Rawlsian agents living in the original position: most of us are not
at all like refugees holed up in a hotel at the airport. More precisely,
Rawlsian agents are not enough like us – the original position is not
enough like our world – for the principles of justice which Rawls
constructs to be The Solution to our moral and political perplexities.

The key difference between the two methods involves Walzer's
previous insistence that we always perceive the world from some
particular point of view. One cannot overemphasize the importance
of this core premise for Walzer's political philosophy: it means that,
for him, morality and politics are always rooted somewhere. Moral
and political life is always experienced in particular places and times,
through the medium of different concrete actions, institutions and
languages. We experience moral and political life, most centrally, in

terms of the values we have here and now, and in terms of how these commitments either compete or cohere with those of others. Reading Rawls, one might get the impression that it is possible to think about morality and politics from no particular point of view, or from everyone's point of view, or at least from one authoritative point of view, for instance that of the most prudent and rational agent. Such disembodiment, such rootlessness, such lack of point of view, is something Walzer rejects utterly. It's not for creatures like us, he suggests, since we are rooted and perspectival, historical and concrete. For Walzer, Rawls's invention is an arid and surreal abstraction, which Walzer seeks to capture by likening it to the controlled and contrived circumstances refugees must endure while having their claims processed. But a hotel is not a home, and ultimately we must look for more than Rawlsian reasoning to provide us with satisfaction in our moral and political lives.

Where should we look for such satisfaction? Which place is most like home? Walzer's ultimate answer, to be discussed in greater detail subsequently, is that we should look to the very moral and political cultures we already inhabit. We should look to our own countries, to the familiar places and people we are already attached to. In a sense, for Walzer we're already home: it's just that we don't know it, or that most political philosophers have done their best to disguise that fact, or to lead us away from it. We have already left the hotel by the airport and have put down roots in a particular community. That is why we do not need a way of merely living – a *modus vivendi* – but a fully-fledged way of life. We need look no further than the ways of life in our own communities for our ultimate source of moral and political guidance in the modern world.

Some readers, at this point, may well wonder about the lack of charity with which Walzer treats discoverers and inventors. There is indeed an air of caricature here, and surely a failure to respond fully to what have often been formidable and complex normative doctrines. Consider, as an example, Walzer's failure to acknowledge Rawls's treatment of the defection issue. Rawls argues that since his principles of justice were generated in a free and fair fashion by agents relevantly like us in being self-interested and rational, it follows that those of us on this side of the veil should still be moved by the terms of the original contract. For Rawls, the abstraction of his method is an advantage, a way to help distance ourselves from particular prejudices which, if unchecked, often produce unfairness and discrimination in the various communities we inhabit. Abstraction helps us to understand what we all share in common, universally and not just in terms of our family, friends and fellow citizens. Furthermore, Rawls is the first to admit that his theory of justice is not designed to answer everyone's questions about the full range of moral and political choices we are confronted with in life. Rawls's principles do not, for example, help one decide whether one should stay faithful to one's spouse during the course of marriage. They are principles explicitly designed to guide the shaping of the most basic social institutions, especially government: no more, no less. They are principles designed to ensure a baseline level of fair treatment for everyone by basic social institutions. Does this fact of focus on how social institutions treat persons suffice to undermine our reasons for finding Rawls's principles persuasive? Since Rawls cannot give us everything, does it follow that we should not take anything from him?

Walzer's engagement with Rawls's theory is neither searching nor sustained, and it seeks through metaphorical suggestion rather than sharp argumentation to establish two main criticisms of Rawls: that Rawls's method of rational choice by prudent persons under ideal and hypothetical conditions is too abstract to be useful in actual political circumstances; and that Rawls does not pay enough attention to the importance of actual communities in people's lives. While some might suggest that such criticisms simply delineate the difference of political opinion between those more inclined to favour individual freedom versus those more inclined to support a close community, such an observation is too simple by half, especially with regard to Walzer. Much more will be said about the complex relation between persons and political communities later. The impression should not be gathered, from these remarks, that Walzer's criticisms of Rawls are not, in the end, legitimate and substantive. The problem is that they are not fully developed. They are merely mentioned, as all but parenthetical observations. Underlying this underdevelopment is the fact that Walzer strongly disagrees with Rawls's understanding of distributive justice, which no doubt colours his rejection of Rawls's broader approach to politics. Our discussion of distributive justice must, however, wait until the next chapter, until after we have finished examining Walzer's interpretative framework for answering such substantive issues of justice.[13]

Interpretation

Walzer continues his appraisal of the three paths in political philosophy by contending that 'neither discovery nor invention is necessary because we already possess what they pretend to provide ... We do not have to discover the moral world because we have always lived there. We do not have to invent it because it has already been invented.' Walzer playfully pokes fun at Nagel's 'discovery of an objective moral principle: that we should not be indifferent to the suffering of other people'. 'I acknowledge the principle', Walzer declares, 'but miss the excitement of revelation. I knew that already.' Furthermore, both discovery and invention are themselves subject to the imperatives of the third path: the need for interpretation. Walzer offers '[a] simple maxim: every discovery and invention ... requires interpretation.' As evidence, he offers age-old disputes over biblical exegesis and the content of the natural law, as well as current disputes over the exact meaning of Rawls's difference principle. Discoverers and inventors cannot escape from the need to interpret what has purportedly been discovered or invented: we must thus acknowledge that the act or procedure of interpretation is at least primary, and perhaps even the only game in town.[14]

'[T]here is no other starting point for moral speculation', Walzer declares. 'We have to start from where we are.' The starting-point of moral and political theory must be reflection upon actually existing moral and political beliefs, which of course will be influenced considerably by the various community contexts in which we find ourselves. But this is *only* the starting-point: the most apt method of moral and political enquiry is to come up with the best interpretation of existing moral and political commitments. Walzer likens the path of interpretation to the judicial branch of government: '[m]oral argument ... closely resembles the work of a lawyer or judge who struggles to find meaning in a morass of conflicting laws and precedents.' But why should theorists start with this morass of actual belief? '[W]hy', Walzer asks rhetorically, 'is this existing morality authoritative – this morality that just *is* [his italics], the product of time, accident, external force, political compromise, fallible and particular intentions?' He offers four answers. The first is that the moral codes offered by discoverers and inventors tend to be 'remarkably similar' to beliefs already present in actual moral and political culture. Second, the process of interpretation gives 'the best understanding' of the experience of moral argument. Third, the paths of discovery and invention are 'efforts at escape' from the realities of our existence. Finally, interpretation 'provides us with everything we need to live a moral life, including the capacity for reflection and criticism'.[15]

In support of the first claim, Walzer points out that many of those often thought of as philosophical revolutionaries, like Kant or Bentham, stress how their moral systems concur with the existing beliefs of the common man. Even the boldest discoverer or inventor is keen on interpreting his theory so that it coheres with fundamental and widespread value commitments, for instance that human happiness or character development be forwarded. Why, then, keep up the pretence that the theory is a discovery or invention when its real value has to do with its degree of acceptance by, and impact upon the behaviour of, ordinary men and women?

Discoverers, for one, would surely respond by arguing that theirs is no pretence but, rather, a sincere claim regarding the nature of moral and political truth. Since one wants the people to understand the truth, one explains to them, in terms they will understand, its precise nature. But Walzer, we have seen, is simply sceptical about all such authoritative truth claims in the realm of moral and political theory. We can hear him asking: 'True in terms of what?' What criteria can we agree on, with regard to what needs to be demonstrated, for one to have 'proved' the truth of a proposition in moral and political theory? For Walzer, the question is rhetorical: the search for timeless and objective standards against which we can measure the truth of normative propositions is futile, and the product of wild ambition. Futile because, on this side of the grave, we mere mortals, tied inescapably to time, place and perspective, will never know whether we have actually got the genuine, true and timeless article; and the product of wild ambition, in that the search is animated not by the modest goal of finding social principles we can live with but by the exalted goal of finding principles we *must* live with, imposed on us from on high, either by God, by nature or by reason itself.

Walzer admits that some moral and political ideas have, in the course of history, seemed to strike with the force of discovery or invention. He cites Marxism, the principle of utility and 'the rights of man'. But he is at pains to show that all these concepts drew on the history of ideas in their own way. Indeed, he insists that genuine and utter newness would condemn an idea to oblivion: outside a tradition of discourse, it would be incomprehensible to those it was addressed to. That kind of conceptual novelty would be greeted by nothing more than sheer perplexity.[16] Walzer, with a hint of understatement or perhaps even sarcasm in his voice, informs us that 'very rarely are we actually called upon to invent new moral principles'. 'Insofar as we can recognize moral progress', he concludes,

> it has less to do with the discovery or invention of new principles than with the inclusion under the old principles of previously excluded men and women. And that is more a matter of (workmanlike) social criticism and political struggle than of (paradigm-shifting) philosophical speculation.[17]

Against Walzer's second argument in favour of the path of interpretation, it might be suggested that interpretation does not provide the best sense of the actual experience of moral argument. For the central appeal in actual argument is to the truth of the matter, as the method of discovery presumes. The concern is not so much with the meaning of the terms as it is with determining what the right thing to do is. The point of moral argument in real life is to guide choices and action, not merely to come to an understanding of the full and precise meaning of moral terms. Real moral argument is concerned with choice and action, with praise and blame, not with pedantic fights over semantic rights. Indeed, it might even be suggested that privileging the path of interpretation is actually a form of special pleading. For if interpretation is the only way to go, then clearly Walzer and his fellow intellectuals – that is, professional thinkers, interpreters and debaters – are going to enjoy considerable status with regard to morality and politics. Perhaps we should be suspicious of such self-serving contentions.

Walzer's response is to prod us into further thought about these claims. What are we doing when we dispute over the right thing to do? What are we doing when we argue over which action to perform, whom to praise or blame? His contention is that, in all these things, we are inescapably involved in an argument over the meaning of moral values. And not merely 'meaning' in the narrow sense of first unpacking all the parts contained within the whole of whatever value we are arguing about, and then understanding what they refer to. We are also arguing over whether the value in question is worthy of being recognized as a value at all, about its proper weight and scope in our general system of values, about whether it is consistent with other values we hold, and so on. In the final analysis, and employing a familiar and resonant phrase, he says that moral discourse is about nothing less than 'the meaning of our way of life'.[18]

Understood in this frame of reference, it is clear that, by 'meaning', Walzer refers to something deep and penetrating indeed. Meaning is not at all exhausted by conceptual analysis or stipulative definitions. It is not fully captured by academic disputes that often seem unduly narrow and technical. Meaning refers to how we understand the universe and our place in it, how we imbue our choices with purpose, how we relate to each other, how we create lives we find worthwhile. It is meaning in this robust sense that must be the ultimate object of all moral and political debate, and Walzer believes that the community is the prime provider of such meaning, or at least the principal arena in which such a search for meaning takes place. It is, above all, our rootedness in our own communities which infuses our lives with import and significance. Thus, frequent appeals to 'the truth', or 'the right thing to do', in actual debate are for Walzer rhetorical devices, designed to impress upon other people the superiority of one's inter-pretation of what it means to be moral and just. But it is the interpretation itself – the conception of meaning, robustly under-stood – which contains all the content and substance. And so it must be the proper object of moral and political theory.

By suggesting in his third argument that discovery and invention are 'efforts at escape', Walzer implies that these paths are animated by 'the hope of finding some external and universal standard with which to judge moral existence'. But Walzer insists that this hope is neither necessary nor realistic. For we already have plausible princi-ples internal to our moral and political discourse. We already have a richly textured existence as moral and political beings. We cannot ever divest ourselves of it completely, so as to stare 'moral reality' straight in the face, nor should we want to.[19] For this existence is, for lack of a better term, our home. It is where we always have been, and where we always will be, regardless of whether or how we prefer to dress it up. One is reminded here of Martha Nussbaum's interesting remark that often the longing for transcendence – for external vali-dation of our beliefs – is animated in part by a shame of being human, as if principles devised by fallible creatures like us somehow fail to be good enough. But, Walzer would ask, who else can we turn to if not ourselves?[20]

Walzer might go even further and suggest that what discoverers and inventors are really trying to escape from is not only the limits of human finitude itself, but also more narrowly the limits of their own personal membership in particular, contingent, fallible and even peculiar communities and cultures. Discovery and invention presuppose a mythology of the heroic and rugged individual, the isolated and exceptional genius who tames nature, or is spoken to by God, or splits the atom, or invents the aeroplane. Romantic as such mythology may be, it also ignores the fact that such exceptional individuals draw on a history of prior discovery and invention, and are as a rule heavily reliant on the supportive work of a whole community of staffers, assistants, researchers, publicists, financiers, family and friends, and so on. There is, in the end, no escape in this life from human sociability and some kind of membership in, or at least connection to, a concrete cultural community.

Walzer's defence of the fourth proposition in favour of interpretation is the most problematic, yet very important. He wants to claim that interpretation is the most fitting normative method because it alone can provide us with everything we need in moral and political life. Critics of Walzer's hermeneutic approach suggest that, to the contrary, interpretation does not provide us with the critical resources necessary for moral and political progress. Interpretation as a method in political philosophy, it is often suggested, is intrinsically conservative, since we can only interpret what already exists. How can we advance beyond the status quo if we are doomed to mere exercises in interpretation, and not permitted to avail ourselves of breakthrough acts of discovery or invention? Furthermore, Josh Cohen contends that the interpretative method ignores the reality of how 'shared interpretations' have come to be that way. In particular, it ignores the role that coercion plays in spreading 'shared ways of life'. To what extent should we remain faithful to principles internal to our discourse if these were generated by questionable means? Why should I treat the values prevailing in my community with such deference and respect if I know that the reason why the majority have come to believe in them was a result of a manipulative, exploitative and ultimately blood-soaked sequence of historical events? Interpretation also confronts a closure problem: how can we ever know that we have reached 'the best interpretation' of the principles of our moral and political discourse, which would enable us to make consistent choices? The interminableness of interpretation works against the imperatives of choice and action.[21]

Walzer is acutely sensitive to the accusation that his interpretative approach to justice is insufficiently critical. At first he feigns puzzlement over this challenge, pointing out that if one reads his works, all of which employ the interpretative method, one can see clearly that his intent is 'nothing if not critical'. *Spheres of Justice*, in particular, is a stinging attack on the status quo of distributive justice in America, especially with regard to money's status as the dominant good, allowing wealthy people to enjoy disproportionate shares of other social goods, like political power, legal justice, fame, leisure time, and so on. He is especially critical of the power of money in America to buy better health care, arguing that this is at odds with the shared meaning of health as a good which ought to be distributed on the basis of medical need. We will return to the fascinating topic of distributive justice in the next chapter.[22]

The other problem Walzer has with this accusation is that it either misunderstands the nature of social criticism, or fails to see how 'immanent critique' can be a potent challenge to the status quo, or both. While acknowledging that effective social criticism requires both emotional and intellectual distance from the object being criticized, Walzer insists that the distance required need not – indeed, cannot – be tantamount to detachment. It need not, because the most successful social critics have never been utterly external to the set of social arrangements they criticize. Consider, for example, Martin Luther King, Jr, and his struggle to lead the civil rights movement for African Americans in the 1960s. More commonly, prominent and powerful social critics have been marginalized within, and thus 'ambiguously connected' to, their societies. And distance cannot equal detachment because the latter is but a myth created by the objectivist's longing for a transcendence, for a guarantee of correctness, that will never come. Walzer concludes that 'criticism depends less on true ... statements about the world than on evocative ... renderings of a common idea'. Social criticism is inescapably 'an inside job'. The sources of social criticism are not detachment and objectivity, rather, they are marginality and opposition to the establishment within a social system. 'It is not connection', Walzer comments, 'but authority and domination from which we must distance ourselves.'[23]

Social criticism, as Walzer sees it, involves a search for the core values within moral and political discourse, an inquiry into the best interpretation available. This interpretation will be coherent and comprehensive. It will be recognized, by the participants within the discourse, as the most compelling account of their own 'socially constructed idealism', which is to say that set of moral and political ideals prevalent in the culture they have created and developed over time. Criticism will thus take its most familiar form as pointing out a failure of persons and institutions to remain faithful to their own ideals. Walzer repeatedly asserts that exposure of hypocrisy is the oldest, and probably most effective, form of social criticism. Pointing out that persons and institutions are betraying their own deepest values is a much more biting form of criticism than denouncing them for failing to live up to some discovered or invented moral code, packaged as representing the objective truth on the matter.[24]

Walzer's hermeneutic method is thus both descriptive and prescriptive. It is descriptive in the sense that its starting-point is a (rich, searching) description of actual moral and political beliefs. Yet the method is prescriptive in that it enables social criticism. In describing a culture's socially constructed idealism, one holds up a normative standard by which people and institutions may – by their own principles – be judged, resulting in either praise or blame, in calls for either staying the course or embarking on reform. The key presuppositions here, which one must assume Walzer holds, are that people and institutions ought to remain faithful to their own deepest commitments and that this norm of fidelity is itself internal to moral and political discourse. To fail to keep one's own deepest commitments is wrong. When unconscious, such failure constitutes ignorance, a lack of self-awareness; when conscious, it constitutes hypocrisy, bad faith, betrayal.

How exactly are we justified in holding particular people responsible for being true to the socially constructed idealism prevalent in their culture? As Georgia Warnke asks, is there not something about the hermeneutic approach to justice that is at odds with individual autonomy and responsibility? Walzer might respond by stressing the fact that all acts of individual moral choice are, inescapably, structured by some cultural tradition, and so it is incorrect to speak of a sharp split between individual and social values. But Warnke could press the point and wonder how we know whether individuals, or institutions for that matter, do in fact hold certain principles as the deepest expression of their socially constructed idealism. By what right can we conclude that the principles in question are, in fact, *theirs*, by which we can judge them *on their own terms?* Walzer's response to this sharpest of critical questions, it seems, is that we know it through their endorsement of the best interpretation of such principles, provided that such endorsement is not the product of 'radical coercion'.[25]

Walzer, after much critical prodding, concedes that interpretations which have come to be shared through means of 'radical coercion' have no normative purchase on our attention. Thus, to respond to a previous question, the communal values of one's culture have little or no claim to one's respect and adherence if they have been produced, or are sustained, by 'radical coercion', for instance through the brutal apparatus of a police state.[26] But this limiting principle, he insists, is not some external standard, employed as a kind of objective check on the extremities of cultural 'group-think', or intersubjective discourse. The ban on radical coercion is itself, he submits, a principle internal to that discourse. We did not deduce the ban on radical coercion from objective principles, any more than we invented it through the set-up of Rawls's original position. The ban on employing violence to coerce agreement during a normative argument is something already present in our discourse. It is something we feel to be unfair, harmful, at odds with the spirit of discourse, and irrelevant to genuine argumentation. We suspect that those who resort to coercion during moral debate do so because they lack the capacity to make persuasive and powerful interpretations of what we should do. It should be noted, however, that Walzer never defines radical coercion, though violence presumably must fall under its rubric. His single explicit example of radical coercion is slavery. But is radical coercion understood solely in terms of violence and slavery, or is some other conception permitted? For example, would an understanding, or a value commitment, inculcated through the mere threat of violence, or through systemic ideological programming, or through fear, be the product of radical coercion and thus illegitimate? What about an understanding endorsed because of a gross lack of positive liberty, such as barred access to elementary education? What about values subscribed to not out of genuine belief and adherence, nor because of radical coercion, but for the sake of what Cohen calls 'strategic selfishness', such as a desire to move up the corporate ladder by joining the boss's political and charitable associations, fund-raising for them, writing on behalf of them, training one's children in their ways, and so on? Are such values in or out of that mixture which can count as part of 'the best interpretation' of existing moral and political beliefs?[27]

We now see that any interpretation endorsed as a result of radical coercion cannot for Walzer count as part of the best interpretation of our socially constructed idealism. Even if we could get clearer on Walzer's definition of radical coercion, we would still be left with the largest question: how exactly do we know when we have come up with the 'best' interpretation? At first, Walzer is almost flippant in assuring us that 'we would know roughly what we were looking for and would have little difficulty excluding a large number of inadequate or bad accounts'.[28] But what exact criteria can we use to determine which of the remaining good accounts is the single most persuasive and powerful interpretation of the principles internal to our moral and political discourse?

The best interpretation

That we have need of a best interpretation is obvious: Walzer does not believe that one person's interpretation of moral discourse is as good as another's. Idiosyncratic readings fail to persuade. He may not be an objectivist, but neither is Walzer a subjectivist, at least in the simplistic sense of asserting that one moral or political code is as good as another. For him, it is all about being intersubjective, best interpreting our shared commitments and values. We also need one best interpretation so as to prioritize, rank and commend our choices and actions. We need a consistent and action-guiding set of imperatives. But, of the various persuasive readings which compete for our attention and commitment, which should we single out as the 'best' one to guide our choices, as the one which definitively captures our own 'socially constructed idealism'? Warnke throws down the gauntlet by suggesting that Walzer cannot do it, that he cannot clearly define for any modern Western country what he means by the best interpretation of its socially constructed idealism. This is so, she says, because any hermeneutic approach to political questions in the contemporary West will run up against the fact that there are two competing yet equally powerful, persuasive and influential 'interpretative keys' regarding moral and social goals or ideals. These two keys are, respectively, the more atomistic and individualistic school of Hobbes, Locke and company, and the more holistic and communitarian school of Aristotle, Hegel, Rousseau and company.[29]

Walzer, unfortunately, is rather elusive about his exact answer to this challenge, preferring in his work to show, instead of to say, what he means by the 'best' interpretation. *Spheres of Justice* is thus offered as a compelling interpretation of the meaning of distributive justice in the United States and perhaps throughout the West more broadly. Likewise, *Just and Unjust Wars* is offered as the most compelling interpretation of the meaning of human thought on the ethics of war and peace. Furthermore, we will see throughout this work that Walzer is dubious of claims that individualism and communitarianism are ideologies which are logically incompatible, 'competing yet equally powerful', ways to interpret social life in contemporary Western civilization. When pressed, however, Walzer does offer a few explicit criteria for determining what counts as the best interpretation. The best reading of our moral discourse, for instance, cannot be gleaned from a public opinion survey; Walzer believes the best reading differs in quality from all its rivals. Thus, Brian Barry's strident criticism of Walzer's method, that it mistakenly substitutes popular acclaim for the truth as its litmus test for justice, misses the mark.[30] The most popular views, at a particular point in time, may not make for the best readings of shared political discourse, especially when we note people's propensity towards a certain amount of either ignorance or hypocrisy, or both.

The best reading, Walzer insists, is the most 'powerful and persuasive'. But to whom? Walzer distinguishes between what he calls 'the interpretive community' and 'the community of experience'. The former is the set of expert social commentators, people who devote their professional lives to moral and political discourse. The latter is much more inclusive, encompassing all who grasp the terms of moral and political discourse. The community of experience includes all who comprehend and employ the basic vocabulary of the discourse in question: essentially every normal, well-developed person in the community at hand. At one point, Walzer seems to privilege the perspective of the interpretative community: 'No discovery or invention can end the argument; no "proof" takes precedence over the (temporary) majority of sages.' Such comments might feed the complaint suggested above about special political pleading on behalf of intellectuals. But it is clear that, for Walzer, the best interpretation must also be recognized by the broader community of experience, which of course includes the interpretative community. While we might expect that the interpretation which stands out as the best will be produced somewhere in the community of experts, if it fails to agree with the community of experience, then it will not survive the scrutiny of judgement. For 'we are all interpreters of the morality we share.'[31]

What counts as evidence that the participants in the discourse have 'endorsed' the principles one contends is the best interpretation? How do we know, to return to Warnke's sharpest question, that the participants 'recognize' the proffered interpretation as the best expression of their own socially constructed idealism? Walzer, we saw, denies majoritarian preference amongst the community of experience. Is it, then, majoritarian preference among the expert participants in the discourse, as the quotation in the last paragraph suggested? Indeed, does the actual preference of either group matter at all, or is it a question of what the participants *would find* most compelling, if they fulfilled certain idealized standards or evaluative criteria? It seems, at first, that it cannot for Walzer be the latter, since it has obvious affinities with the invented kind of procedure employed by Rawls. Essentially, Rawls suggests that we find most authoritative those principles of justice that prudent, self-interested rational agents would agree to in the context of a free and fair bargaining session. Yet Walzer's disclaimers about radical coercion cloud the picture: those whose vote matters, so to speak, in determining what counts as the best interpretation must not have been subjected to radical coercion. They must, at the least, fulfil that one evaluative criterion.

This raises a very deep question about Walzer's method of interpretation, and may help explain the verbal hostility he displays against Rawls's method: is interpretation really different in kind from invention? Does Walzer protest too much when he objects to Rawls? Is his a dislike born of an underlying recognition of similarity, an over-the-top attempt to demarcate himself from a close competitor offering a barely distinguishable product? Consider that the two methods are both socially constructed doctrines, in the sense that there is no commitment to the idea of an objective normative truth just waiting for us to uncover it, as the discoverer would have it. Both insist we have to rely on our own resources and agreements to shape the terms of social co-operation. Both methods are modern doctrines that have to be explained to the people, and each enables social criticism in its own way, as Walzer nimbly demonstrates. And interpretation cannot escape from the need to privilege one kind of best interpretation, so as to exclude obscure and partisan readings and to provide an effective guide to action. In short, is it not true that the best interpretation is a kind of invention? After all, Walzer himself admits that it does not just stare us in the face. The best interpretation is a sophisticated and deliberate reading of communal values which has to be put together, probably by a gifted expert, out of the old parts, privileging some and discarding others. Also like an invention, it has to be sold to the buying public, in that it must win their endorsement, though what counts as such endorsement is something Walzer, to the disappointment of Warnke, fails to disclose fully.

Walzer suggests that such endorsement is had when the participants 'recognize themselves' in the terms of the reading, and presumably, if one wants to add in a charitable fashion to Walzer's oblique remarks, when the participants also take some kind of action on the basis of such 'recognition', to make their commitment real. The participants may not always adhere to the precise terms of the best reading, but they praise and blame in accord with such terms, and make some kind of deliberate effort to structure their social institutions so that they respect such terms. Thus, we 'know' that the participants endorse such principles as their own when, without being subjected to radical coercion, they identify with the principles, praise and blame in accord with them and try, in some sense, to act consistently with them and to shape social institutions accordingly.

The best interpretation, whether in the end an invention or not, will not be permanent. We do not, Walzer submits, have one Rosetta Stone of interpretation which will stand as the timeless 'decoder' of our moral discourse. The world changes rapidly, and sometimes our moral valuations will follow it. New technology, new events, new experiences, new people: all provide fresh fodder for our interpretative skills. All of them test, and at times expand, the limits of our moral meanings. There will be no end to the process of interpretation, only temporary stopping-points of consensual judgement. Ronald Dworkin has suggested, in opposition to Walzer, that without a correct moral theory (either discovered or invented), we will never agree on which interpretation is best.[32] Walzer disagrees. The best interpretation – at a particular moment – will be the one which makes the most sense to the community of experience;

members of that community will freely recognize themselves in its terms. The best reading will cohere the most with other elements of that community's discourse; and it will describe and order the core principles of that community's discourse. The best reading will make moral discourse 'the most fully understood'; it will study 'the pattern of the whole', 'reaching for its deepest reasons'. Above all, the best interpretation will be that account which participants in the discourse freely agree constitutes the fullest and most persuasive expression of their own socially constructed idealism.[33]

Where precisely does this leave us with regard to recognizing the best interpretation of our shared, existing moral commitments? The best interpretation cannot be the product of radical coercion. It must be logically consistent and take broad account of other commitments in the culture. It must offer an ordered set of values by which people and institutions can make important moral and political choices. Even though the best interpretation will probably be offered by a member of the expert interpretative community, all members of the community of experience must be able to recognize themselves in it. Whether they actually endorse it or not may be a separate issue, but the actual consent of the majority of experts might suffice to diagnose it, at least in outline and for the time being. Then the world will change in important ways and we will be forced to begin the process anew. In general, the best interpretation will speak better than all its competitors to the identity and self-understanding of the community in question, and evidence of commitment to its norms can be found by examining what gets most widely *and* deeply praised and blamed in that community, how the individual members strive to act, how they justify their actions, and especially through how they try to structure such basic social institutions as government.

Summary

Walzer's just war work is situated within his general theory of justice. The method of this general theory is hermeneutic, mandating that we best interpret our existing beliefs and commitments, which are influenced and affected by our membership in cultural communities. Walzer dismisses rival methods of discovery and invention, singling out Rawls's method of idealized rational choice for its abstractness and lack of recognition of our historical attachment to particular societies. Walzer offers the method of interpretation as the most plausible, serviceable and potent method for moral and political philosophy. While he offers spirited and substantive argumentation in support of such claims, ambiguities and difficulties remain. Among them are: whether interpretation as a method is really different in kind from invention; what exactly counts as the best interpretation; and how we are to know whether we 'recognize', or consent to, or identify with, the principles outlined in the best interpretation, which is what enables the process of 'immanent critique' Walzer so staunchly defends. No normative system, of course, is flawless, and Walzer probably offers the most resourceful and thoughtful defence of conventionalism as yet on offer. The next logical step in our inquiry must be to discern more clearly what exact content Walzer uses to fill in the form of his general theory of justice. If we follow his conventionalist method, what substantive principles of justice are we going to arrive at?

2 • Thick and Thin: The Content of Walzer's General Theory of Justice

[T]here is a thin man inside every fat man.

Walzer, paraphrasing George Orwell[1]

Walzer argues that, if we apply his interpretative method to contemporary issues in moral and political philosophy, the most defensible conclusion we shall reach is that we are all committed to both thin and thick codes of conduct and social organization. For Walzer, we start off with an interpretative framework or procedure, and we end up, as the best interpretation, with two substantive sets of values, the one being nested within the other. This idea, of the thin being contained within the thick, is captured in the epigraph above. The purpose of this chapter is to explain and examine in detail exactly what these thin and thick values of Walzer's general theory of justice are, how they are related, what different sets of action they apply to, and what import they have for his just war theory, which remains our major concern.

The big picture

Walzer believes that the best interpretation of justice in general must acknowledge that we are all committed to both thin and thick norms of conduct. The thin general theory of justice is, in his words, 'minimal and universal'. Significantly, he hastens to add: 'I should say almost universal, just to protect myself against the odd anthropological example.' This thin theory of justice is rudimentary and 'largely negative', consisting of prohibitions against 'the grossest injustices', like 'murder, deception, betrayal, gross cruelty', 'radical coercion', 'brutal repression' and 'torture, oppression and tyranny'. It also enshrines human rights to life and liberty, with correlative duties of non-violation. Though the language of human rights is Western in origin, Walzer comments confidently: 'I assume that it is translatable', and thus that nearly identical concepts and values are at play in non-Western cultures too. He even refers, in terms jarring for a conventionalist, to these elemental prohibitions as 'moral facts', 'immediately available to our understanding'. This 'minimal and universal moral code ... regulates our conduct with all humanity'. Just war theory falls under the purview of this thin theory of minimal morality.[2]

Walzer emphasizes that the thin theory of minimal morality is universal *only* in the sense of the scope of those who endorse it. It is *not* the objective truth of morality, either discovered or invented; rather, it is nothing more (nor less) than that core set of values we find reiterated in every substantive moral and political code. Thin morality is universal only in the sense of being 'reiteratively particularist', 'the sum of [common] recognitions', that set of 'overlapping outcomes' shared by diverse moral codes. Thin morality, in short, consists of those basic moral rules everyone believes in. We all endorse the thin norms as part of our socially constructed idealism. The thin code is not externally imposed; rather, our interpretative skills lead us to the conclusion that it is immanent in every actual moral system.[3]

Minimal morality is 'embedded' in maximal morality, which is not universal in scope but rather is radically particularist. Maximal morality is not shared with all humanity; it is utterly relative to one's cultural surroundings. Distributive justice is Walzer's foremost example of maximal morality, for it deals with the distribution of social goods – like food, wealth, employment, health care and education – and the meaning of such goods varies from culture to culture, and sharply so. All discourse surrounding distributive justice, Walzer asserts, 'will be idiomatic in its language, particularist in its cultural reference ... historically dependent and factually detailed'.[4]

Walzer believes it crucial to note that the world's many maximal moralities cannot be deduced from the one thin theory they all share. Minimal morality is 'not the foundation' of all the maximal moralities; rather, it is 'only a piece' of them. Furthermore, it is not as though maximal moralities developed historically out of the one thin theory shared originally by our primordial ancestors. It is not as though minimal morality is more essentially human, or natural, or authoritative, *simply because* it is more universal in scope. Being more widely shared does not make it more true or real.[5]

Walzer is adamant that morality always confronts us first in the maximal sense, and that the minimal sense can only be arrived at through interpretation and the search for commonalities amongst the world's many maximal doctrines. If anything, it is maximalism which is the most natural, for that is how we first learn and experience normative phenomena: from within the confines of a particular moral and political culture. Morality is always, first and foremost, maximal: thick, robust, resonant, culturally particular, close to home. Minimal morality, Walzer says, comes to the fore only during times of crisis. The spur for thin morality's 'liberation from its embedding' in maximal morality – the reason for its occasional assertion of itself as most in need of attention – is not a common culture shared by all humanity; rather, it is the presence of a common enemy, like a tyrannical government launching an aggressive war.[6]

Walzer does believe, importantly, that thin morality constitutes a check on thick morality. For instance, any government which violates the dictates of thin morality can only be seen as deficient and unjust. Appeal to thick cultural particularities *cannot* justify violations of the thin moral code. Appealing to local customs and traditions can never outweigh appeals to be free from torture and gross cruelty. Once more, this is not because the thin code stands as the objective litmus test, disclosed to us by reason or revelation; rather, it is because of the elemental meaning of the thin code already embedded in every thick one. That meaning contains the information that, for all of us, no grosser injustices exist than violations of the thin prohibitions on murder, tyranny, coercion, oppression, cruelty, and so on. Minimal morality is 'morality close to the bone' and as such is simple, universal and intensely held. Maximal morality, by contrast, is a richly articulated cultural code, complicated, qualified and full of such subtle nuance that non-participants in the culture can find difficulty grasping, much less endorsing, it. Maximal morality has to be 'read, rendered, construed, glossed, elucidated'.[7]

Reflecting critically on Walzer's contentions, we might ask: is minimal morality really more intensely held than maximal morality? After all, by Walzer's own admission, people identify first in the ordinary course of their lives with the thick morality of their own culture. Home is where the heart is. Furthermore, it is not implausible to suggest that, during times of crisis, the socially constructed idealism of many people is to attend to the thin moral code only *vis-à-vis* their fellow citizens, and not necessarily with regard to outsiders, especially if those others brought on the crisis, as in the case of war. Do all maximal moralities truly contain the thin one, and is it anything other than convenient that the content of the thin morality turns out by Walzer's lights so brightly, so happily?

On the one hand, there is no denying that the thin norms as Walzer describes them appear very broadly endorsed indeed, at least in general outline. This is surely related to the fundamental interests that rational human beings see well protected by norms forbidding torture, murder and tyranny. Such fundamental interests seem to revolve around an elemental need for security: protection of one's life and limb, freedom from domination at the hands of another. We all have obvious and vital interests in each having reliable security. Such seems a necessary condition, in general, for the pursuit of whatever else we might personally find desirable in life. At the same time, we note Walzer's reluctance to declare such fundamental interests universally true or advantageous, full stop.

We might also wonder whether the thin norms are so abstractly put by him that they leave considerable space for different interpretations of the same phenomena. Granted that nobody is going explicitly to endorse 'murder', 'torture' and 'gross cruelty', can Walzer simply leave it there without acknowledging residual ambiguity with regard to how people – even interpretative experts – understand such activity? For instance, is the death penalty gross cruelty, or abortion murder? What about breeding and slaughtering animals for human consumption? Or torturing a terrorist to gain needed information about his confederates? Think now of such thin prohibitions on 'tyranny', 'betrayal' and 'oppression', and whether there is a globally shared, socially constructed idealism disclosing their content. Walzer refers quite breezily, almost off-handedly, to the content of minimal morality, presumably owing to his view that we all know more or less what he is referring to. But do we really? Is the 'more or less' enough to provide firm guidance in difficult situations, such as wartime?

Here is where the methods of discovery and invention may show up that of interpretation, even on Walzer's own terms. While we saw in the last chapter that his critics overstated their case with regard to interpretation being insufficiently critical, they may be able to claim that they can better guarantee universality. They might ask: are we genuinely assured by Walzer's quick declarations that his thin norms are actually shared by everyone, at least at the level of socially constructed idealism? Or are we more assured by the substantive universality of such non-interpretative norms as Rawls's principles of justice, or Kant's categorical imperative, or even the principle of utility? An uncharitable discoverer or inventor might observe that interpretation may disclose a universally shared thin moral *vocabulary* but not so clearly a universally shared *understanding of what that vocabulary refers to*. The universally shared core, as described by Walzer, may turn out to be not only thin but hollow.

Walzer's just war theory a kind of minimal morality

Walzer's methodology in *Just and Unjust Wars* exemplifies his interpretive, conventionalist approach to moral and political philosophy: 'For as long as men and women have talked about war, they have talked about it in terms of right and wrong.'[8] His starting-point is to examine this common way of talking about the ethics of war and peace. This discourse is based on a shared moral vocabulary regarding war. Walzer suggests that this vocabulary – aggression, defence, neutrality, surrender, massacre, etc. – is not only universally shared amongst divergent thick moralities in the present; it also has remained 'remarkably persistent' over the centuries. Some scholars are inclined to dismiss just war theory as Eurocentric, citing its clear links to the system of international law first developed in Europe. In response, Walzer cites many examples of cross-cultural, cross-temporal concurrence with most of the central norms of just war theory, such as those critical of interstate aggression and permissive of a state resorting to self-defence in response.[9]

Extensive as these citations may be, one cannot help but wonder whether they sufficiently ground Walzer's claims of a genuine universality with regard to a shared moral vocabulary regarding war. After all, Walzer himself concedes: '[n]o doubt the moral reality of war is not the same for us as it was for Genghis Khan.' Perhaps this is why Walzer generally eschews talk of universality in favour of related locutions like 'very broadly shared', and why he shies away from proclaiming the changelessness of moral propositions about war over time in favour of referring to their 'remarkable persistence'. At one point, he even admits that his claims of universality and identity are 'not always true' yet insists that they are still 'true enough . . . to give stability and coherence to our moral lives'.[10]

It is crucial to note that, by a shared vocabulary and discourse, Walzer is not referring to widespread agreement as to *judgements about* the (in)justice of particular wars or wartime tactics. He is referring to widespread agreements as to the *intelligibility of* claims as to what constitutes an (un)just war or tactic. Obviously, there is nothing approaching universality regarding actual judgements people make about the (in)justice of particular wars; but there is something approaching universality regarding modes of discourse for talking about war. All people, Walzer submits, understand what is an appropriate, and what an inappropriate, way of talking about the ethics of war and peace. Even though there are sharp disagreements as to which wars and tactics are just, everyone employs the same moral vocabulary in attempting to justify or criticize wars and tactics. Everyone employs the language of aggression and defence, of the value of political community, of the need to protect their own people, of the need to avoid civilian casualties and excess cruelties, and so on. Indeed, the diverse nations of the world have structured international law around these shared terms and concepts. In other words, we *necessarily share discourse* about war and thin justice in general but we only *contingently share judgement* about the justice of particular wars. Walzer observes that '. . . our sharpest disagreements [about war] are structured and organized by our underlying agreements, by the meanings we share'.[11]

So for Walzer there is a thin, reiterated, universal moral code with regard to the ethics of war and peace. Walzer asserts that this code is 'made obligatory by the general consent of mankind'. Justice in wartime consists of adhering to the terms of this thin code; it constitutes what Walzer calls 'the moral reality of war'. Walzer insists that the code is a moral one. Though there is a body of international law surrounding armed conflict which reflects this code to a considerable degree, the code is first and foremost a set of moral terms and concepts. Thus, the 'text' to interpret in order to glean the best reading of this code cannot be limited to international law, though it should include it.[12]

The thin moral code on war also 'refers in its own way to the real world'. By this Walzer means that it is possible to gather evidence, and enumerate arguments based on that evidence, which can enable us to judge – in a non-idiosyncratic or partisan way – whether particular wars and tactics are just or unjust. The thin moral code is thought to be not only universal and public in terms of intelligibility and shared meanings of terms; it is also public in the sense of enabling the sober and intersubjective judgement of real wars *vis-à-vis* its standards. It is a manifestly applicable code, designed to facilitate, not obfuscate, well-grounded judgements about the (in)justice of real wartime decisions. The code is designed to offer us the core values by which to make moral judgements in wartime, as well as to point out what kind of evidence is required to make those judgements compelling and authoritative.[13]

What exactly is Walzer's reading of the best, most authoritative interpretation of this universally shared, thin moral code with regard to justice in wartime? 'I want to suggest', he answers,

> that the arguments we make about war are most fully understood (though other understandings are possible) as efforts to recognize and respect the rights of individual and associated men and women. The morality I shall expound is in its philosophical form a doctrine of human rights . . .

Though 'considerations of utility play into the structure at many points . . . they cannot account for it as a whole. Their part is secondary to that of rights; it is constrained by rights.' 'At every point', he concludes, 'the judgments we make [about war] are best accounted for if we regard life and liberty as something like absolute values and then try to understand the moral and political processes through which these values are challenged and defended.' The rest of this book, by and large, will be devoted to explaining, and critically evaluating, what Walzer means by these remarks regarding human rights protection in wartime.[14]

Before we get to that task, the main one of this study, it will be beneficial for the remainder of the present chapter to look at Walzer's account of distributive justice, even though it has already been discussed in detail in the academic literature. This is true for at least two reasons. The first is that it will help us grasp more fully his general theory of justice, within which his just war theory is located. It will aid us in understanding how thick and thin codes interact, since distributive justice is for him the foremost example of thick morality. More importantly, it will help us to understand Walzer's own political commitments, and especially the central role that the community plays in his social philosophy. Since political communities are the main actors during wartime, it follows that anything which sheds further light on Walzer's understanding of them will be worth our while.

Distributive justice a kind of maximal morality

Walzer insists that the context for all questions of distributive justice is the political community. The question of who gets what resource, which group of people gets what amount of that good or that benefit, is an issue to be settled within the confines of the good old-fashioned nation-state. Why is this the case? Walzer offers the following argument:

1. Distributive justice is concerned with distributing social goods. A social good is a benefit that can only be enjoyed in an interpersonal context. Peace of mind, for instance, would be what we might call a personal, not a social, good. There are also goods we might call idiosyncratic, which might also presuppose a social context but which particular persons value out of all proportion. Think, for example, of an obsessive stamp collector, or a gambling addict. The social goods which Walzer is concerned with, as a matter of distributive justice, presuppose an interpersonal context yet carry with them undeniable use and value, for every normal person. Key social goods include money, political power, fame, education, health care, awards, honours and opportunities for both employment and leisure.

2. Social goods have no essential or intrinsic nature, either as a matter of discovery or invention. The value social goods have is derived entirely from the place, significance and meaning they occupy within people's lives.

3. The meaning social goods have within people's lives varies from culture to culture, from community to community. Some cultures, for example, place high value on education, others on money, fame, or political power.

4. Therefore, distributive justice is about how to distribute social goods within various cultures and communities, according to the various meanings such goods have within each of them. Distributive justice, Walzer submits, is thus 'surely misrepresented when it is described . . . as if it had been guided from the beginning by a single, comprehensive and universal principle'. The political community is 'the appropriate setting' for distributive justice, since it is 'the closest we can come to a world of common meanings. Language, history and culture come together . . . to produce a collective consciousness.' What counts as justice in distributions will vary from culture to culture, in both time and place, according to the shifts in collective

consciousness. Walzer summarizes this four-step argument with one of his most-cited quotations: 'A given society is just if its substantive life is lived in a certain way – that is, in a way faithful to the shared understandings of its members.'[15]

Take, as an illustration, Walzer's own 'favourite example': health care in Western civilization. Walzer suggests that applying his method of interpretation will tell us that, from medieval to modern times, there has been a shift in what the majority of Westerners have believed about health care, a 'transition from cure of souls to cure of bodies'. During the medieval period, the prevailing idea of health care was that of care for one's soul, the most precious thing about oneself according to Christian theology, itself the fountainhead of the medieval world-view. So important and meaningful was the idea that one's soul could be saved, either through God's grace or good works, that care for souls 'was socialized in distribution', made 'universally available'. Churches were built everywhere, priests made available to even the smallest population centres. Churches were always kept open and the whole system was 'publicly funded' by tithing everyone's income. By contrast, the cure of bodies was left in private hands, and was much harder to access than soul care. Midwives, doctors and 'barbers'/surgeons all had to be paid for, and few people had the money to do so. As a result, people tended either to look after their own physical health or to resign it to fate. But they were sure that their soul was always well tended, or at least could be well tended, if they were believers. We should not, in light of these realities, be surprised that so much of medieval medicine was appallingly crude and underdeveloped: it was not valued enough for communities to invest in it so that it could have made progress.[16]

Walzer argues that very few people, at the time, complained about physical health care being so narrowly distributed, left in private hands animated by the profit motive. But as soon as the smallest number of people got together to form a village, there arose a loud hue and cry for a church to be built to look after the welfare of their immortal souls. This was so, he asserts, *not* because of the Church's own pursuit of power, *nor* out of sour grapes on the part of those who did not have health care, *nor* because those who might have complained probably could not have made an impression on the historical record anyway (e.g. by writing books, since so many were illiterate). The real reason why, he claims, was because the medievals conceived of the meaning of health care in a radically different way from us moderns. They wanted soul care for all, and health care only for those who could pay for it. He argues that

> [n]one of this seems unjust to me . . . what we have here is a maximalist morality, a thick understanding of life and death, a human culture. To this we ought certainly to defer, for it makes no moral sense to wag our finger at medieval Christians, insisting that they *should have had* [his italics] our understanding of life and death.[17]

Over time, people in the West came to reinterpret the meaning of health care. Specifically, they came to value 'longevity over eternity', thus devaluing the need to keep making universally available the means of soul care, the tools of religious salvation. A switch in meanings occurred, calling for the privatization of soul care and the socialization of health care. This, Walzer suggests, is where we now stand today in the West: religious institutions are privately funded through gifts of voluntary members pursuing their vision of soul care, whereas the state has been empowered, through our consent, to raise taxes from everyone to build, staff and fund health care systems which are, to varying degrees, responsive to the physical ailments of everyone. '[N]o case can be made', Walzer declares, 'for the disengagement of the state from the cure of bodies' in contemporary Western countries, owing to the new shared meaning of the social good of health care. Mind you, 'the precise form of socialized [physical health] care is still subject to debate but not the principle that there should be such care.' Such debate about the precise form of care is 'necessarily local in character', and is up to particular Western nations, and sometimes to sub-state units like provinces or even municipalities, to resolve in practical terms. Walzer insists that, according to their own values, such localities cannot, on pain of hypocrisy and criticism, betray the core shared principle of physical healthcare being made available to everyone who needs it. In Walzer's view as an American, the United States has betrayed its deepest, shared commitment to universal access to health care by allowing too much control over the American health-care system to rest in the hands of private, profit-motivated hospitals and insurance companies. The result: tens of millions of Americans lack any health insurance, and have only the most rudimentary claims on the health care system.[18]

This example highlights a vital premise of Walzer's theory of distributive justice: the idea that the shared meaning of any given social good contains the criteria which ought to govern its distribution in the society in question. '[I]f we understand what it is, what it means to people', Walzer suggests, 'we understand how, by whom and for what reasons it ought to be distributed.' *The shared meaning of the good contains the ideal method for its social distribution.* For example, in the contemporary West, the very meaning of health care purportedly informs us that it ought to be distributed, in Western societies, solely on the basis of medical need. Such is either a part, or a direct consequence, of the very meaning of health care. Much of Walzer's *Spheres of Justice* is devoted to looking at particular social goods – like money, power, education and welfare – and discerning what distributive criteria are present in their shared cultural meaning. How is such discernment to be had? By employing hermeneutics, as discussed in the last chapter, to arrive at the best interpretation of the shared meaning of the particular good in that particular culture.[19]

Spheres of justice and socialism

It is beyond the ambit of this work to consider in detail how Walzer arrives at the various distributive criteria for various social goods by applying his method of interpretation. What is relevant for us is that Walzer understands the various criteria for the most critical social goods all interlocking together, pointing towards a coherent and definitive arrangement for distribution in Western societies in general, and in the United States in particular. He is worth quoting at length on this point:

> The appropriate arrangements in our own society are those, I think, of a decentralized democratic socialism; a strong welfare state run, in part at least, by local and amateur officials; a constrained market; an open and demystified civil service; independent public schools; the sharing of hard work and free time; the protection of religious and family life; a system of public honouring and dishonouring free from all considerations of rank or class; workers' control of companies and factories; a politics of parties, movements, meeting and public debate.[20]

This claim raises interesting questions and observations, first raised in the last chapter, about Walzer's interpretative method. We witness here the degree of prescriptivity involved in the interpretation, and it raises the question as to what degree it can be called an interpretation of an existing commitment and not, say, an invention offered for fresh commitment. Consider, as an example, how far from the *prima facie* understanding of actual American values is the idea that the best interpretation of corporate governance in the United States is that the workers should be in control, or that hard and dirty work, like garbage collection, should be shared equally on a rotating basis. Indeed, do American values and democratic socialism mix at all? Is there any descriptive ground here for Walzer's prescriptive judgements, such that we can still meaningfully refer to such claims as ones of interpretation? In a telling concession, Walzer actually admits that his view that hard and dirty work should be shared equally on a rotating basis 'goes against the grain' of the shared social meaning of that good. He admits that, in most cultures, hard and dirty work is thought to be fit for, and thus goes to, 'hard and dirty people', who are then socially stigmatized for it. To what extent, then, can we refer to the norm of equally sharing hard work as being self-imposed, one of our own deepest shared commitments? In this case, it is a rhetorical question, and it reveals a real gap in Walzer's account of distributive justice.[21]

Presumably, though, Walzer would not see it as a gap. Why not? The answer is that his interpretative process is as much 'top-down', drawing on large-scale social values and political commitments during the process of interpreting the meaning of particular social goods, as it is 'bottom-up', moving from a discernment of particular meanings to a wide-ranging political prescription for the whole of society. This emphasis on achieving one overarching and interconnecting interpretation is Walzer's version of 'the hermeneutic circle', according to which the interpretation of the parts is influenced by that of the whole, and vice versa. This holistic approach may allow one to fill in gaps, so to speak, and perhaps even override the analysis of one or two of the parts if the bulk of the whole points in an opposing direction. Thus, we can presumably ignore the meaning of dirty work pointing towards an unequal and stigmatized distribution because its own unique and isolated meaning gets overwhelmed by the overarching 'best interpretation' of a more equal distribution of all goods society-wide.[22]

Ronald Dworkin has refused to let this important point go, and focuses on Walzer's favourite example of health care. Dworkin's core accusation is that Walzer is not so much engaged in interpretation, whether holistic or otherwise, as he is in advocating on behalf of his own invented commitments, namely, those of democratic socialism. It is Walzer, and not the discoverer or inventor, who is relying most heavily on rhetorical devices for persuasive effect. It is Walzer who disguises his preferred political inventions in the comfortable garb of 'our deepest shared commitments', 'our community values', 'the meanings we share'. We have seen that Walzer argues that the deepest shared meaning of health care in the West is that it ought to be distributed by the public sector solely on the basis of medical need. Dworkin responds that, if Walzer were really engaged in interpretation, and if he applied that interpretative method to the United States, the result would be a more complex yet accurate reading of American culture. This reading would be that America is committed to universal access only with regard to a very basic minimum of health care for all who medically need it (basic preventative care for children, emergency care for adults) and, beyond that very thin threshold, to medical distribution based on the ability to pay, whether out-of-pocket or through private insurance coverage.[23]

Dworkin's criticism, of course, does not get to the substance of Walzer's health care recommendations but, rather, to the idea that this substance can be arrived at using the interpretative method he claims to be using. Dworkin doubts it, and stresses the importance of this fact: if you are going to hold people up to the standards of 'their own shared principles', you'd better get it right with regard to what exactly those principles are. The evaluative element in the interpretative process cannot be utterly at odds with, or unhinged from, an accurate description of the thing being interpreted. For Dworkin, Walzer has stepped over that line in this case, and perhaps more broadly. For Dworkin, Walzer offers an inaccurate reading of the health care values of Americans, and thus cannot suggest policy reform in the direction of greater socialization of health care *on the grounds that* failure so to reform is a betrayal of principles already accepted. Socialized health care is simply not a principle Americans are committed to, no matter how 'deep' or 'compelling' or 'coherent' the so-called interpretation of their values is. It is just not there; Walzer has 'read it in' to the culture. More precisely, in Dworkin's view, Walzer is himself the author of the principle. What could animate such criticism and call for reform in the direction of socialized care, then? The answer, in terms of options Walzer acknowledges, would be either a discovered or an invented one. This ties back in forcefully to the suggestion made in the last chapter that Walzer may not, in the end, be able to sustain a sharp distinction between the methods of interpretation and invention.[24]

Not only does Walzer believe that the meaning of any given social good contains its own distributive criterion; he moreover believes that this criterion will not be the same between different social goods. Different goods have different meanings, and thus different criteria governing their distribution. This is the case even if, in the end, all the different meanings add up to a society-wide democratic socialist distribution. For instance, the criterion which should govern the distribution of money will not end up being the exact same criterion as that which should govern the distribution of political power. Walzer takes this assertion as a fact of social valuation which can be revealed through interpretation, and approves of it more generally. Why? Because, if it is respected – if different goods are distributed to different people according to different meanings – then it will reduce or even eliminate domination and tyranny, and enable the creation of a social world characterized by what he calls 'complex equality', his preferred shorthand term for a democratic socialist society.[25]

For Walzer, the height of injustice in distributions occurs when the possession of one social good, X, allows a person or a group of people to possess another social good, Y, *simply because they have X and without regard to the meaning of Y in their culture*. This reality he calls domination, and he says it is the handmaiden of tyranny. Tyranny he defines as a condition wherein a very small number of people come to control all that is most valued and precious in the social world they share (though they would prefer not to) with everyone else. A dominant good is one whose possession translates, either automatically or at least all too readily, into possession of other valued social goods, irrespective of their meaning. One of the most obvious dominant goods in contemporary society, on which Walzer dwells at length, is money. The wealthy have ready access, on the basis of their wealth alone, to a better education, a better shot at winning public office, etc. The critical force of Walzer's theory of distributive justice is precisely to resist the easy 'convertibility' of dominant goods into other valued benefits, and in so doing to resist the rule of tyrants, whether they be autocrats or plutocrats.[26]

The problem with such easy convertibility, of one social good into another, is that it is at odds with our deepest commitments and ideals. The injustice arises from the violation of shared meaning.

Each social good, Walzer says, has its own unique and independent criterion of distribution, along with its own 'separate set of legitimate claimants'. Different goods mean different things and thus imply different – not homogeneous – distributive criteria. Health care has, as part or consequence of its meaning, the distributive criterion that it ought to go to the sick. Love has, as part of its meaning, the distributive criterion that it ought to go, as a matter of free choice, to those objects of affection who can love back in return. Professorships have, as part of their meaning, the distributive criterion that they ought to go to those most demonstrating academic talent. And so on.[27]

There is no overall hierarchy of social goods for Walzer, any more than there is one objective 'greatest good'. Social goods are each autonomous: they have separate meanings within a culture, and also different meanings across various cultures. It is crucial to respect such autonomy, for two reasons. The first is the fact that 'autonomy is a basic distributive principle, itself entailed by the differentiation of goods'. Separate goods have separate meanings and thus different distributive principles. The second reason is that respecting autonomy avoids, perhaps even eliminates, domination and tyranny, something enjoined upon us by the thin universal morality we all share. 'No one good', Walzer submits, as matter of both fact and value, 'rules over all the others, such that possessing it brings everything else in train. Justice requires the defense of differences – different goods distributed for different reasons among different groups of people.' Hence the title metaphor in *Spheres of Justice*: each social good has its own social meaning, its own 'sphere'. Within that sphere the good ought to be distributed solely according to the meaning it has in that culture. We should resist strongly the claims of those people who want to shatter the spheres, to disrespect the boundaries of shared meaning which keep social goods apart. Such people are asserting their dominance, seeking to convert their control over one social good (say, money) into control over other social goods (like health care or political power) without regard to the meaning those other goods have within the culture. Such people are aggressors, crossing borders and invading protected spaces without the consent of those affected and in violation of the meaning of the life they share with others. Walzer employs very similar imagery and language when dealing with the problem of war. In reading Walzer, one can never go wrong in remembering that, for him, one of the core political themes is about defending protected spaces from outside invasion, from non-consensual boundary crossings.[28]

Tyrannies on the right and left

Walzer, in more recent works, describes and criticizes two contemporary forms of social dominance and tyranny, one from the right of the political spectrum, the other from the left. The one from the right regards money as the dominant social good, viewing all of society as one big market – one enormous network of supply and demand – within which individuals and groups ought to be free to strike up whatever deals and exchanges they both want and are able to carry out. This rightist perspective, combining rational-choice economic theory with the practice of libertarian politics, asserts that all supposed boundaries between social goods must fall in favour of the dominance of money, which they often insist is the one universal standard of social value in any event. Walzer disagrees, contending that the fact that we employ 'blocked exchanges' in a number of areas shows that, in the final analysis, we do not buy into this superficially tempting idea of money being the one universal social good, into which all others can be measured, converted, supplied and demanded.

What is a blocked exchange? It is an area of social life into which we bar the intrusion of money. An example would be the fact that we have made it illegal to bribe a judge or jury in order to secure a favoured verdict in a court of law. Of course, sometimes such blocked exchanges fail, but that is not the point for Walzer: the point is that we are still committed to blocked exchanges as a matter of our socially constructed idealism: as a feature of the kind of social world we should like to be a part of, not merely the kind of social world we happen to be subjected to. The deepest meaning of a social good can be discerned only through seeking out the best interpretation of it, which we have seen combines both descriptive and prescriptive elements. The best interpretation of social goods in the West, Walzer claims, will not endorse the dominance of any one social good, not even that of money. In fact, Walzer devotes considerable attention to criticizing the status of money in contemporary Western societies. He declares that money is clearly the most dominant good and that its possession is all too readily converted into other social goods, like education, health care and public office, goods whose meaning has nothing whatsoever to do with market values. 'Money doesn't talk', Bob Dylan once sang; 'it screams.' Walzer agrees but is keen to establish clear and firm sound barriers between it and the other social goods we value.[29]

The leftist form of social dominance and tyranny which Walzer discerns, and is keen to criticize, views political power as the dominant social good. Society is wholly political, according to this view: it is all one big network within which people seek control over others, under various guises and strategies. Since political power is the dominant good, allowing its holders to enjoy all the other social goods, it follows that it is not the market but rather the state which is the crucial site for struggle and recognition. Leftists accordingly favour the state as the dominant social institution, and argue that it ought to distribute power among citizens as equally as possible.

Walzer criticizes this view, in spite of the salient fact that his own political commitments are clearly on the left. His main criticism is this: it simply is not true that all of social existence can be adequately explained as the struggle over power. Such is a fashionable reading in many circles – particularly in academe – but it remains incorrect, as much a false generalization about life as the rightist claim that it is all about money. Indeed, Walzer notes with some irony that this leftist tyranny of the state is really, and merely, the inverse of the rightist tyranny of the market: they are both aimed at blocking, or eliminating, the other. The rightists want to beat back the state, so that they are free to make more money, and the leftists want to do the same to the market, so that they can pursue more social equality. In doing so, both groups reveal that they have the spirit of aggressors, seeking to invade boundaries, disrespect difference, and impose a merciless policy of social assimilation, whether in the name of free enterprise or the brotherhood of man. Walzer argues that social life, as any accurate reading of culture will tell you, is not unified by any one underlying principle or dominant good; it is naturally divided according to the diversity of social goods at play within it. The 'totalizing' ambitions of those seeking one unified general theory of social goods are doomed to be disappointed; they will crash into the rocks of a more complex and variegated social reality. Moreover, this social division and plurality is mirrored in our personal lives.[30]

Identity and difference

We are, as persons, neither pure examples of market participants seeking to maximize expected utility, nor of activist citizens enthusiastically engaged in the equal exercise of political power. Both are undeniable facets of our lives, as members of contemporary Western democracies, but they remain just that: they are parts, not the whole, of our identity and existence. This is both fact and value: our personalities are not so one-dimensional as a matter of fact, nor do we aspire to be so narrow in terms of our own deepest commitments and ideals. Beyond money and power, we also care about love, friendship, family ties, education, health care, reputation, leisure activities, personal hobbies, etc. We cannot plausibly reduce the latter set of goods, activities and interests to either of the first two, or even to both of them put together. And this is leaving unsaid our diverse attitudes towards personal goods, such as peace of mind, reflectiveness, happiness and desire for self-improvement. Ditto for those social goods some of us value out of all proportion, such as fine art or high fashion. 'Selves are more naturally divided', Walzer concludes.[31]

It proves impossible to fit any of us into neat and narrow slots in terms of our fundamental interests and identities. We each have multiple layers of passions, roles, concerns, tasks, memberships and self-understandings. Walzer refers, as an example of this multiplicity, to himself as an American, a Jew, a professor, an East Coaster, an author, a family man and a democratic socialist. Instead of working for a society which grinds against all these natural divisions and multiple identities of the self – by seeking to bring all social goods under the dominance of one single good controlled by a small set of ultra-privileged people – Walzer insists: 'I must work for a society that makes room for this divided self.' Divided selves, which are the selves we both have and want, are 'best accommodated by complex equality', defined as 'a social condition where no one group of claimants dominates the different distributive processes' and such distributions are guided by the separate and internal meanings of each of the social goods.[32]

What is Walzer's precise relationship with his comrades on the left, if he subjects them to such searing criticism, accusing them of ignoring the very bases of personal identity? The relationship is, no doubt, an ambiguous and highly personal one; the fact that he refers to it not infrequently throughout his work reveals its significance for him.

And it is not just his academic writings that speak to this attachment. Walzer's high-profile involvement with the American left led him to be a Vietnam War protester in the 1960s and 1970s, along with one of his current roles as editor-in-chief of *Dissent* magazine. Walzer's commitments with regard to distributive justice place him firmly on the left; of that there can be no doubt. The best distributive scheme, he insists, is that of a democratic socialist regime, with its stress on extensive state intervention, public ownership, political activism and equality across classes and persons. But Walzer believes that leftists have, historically, ignored the role and vitality that participation in cultural tradition and membership in national communities play in people's lives. He puts this rather colourfully, suggesting bluntly that '[t]he left has never understood the tribes'. One way of putting this relationship would be to say that Walzer remains a democratic socialist, stressing equality and strong public-sector involvement in distributions, yet he also values group identities and private personal attachments, and tolerates the resulting pluralism and social difference. If the distinction between Walzer and the left could be summarized in one word, it would probably be 'tolerance': Walzer views the left in general as far too assimilative and universal in its ambitions, far too dismissive of the cultural and personal differences that add spice and significance to life.[33]

Walzer's attempt to link leftist politics with 'the politics of difference' is captured in his rewriting of Karl Marx's famous declaration on distribution. Instead of saying, 'From each according to ability, to each according to need', Walzer submits that the principle really ought to be: 'From each according to ability, to each according to *shared, socially-recognized* needs [emphasis added].' Walzer, we have seen, is sceptical of universal claims to all but the most basic and minimal, 'thin' protections. In general, he favours talking about how the very idea of 'need' gets constructed and culturally interpreted, how we are as much creatures of context and shared meaning as we are of flesh and bone, or of rational agency for that matter. There is no one single overall 'human need', stamped on us all as if by a cosmic cookie-cutter. There is, rather, a plurality of goods, benefits, opportunities and protections we all require – each in our own way, pending the time and place of our personal context – if we are to be treated properly by way of distribution. A just community, then, is one wherein there is a background of broadly shared valuations with regard to social goods, and a pair of core commitments: the first to active participation in social life; the second to providing all members with those goods recognized as objects of need in that community. Walzer puts it thus: 'The social contract is an agreement to reach decisions together about what goods are necessary to our common life, and then to provide these goods for one another.' This 'contract is a moral bond . . . creating a union that transcends all differences of interest, drawing its strength from history, culture, etc.'[34]

Politics and dominance

There is one lurking complexity, and potential problem, for Walzer here. The emphasis he puts on public-sector involvement, in ensuring distributions according to shared meaning, means that he may have trouble avoiding the accusation that, when push comes to shove, political power is for him the dominant good. Political power, of course, is about holding a public office which exerts influence and authority over one's fellow citizens. Walzer argues that the deepest shared meaning of political power, at least in the West, tells us that it ought to be distributed solely on the basis of the consent of the citizens. But the political sphere is for Walzer a 'double-sphere'. The political power concentrated in the state must, in his ideal society of complex equality: (1) enforce and police the boundaries of other social goods, ensuring separation, difference and non-dominance; yet (2) itself be distributed as a social good on the basis of the consent of the governed. Thus political power is, in Walzer's own words, 'specially extended' and 'probably the most important' sphere of social activity. Most clearly: the state for Walzer is and ought to be 'enormously powerful'. Indeed, in almost textbook declaration of leftist ideology, Walzer at one point suggests that '[r]esistance will require at some point a concentration of political power that matches the concentration of plutocratic power – hence a movement or a party that seizes or, at least, uses the state'.[35]

What guarantee can Walzer give that political power will not become a dominant good in his ideal society, allowing those who possess it to convert it automatically into other goods, like fame or wealth, as so many politicians are currently able to do? The sheer pervasiveness of state power, as Walzer sees it, and its uniquely privileged position as the guardian of all other spheres would seem to make it ripe for abuse. After all, why would politicians in Walzer's ideal society hold back from converting their good into others? What would prevent them from skewing the boundaries to benefit themselves? Walzer seems to believe that the very nature of political activity in a complex egalitarian society would function as a constraint on political power. The essential contestedness of who gets political power would, it seems, function as a sort of internally limiting principle on political power. Walzer's vision here, inspired by Rousseau, is of an activist citizenry distributing power between themselves based on the persuasiveness of political arguments and the shared spirit of tending to the general will. Walzer even summarizes his version of the just society as one wherein citizenship becomes the dominant good. But, he insists, such domination would mark not another, but rather the end of, tyranny. An effective state, empowered by its own citizens, will ensure that the spheres of justice are kept separate, and thereby remain faithful to shared understandings in the community.[36]

I am not so sure of Walzer's confidence in this regard. Falling back on the activism and public spirit of the citizens, as effective checks on political power, seems too intellectualized. Activism, participation and debate – even at augmented levels from what they are now – all seem to be compatible with the domination of political power. Indeed, one could contend that such activism in Walzer's ideal society would be augmented *precisely because* it would be the dominant good. But this augmented activism would not, of itself, suffice to limit state power within its own proper sphere; it would just make it more fiercely contested over and competed for. And if it does become more fiercely fought over, why would the victors not want more spoils than are already available to those currently on top? It is not at all clear that the dominion of citizenship, the rediscovery of Rousseau's republican virtue,[37] would not, or at least could not, become yet another tyranny. Walzer does not provide sufficient assurances that, in his ideal society, political power will not simply replace money as the dominant good. At the very least, he needs to construct in detail effective mechanisms whereby the state, in his just society, could be assured of remaining true to the shared meanings of its proper function. Here is where a more procedural, as opposed to substantive, understanding of distributive justice might prove more useful, detailing for example the need for constitutional checks and balances, a division of governing power, and so on.

Proceduralism and fairness

It is both interesting and important to note that, although Walzer in general is hostile to a proceduralist conception of distributive justice – since most often it is not rooted in culturally relative meanings but, rather, in universal ambitions – at times he makes significant concessions to it. For instance, at the very end of *Spheres of Justice,* he considers the following challenge: what happens when there is no one best interpretation of the shared meaning of a social good or goods? What if, all things considered, interpretative conflict about a certain good, during a certain era, remains intractable? Walzer admits that, here, distributive justice can no longer reside in being faithful to the good's meaning; it will reside, rather, in 'being faithful to the disagreements, providing institutional channels for their expression, adjudicative mechanisms and alternative distributions'.[38] At first glance, this seems a modest concession, at most providing for a ranking of distributive principles: first tend to the best substantive interpretation and, failing that, resort to some proceduralist, dispute-resolution mechanism. But more thought suggests that the concession may be deeper than it seems, and ends up raising more questions than it answers. For according to what values and principles should the procedures themselves be guided? Are the procedures somehow seen as value-neutral? If so, and if they can provide adequate distributions, then why not talk about distributive justice in purely procedural terms right from the start? What role would be left for appeals to cultural meaning when our time would be spent constructing free and fair institutions to settle disputes according to a set process? If the procedures are not seen as value-neutral, then whose values are to prevail, and why? If the meaning of the good in question is so contested and disputed, then why should we believe there will be broad-based agreement about the procedure for distributing it? Must we then appeal to reason, or some 'higher interest', or should we rather let the rival factions fight it out, and establish the primacy of one interpretation in that sense, or perhaps even split the community itself into parts which do have shared meanings? Walzer fails to confront these potent questions about proceduralism and how it may constitute a serious challenge to his own conception of both distributive justice and the limits of state power.

Walzer has engaged more directly the issues arising from a somewhat related concession. In *Spheres of Justice*, Walzer's enthusiasm for distribution according to culturally relative meaning leads him to admit that, on his theory's terms, a caste system could be seen as just, in spite of the fact that, in it, one ultra-privileged group comes to control all the valued social goods. '(I)t's not impossible', he concedes, 'to imagine a society where dominance and monopoly are not violations but enactments of meaning, where social goods are conceived in hierarchical terms.' In the India of yesteryear, for example, the Brahmins were the dominant élite, flush with wealth, power and privilege, while the so-called 'untouchables' were systematically shamed and utterly deprived. Walzer puts the matter with uncharacteristic abstraction: 'In a society where social meanings are integrated and hierarchical, justice will come to the aid of inequality' in spite of the fact that justice should only come to the aid of equality, preferably of his complex kind.[39]

Many critics pounced on Walzer's admission, arguing that it laid bare not only internal tensions within Walzer's theory but also the external dangers of making justice in any sense relative to supposedly shared meanings within a certain culture at a certain time.[40] What does distributive justice have to do with meaning at all, especially if it can be reinterpreted to serve the ends of gross, grinding inequality? Why not stick with the old tried-and-true insistence that distributive justice is about pursuing equality and fairness, using neutral institutions, instead of propping up customary ways of life? In my view, the most burning question here for Walzer would be this: *what is fair about distribution according to cultural meaning?* Where is the fairness in Walzer's proposal?

Fans of John Rawls's conception of distributive justice were especially appalled by Walzer's concessions to caste systems, seeing that Rawls's system is designed to secure, among other things, the best possible set of goods for the least advantaged position in society. Comparing Rawls's difference principle with Walzer's admission that he might have to condone caste systems seemed to make the choice clear, especially to those to the middle and left of the political spectrum. Which system to endorse: one calling for individual rights to liberty and equality of opportunity, set within a social context ensuring that the least advantaged position is the best it can be, *or* one wherein individual rights are absent and the only guarantee against gross inequality and systemic deprivation is the hope that one lives in a culture where such things are not broadly endorsed? If you were an 'untouchable', would you rather live in Rawls's, or Walzer's, ideal society? Which option seems more fair? In my view, it is a fact of some irony that, for Walzer the socialist, there are no distributive guarantees for the worst-off in certain cultures.[41]

Distribution and rights

Why does Walzer not frame the question of distributive justice in terms of rights? It is an important question that, at first, gets an odd response from him. In his earlier work, he submits that there is 'no sense' in 'multiplying rights' beyond the thin threshold of life and liberty to whatever else we might want in terms of social goods. I suppose it is important to resist 'rights inflation', limiting rights claims to that precious handful of objects we vitally need as human beings and that deserve such a weighty term as 'rights'. But it seems a leap to move from that observation to the conclusion that it makes 'no sense' to frame distributive justice in terms of rights. Indeed, Walzer's own conventionalism might have led him naturally down that road right from the start: it is very commonplace, in our culture, to speak of rights to social goods like employment opportunities, health care, access to political power, a minimal level of income, or welfare in the event of unemployment, and so on. Do such rights claims, in spite of their prevalence, do no work at all with regard to setting out the nature and limits of distributive justice?

Walzer resists rights talk about distributive justice for two additional reasons. The first, I think, is personal. He published *Spheres of Justice* in the early 1980s, and was keen on making an original statement with impact. Had he chosen the rights route, he would have had a hard time distinguishing himself, since the discourse on distributive justice at that time was dominated by two powerful accounts, both prominently featuring rights claims. These accounts, of course, were Rawls's *Theory of Justice* and Robert Nozick's *Anarchy, State and Utopia*. It is revealing that Walzer says that *Spheres of Justice* was written in response to Nozick, and so perhaps Nozick's right-wing rights talk, with its staunch individualism and ultra-minimal government, scared Walzer off rights talk, and on to the search for a more flexible, communal and left-leaning approach to distribution.[42] The second, more substantive, reason why Walzer resists framing distributive justice in terms of rights is that, if he went down that road, he might have feared that the line between his thin and thick accounts would become too blurred. A unitary approach to all questions of justice might then appear on the horizon, bringing with it what, for Walzer, would be disagreeable airs of objectivity, universality and lack of tolerance for pluralism.

In his more recent work, though, Walzer has come to more inclusive terms with rights, in part to deal with the caste system problem. He now stresses that, when he says that distributive justice is relative to cultural meanings, he means *'not relative simply* [his italics], for justice in distributions is a maximalist morality, and it takes shape along with, constrained by, a reiterated minimalism – the very idea of "justice", which provides a critical perspective'. He now appears to view caste systems as violating universally shared thin injunctions against violating human liberty. He also says that statements like, 'That's no way to treat a human being', have real force in arguments over distributive justice, in every cultural context. Finally, he points attention to the other 'constraint built into my "relativist" maxim', namely, the ban on radical coercion discussed in the last chapter. The underclass in a caste system, much like slaves in a slave society, 'endorse' the shared meanings which justify their oppression only as a result of radical coercion, and thus the endorsement carries with it no normative strength.[43]

Walzer is now of the more defensible view that 'there are minimalist versions' of distributive justice which limit what is permissible on the maximalist, culturally relative front. One of the most plausible of these minimalist versions involves universal rights claims, 'the minimal rights of all', in particular those to membership in some human community, to 'security and welfare', and to whatever is defined as a need within the community one is attached to. We are all entitled, through thin justice, to claim as a matter of right an equal distribution of such crucial social goods.[44] Which exact set of goods is referred to, though, in this terribly abstract list is not entirely clear. For instance, is access to housing, or to clean water, or to some leisure time, a right under the rubric of welfare? Is gun ownership part of the right to security? The role of rights in distributive justice has been only very recently, and just barely, recognized by Walzer; he has yet to detail either its extent or content.

Back home

This returns us, much as the earth moves ever round the sun, back to Walzer's core interest in human communities. Walzer's references to community, to the centrality of the state, and even to identity and self-understanding, naturally make one mindful of the philosophical heritage of Hegel.[45] While Walzer only sparingly cites Hegel, he does share substantive motifs with the controversial and influential German philosopher. Like Hegel, Walzer views self-understanding, identity and recognition from others as key elements in political life, indeed in human existence more broadly conceived. At the close of *Spheres of Justice*, for example, he comments that '[m]utual respect and a shared self-respect are the deep strengths of complex equality, and together they are the source of its possible endurance'. A society which permits domination and tyranny is a society which is at odds with the value of self-respect, and thus not only normatively deficient but perhaps also factually unstable over the long term. He also refers approvingly to the work of Charles Taylor, a well-known contemporary exponent of Hegelian themes in political philosophy, especially the so-called 'politics of recognition', which emphasize the maintenance of plurality and cultural difference within autonomous political structures that all agents acknowledge as legitimate, natural and healthy.[46]

Like Hegel, Walzer emphasizes the active, constitutive role that ideas and values play in life, and that one cannot meaningfully speak of things like justice, whether in distributions or in war, outside the flow of history. Social goods, he insists, do not come with pre-packaged purposes or values to them: we imbue them with purpose and values through our processes of creating them, using them, telling stories and making arguments about their proper role in our lives. 'People conceive and create goods', he stresses, 'which they then distribute among themselves.' And it is not merely goods which we create and conceive, on which we deploy our constitutive powers of thought, but our personal identities themselves: '[m]en and women take on concrete identities because of the way they conceive and create, and then possess and employ, social goods.' History, in this sense, may indeed for Walzer be about a process of thinking and self-understanding, though of course of ourselves and not of the mysteriously metaphysical *Geist* of Hegel. Walzer refers vaguely to 'a certain attitude of mind' underlying his theory of justice, namely, one of a 'decent respect for the opinions of mankind'. 'Not the opinions of this or that individual', mind you, but 'those deeper opinions that are reflections in individuals' minds, shaped also by individual thought, of the social meanings that constitute our common life'.[47]

The reference to 'our common life' makes one mindful of the largest shared motif between Hegel and Walzer: the understanding of social life in general, and of politics in particular, as being rooted in a particular state, in a concrete community at a particular place and time, thoroughly contextualized in the flow of historical events. For Walzer, the political community is 'the appropriate setting' for his theory of justice because 'it is the closest we can come to a world of common meanings. Language, history and culture come together . . . to produce a collective consciousness.' 'The sharing of sensibilities and intuitions among the members of a historical community', he says, 'is a fact of life.' We recall his remarks, from the last chapter, that we all inescapably perceive and interpret from where we are, and where we are is always a matter of belonging to a political community. In this community, we receive our earliest ethical education, we feel our first emotional responses, and eventually we frame our first considered arguments regarding the world and how it should be shaped. We are, as a matter of fact, not merely physically and emotionally but even cognitively rooted in a particular community, or at least a finite set of communities. We have a point of view, with a definite orientation. Furthermore, for Walzer as for Hegel this rootedness is a happy fact, since it implies belonging, recognition and membership with one's fellows. It orders one's place in the universe, in the best sense of providing a home, a familiar place from which to start out in life.

Walzer's valuation of the role that concrete and historical communities occupy in our lives helps illuminate further his differences with Rawls. Rawls, of course, models his theory of justice as a problem to be solved through the thought experiment of individual persons making self-interested rational choices under highly idealized, and utterly ahistorical, conditions. History and current political affiliation, Rawls would say, are irrelevant to the moral point of view. They are mere contingent facts, not abiding moral principles. History and membership are parochial things which we must put aside if we are to access the appropriate mind-set of justice as fairness: paying attention to them can only result in importing into our negotiations elements which will poison the social contract and slant the results.

Other than philosophy, the two disciplines which Rawls draws upon are economics and psychology, whereas for Walzer the comparable disciplines are history and anthropology. Walzer believes we cannot carry moral and political discourse so far that we abstract utterly from the kinds of creatures we obviously are: not merely self-interested rational agents but also contingent social animals who have perspectives and who belong to particular groups which have histories and shared meanings. Whatever the convergences that may exist between the methods of invention and interpretation, it is a clear and substantive divergence between Rawls and Walzer that, for one, history and community attachment are allowed no appeal, whereas for the other, they are the necessary context, without which political argumentation and struggle lack all reality and bite.

We will see, throughout the course of this study, that it is probably impossible to overstate the significance and resonance of community for Walzer's social philosophy. This is not to say that he is a 'communitarian' in the sense that he consistently privileges collective goals – like public welfare, or the preservation of cultural tradition – over individual rights and personal freedom of choice. Such a claim would be not merely an exaggeration but a falsification. Walzer is keen to defend both 'the politics of difference and, at the same time ... a certain sort of universalism' which affords all individual persons basic protections.[48] Hence his distinction between thick and thin moralities, accessible through interpretation and inextricably interwoven, though with application to different questions and issues. It is relevant to note here, by way of example, that Walzer does not believe that communities should resort to war so as to fire the hearts of patriots and solidify national identity through violent contrast with an alien 'other'. Much of Walzer's just war theory, we will shortly see, is concerned with protecting individual human rights, regardless of national membership, when political communities come into armed conflict. And, of course, we have just seen that even in distributive justice, Walzer feels compelled to impose constraints on communal choice in the interests of individual protection, owing to 'the very idea of "justice" itself'.[49]

Though it is false that Walzer is a communitarian in the above sense, it is true that Walzer is not a 'cosmopolitan' in the sense that particular and concrete communities are to be ignored, or abstracted from, or consistently devalued, in the face of claims of personal freedom or a universal super-state with global reach. More on the question of global governance in chapter 7; for now, we note with emphasis that Walzer is committed to cultural difference and communal plurality, believing that respect for our identity as political animals rooted in time and place need not come at the price of disrespect for our most private projects and personal protections. The relationship between the self and the state looms as one of the largest questions for Walzer, and in a sense all of his political theory is devoted to exploring its contours and appreciating its full import. It is a relationship which will be touched upon, and discussed, numerous times throughout the rest of this work.

'The primary good', Walzer suggests, 'that we distribute to one another is membership in some human community.' Contrary to his earlier comments, this seems one essential, natural and foremost good for all of us. For non-members are outsiders in the worst sense of the word: desperate nomads with 'no guarantees of anything'. 'Statelessness', he writes, is 'a condition of infinite danger.' It is only in community contexts that we can participate in the distribution of social goods, that we can engage in the processes of conception and creation that not only provide for our material subsistence but also help fashion our own personal identity. 'The deepest purpose of the state', he insists, 'is defence', providing reliable security guarantees, both to its citizens individually as well as to the communal life, or civil society, they share collectively. The state is *the* necessary condition for that provision of shared, socially recognized needs that Walzer views as both the hallmark and the pinnacle of a just political existence. This focus on the state's role as the defender, of both life and ways of life, makes for a natural transition to Walzer's just war theory, in which this role is tested and examined on a number of important fronts.[50]

Summary

This chapter sought to complete the discussion of Walzer's general theory of justice before focusing on his acclaimed just war theory. If we apply the method of interpretation to questions of justice, Walzer believes that we will come to see that we have commitments to both thin and thick kinds of morality. Thin morality is universally shared, and enshrines a set of human rights: rights to life and liberty, rights not to be subjected to things like murder, torture and tyranny. Thin morality is neither objective nor does it form the moral truth; it is simply that moral code we witness everyone endorsing. Thin morality is the minimal code shared by all the world's maximal codes. Just war theory is part of thin morality, and it regulates our conduct with all humanity. Distributive justice, by contrast, is part of maximal morality, which is culturally relative. We looked at Walzer's theory of distributive justice in considerable detail, and critically, for two reasons: to discern the interaction between thick and thin morality more fully; and to understand Walzer's own political commitments. We know now that his commitments combine a respect for cultural difference worldwide with a preference for democratic socialism back home, and that they mix a concern with individual human rights everywhere with the maintenance of some degree of national pluralism and rootedness in history and political membership.

3 • Walzer on Alternatives to Just War Theory

It is common to criticize authors for devoting too much time to refuting rival theories and too little time to developing their own. Walzer has incurred the lesser fault of devoting too much time to his own ideas and too little time to reflection on alternatives.

Douglas Lackey[1]

Before exploring the substance of Walzer's just war theory, we should consider his most controversial presuppositions. The first is that the thin, universally shared moral code commits us to the idea that wars can sometimes be just. The second is that this just war code, when best interpreted, enshrines human rights protection. The first claim has been called into question by competing doctrines of realism and pacifism, the second by rival conceptions of justice in wartime, particularly utilitarianism.

Realism's challenge

Walzer's just war theory is rooted in his conventionalist methodology, according to which we must examine, and best explain, our shared public discourse on the ethics of war and peace. Walzer acknowledges that, for as long as there has been talk about the ethics of war and peace, there have been those who have 'derided such talk', calling it a 'charade', insisting that 'war lies beyond (or beneath) moral judgment'.[2] These doubters are usually called 'realists'. Prominent classical realists often mentioned include Thucydides, Machiavelli and Hobbes. Modern realists include Hans Morgenthau, George Kennan, Reinhold Niebuhr and Henry Kissinger, as well as so-called 'neo-realists', such as Kenneth Waltz and Robert Keohane. While realism is a complex and often sophisticated doctrine, its core propositions express a strong suspicion about applying moral concepts, like justice, to the conduct of international affairs. Realists believe that moral concepts should be employed neither as descriptions of, nor as prescriptions for, state behaviour on the international plane. Realists emphasize power and security issues, the need for a state to maximize its expected self-interest and, above all, their view of the international arena as a kind of anarchy, in which the will to power enjoys primacy. Referring specifically to war, realists believe that it is an intractable part of an anarchical world system; that it ought to be resorted to only if it makes sense in terms of national self-interest; and that, once war has begun, a state ought to do whatever it can to win. So if adhering to the rules of 'just war theory' hinders a state in this regard, it should disregard them and stick steadfastly to its fundamental interests in power and security.[3]

Walzer says realists view war as 'a world apart', where 'self-interest and necessity prevail. Here men and women do what they must to save themselves and their communities, and morality and law have no place.' '[R]ealism', he observes, 'imposes no moral requirements.' Just war theory, designed to limit war's destructiveness and to protect rights during armed conflict, is viewed by realists as mere 'idle chatter, a mask of noise with which we conceal . . . the awful truth'. This truth is that we are essentially 'fearful, self-concerned, driven, murderous', and war brings all these ugly traits to the surface. If realists endorse any universal rule at all with regard to wartime behaviour, it is the old proverb, 'All's fair in love and war.' In war's desperate circumstances, 'anything goes.'[4]

Thucydides' 'Melian Dialogue' offers a frank expression of realism. This memorable, well-known piece describes a historical meeting between Athenian generals and the leaders of Melos, a Greek island. The expansionist Athenians want to annex Melos and supplement their power, the Melians to preserve their independence and protect their own way of life. The generals suggest that 'all fine talk of justice' be put aside and that everyone stare reality square in the face. This reality is that 'they that have odds of power exact as much as they can, and the weak yield to such conditions as they can get'. Walzer encapsulates this view in a maxim of realism: 'The narrow necessity of inter-state politics [is] reign or be subject.' The Melians refused to play ball, citing their right as an independent and peaceful community not to be invaded, and were subsequently crushed by the Athenians.[5]

Walzer suggests that the systematic amorality of realism, exemplified in the dialogue, is grounded in three propositions: (1) there is no freedom to choose morally in the international arena; (2) moral argument with regard to international affairs is meaningless; and (3) any link between morality and armed force will result in greater destruction than an amoral stance. Walzer undercuts the first realist proposition by insisting that, in Marx's words, it is 'a piece of mystification'. Appealing to the necessity of *realpolitik* is more rhetorical than real. Walzer points out that the day-to-day experience of international affairs is more a matter of strategic risk-taking than it is of succumbing to strict necessity. The reality on the ground of global politics is not constant confrontation with the dark decision between survival and extinction but, rather, the more familiar choice between various policy options, each facing its own trade-off between risk and reward. States are much more free to choose between alternative courses of action than realists contend. This means that states are free, should they choose, to act on the basis of moral commitments and conceptions of justice. The Athenian generals, for example, were not actually forced to 'reign or be subject'; rather, they carried out a deliberate policy of aggressive expansion that was authorized by the Athenian assembly. The crushing of the Melians was not a 'necessity of nature' but rather the brutal outcome of a free collective decision by a group of Athenians giddy with power and lusting for more. Walzer notes that Thucydides omits these prior debates and decisions in his Dialogue. Walzer suggests that war is the inevitable product neither of the structure of nature nor of the international system; rather, war is 'a human action, purposive and premeditated, for whose effects someone is responsible'.[6]

Walzer revisits this last point in subsequent work. He cites Edmund Wilson who, in a vivid image, likens interstate relations to relations between a sea slug and surrounding organisms. Just as a sea slug devours all it can, so states will 'ingurgitate' all they can, animated by 'the exact same instincts'. Walzer denies this realist description, insisting that there is nothing like what we might call the monocausality of state behaviour in terms of pursuing power. If we look at the history of states, Walzer suggests that 'we will not get anything like uniform voraciousness'. States 'behave very differently according to their . . . understandings of themselves and their place in the world'. The realist conception of state motivation in terms of a primal drive for dominance is not the best interpretation of the phenomena, since it ignores the constitutive, Hegelian role that reflection upon meaning plays in our lives. Walzer claims that a state with only self-preservation and self-assertion as its goals would not last long. A collective association can endure only if there is a shared 'commitment to the kind of belief or value that might inspire and sustain a common life and lift it out of mere existence'. 'It isn't really prudent', he says, 'to assume the malign intent of one's neighbours; it is merely cynical, an example of the worldly wisdom which no one lives by or could live by.' We have, of course, to tend to our elemental Hobbesian claims to physical security. But this is not all we want, nor all we can expect. Our fuller desires and hopes reside in inhabiting a community in which our values are reflected, in which we enjoy equal membership and fellow feeling. We do not merely desire personal security, or even political expansion; we also want a place we can call our own, a political home.[7]

There is a tight link between realism's first two propositions, as outlined above: if there is no freedom to choose morally in foreign policy, then appealing to justice in wartime is beside the point. Walzer paraphrases the realists: real talk is interest talk. All discourse about morality and justice refers to nothing real in the international arena, which is a domain given over completely to the pursuit of power and self-interest. At best, moral discourse about international relations is itself a disguised play for more power, usually employed by less powerful states to constrain their more forceful neighbours. Morality, realists often say in their more Nietzschean moments, is for the weak; it's the only card left for the powerless to play in the harsh realm of global politics. Walzer insists, in response, that '[w]e don't have to translate moral talk into interest talk in order to understand it; morality refers in its own way to the real world'. The publicly shared discourse we have about international affairs, as a matter of fact, commits us to such concepts as the possibility of an unjust use of force. It commits us to telling 'a very special kind of story' about such a use of force, employing vocabulary and evidence that others can make sense of and evaluate. He makes his case eloquently:

> I am going to assume throughout that we really do act within a moral world; that particular decisions really are difficult, problematic, agonizing, and that this has to do with the structure of that world; that language reflects the moral world and gives us access to it; and finally that our understanding of the vocabulary is sufficiently common and stable so that shared judgments are possible.[8]

Walzer's contention is that the realist either misunderstands the nature of our shared discourse on war or understands it, yet prefers to subvert it. One reason why a realist might do the latter is, like the Athenian generals, to rationalize behaviour which would roundly be condemned by the judgements we share. 'The proverb, all's fair, is invoked in defence of conduct that appears to be unfair.' 'The moral posture of mankind', Walzer argues, 'is not well represented by that popular proverb about love and war.' After all, he says, 'aggressors can be realists, too'.[9] Intriguingly, Walzer claims that this strategy of subverting our shared discourse on war is, in fact, indirect proof of its very existence and import. 'The clearest evidence for the stability of our values over time', he suggests, 'is the unchanging character of the lies soldiers and statesmen tell. They lie in order to justify themselves, and so they describe for us the lineaments of justice.' Walzer notes that rarely in history have there been those who have spoken with the bluntness of the Athenian generals. The reason why, he supposes, is precisely because realism is not generally recognized as the best interpretation of the ethics of war and peace: '[T]he truth is that one of the things most of us want, even in war, is to act or to seem to act morally. And we want that, most simply, because we know what morality means.' Thus, the amorality of realism runs afoul of the fact that 'we are still committed to a moral world'. The norm here is not to appeal to realism but rather to justify one's behaviour in terms of our shared wartime judgements, even when one's behaviour fails to live up to them.[10]

Walzer is the first to admit that, often, states and individuals 'lack the courage' of their own moral judgements. We often fail to abide by the principles of our own socially constructed idealism. Any cursory glance at the history of warfare reveals how often we betray the war convention Walzer asserts we share. But, Walzer insists, it does not refute the claim that there exists such a convention, 'rich with moral meaning', which constitutes a thin and universal understanding of how wars should be evaluated. The cursory glance does not prove, as the realists argue, that there is nothing to say about the ethics of war and peace, that we can neither praise nor blame state conduct during wartime and thus would be better off remaining silent. For as a matter of fact we do not remain silent with regard to wartime judgements, we can indeed make sense of such judgements (even when we do not share them or meet them) and, moreover, we understand what criteria must be fulfilled for a good judgement in this regard. These criteria are best seen as the rules of just war theory. A just war, for Walzer, is 'one that it is morally urgent to win . . .

[c]ritical values are at stake: political independence, communal liberty, human life.' And the goals of a just war include 'resistance . . . [and] reasonable prevention' of precisely the kind of violent aggression displayed by the Athenians in the 'Melian Dialogue'.[11]

Further evidence of the weakness of realism's claim that moral talk in wartime is meaningless concerns the similarities between morality and military strategy. Both discourses are devoted to evaluating courses of action, enabling justification and criticism. Both discourses offer firm, action-guiding rules, such as (morality) 'Do not directly attack civilians' and (strategy) 'Do not launch a frontal attack on a protected position'. Both discourses presuppose a shared vocabulary, appeal to public evidence for support and recognize the risks attending alternative courses of action. Both discourses presuppose that the alternatives in question are real and not merely apparent: the actors are genuinely confronted with free choices. Both offer norms for action which are frequently ignored on the ground during the heat of battle but this does not detract from the intelligibility of the norms, nor even (perhaps) the overall commitment to adhere to them. In light of these profound similarities between morality and strategy, Walzer asks rhetorically, how can the realist deny the salience of one while emphasizing the import of the other? How can the realist exalt the importance of smart strategy during wartime while shouting down those who dare to forward moral arguments about military conduct?[12]

Even though Walzer denies the first two of realism's core propositions, he does believe that the third constitutes 'a powerful argument'. This argument, once more, is that it is a mistake to link justice with war because doing so can only increase war's destructiveness. Better to have a detached, amoral, even cynical understanding of the use of international armed force: it will then be easier to control than a process of violence fuelled by the fanatical pursuit of some conception of justice. Just war theorists, on this understanding, 'sow justice and reap death'.[13] Though this is a relevant and disturbing insight, Walzer argues that it is animated most deeply not by realist amorality but rather by genuine moral concern: 'The remedy the realists proposed was to give up justice and aim at more modest outcomes. The remedy I propose instead is to understand better the justice at which we cannot help aiming.' The aim of our shared wartime discourse must be justice, but this does not mean that we are committed, as the saying goes, to seeing justice done though the heavens fall. It does not commit us to fighting unlimited crusades in the pursuit of Pure Justice. Just wars, Walzer stresses, 'are limited wars; there are moral reasons for the statesmen and soldiers who fight them to be prudent and realistic.' Such moral reasons include, perhaps above all, the need to minimize human suffering.[14]

Many have praised Walzer's refutation of realism as one of the most trenchant on offer. I concur with this judgement; however, I believe that it applies mainly to the descriptive form of realism. Descriptive realism is the claim that states, as a matter of fact, do not (or cannot) behave morally, and thus moral discourse surrounding interstate conduct is empty, the product of a category mistake. Prescriptive realism, though, need not be rooted in any form of descriptive realism. Prescriptive realism is the claim that a state ought *(prudential* 'ought') to behave amorally in the international arena. A state should, for prudence's sake, adhere to an amoral policy of smart self-regard in international affairs. Walzer seems blind to this distinction, and it shows. For as soon as we see it, we realize that Walzer's argument against realism's third proposition is weak. For the concern this proposition expresses, about linking morality with armed force, need not be thought of itself as being moral, as Walzer claims. The proposition can be recast as a purely prudential concern: don't link justice with warfare because then the war will get out of control, thus making it harder to secure one's interests. A different, better argument needs to be offered here by a just war theorist, mindful of the distinction.[15]

One such argument would be the following. Prescriptive realism likes to portray itself as being more sober and stabilizing to the international system than any morality-based account, since it is based on rational choice and not on hot feelings about justice. But consider this. According to prescriptive realism, every state should be a self-interested entity keen on forwarding its own power and security. We can see, on this basis, how prescriptive realism might recommend more aggressive foreign policies – perhaps even more wars – than, say, a justice-based account of foreign policy. This is especially the case for a powerful state, which has less to lose and more to gain, in relative terms, by forcefully exercising its influence. This is not merely an idle thought experiment; even a cursory glance at the historical record shows the deleterious consequences of states basing their mutual dealings solely on the basis of national egoism and the strategic struggle for power. Indeed, to the extent to which prescriptive realism recommends national egoism – and to the extent to which such egoism is the cause of the assurance problem at the heart of the anarchical world system – prescriptive realism appears itself to undermine the security of the interstate system. This is a version of the familiar prisoner's dilemma: co-operation in the solution of a common problem predictably leads to greater benefits than the narrow pursuit of egoism. Yet, in the absence of assurance or mutual trust between the actors, the rational choice they will each make will be the egoistic option, thereby placing them all in a worse-off position. Far from saving us from morally charged military adventurism, prescriptive realism may well condemn us to another kind of military adventurism, a prudential or strategic one, whose costs would seem not predictably less than those of the putative first kind. So, prescriptive realism has serious questions of its own to face with regard to whether adhering to it would really produce better consequences than not.[16]

Walzer's failure to appreciate the pluralism in realism accounts for his failure to see how a prescriptive realist might, in the end, actually endorse international rules much like those offered by just war theory. These rules include: 'Wars should only be fought in response to aggression'; and 'During war, non-combatants should not be directly targeted with lethal violence'. Of course, the reason why a prescriptive realist might endorse such rules would be very different from the reasons offered by the just war theorist: the latter would talk about abiding moral values whereas the former would refer to useful rules which help establish expectations of behaviour and solve co-ordination problems, and to which prudent bargainers would consent. Just war rules, the prescriptive realist might claim, do not have independent moral purchase on the attention of states. These rules are what Lackey calls 'salient equilibria', stable conventions limiting war's destructiveness which all prudent states can agree on, assuming general compliance. Prescriptive realists might go farther and assert that the reason why so many just war rules have been codified into international law is not so much owing to the resonance of our shared moral discourse about war but rather because international law is the product of rational-choice bargaining sessions between self-interested state parties. Which is the best, thickest and most robust interpretation of the phenomena?[17]

Pacifism's challenge

While Walzer's response to (descriptive) realism is strong, his response to pacifism is less satisfying. He admits this, conceding that a full response to pacifism 'would require another book' whereas his response is a mere six-page 'Afterword', a 'partial and tentative analysis' appended to *Just and Unjust Wars*. It is interesting that, since *Wars* first appeared in 1977, Walzer has chosen not to shoulder the burdens of a full response.[18]

Pacifism is the view that no war is, or could be, just. As Jenny Teichman says, 'Pacifism is anti-war-ism.' Pacifists categorically oppose war, though their reasons vary. An extreme version eschews any kind of violence (especially killing) as an intrinsic wrong, whereas a more moderate version contends that it is *the kind and scale* of violence (especially killing) which war involves that cannot be justified. So, unlike most realists, pacifists do believe that it is both possible and meaningful to apply ethical judgement to international relations. In this they agree with just war theorists. But pacifists differ from just war theorists by contending that such judgement commits us never to resort to war.[19]

Pacifism poses a problem for Walzer's conventionalist methodology. It seems easier for him to point out that our socially constructed idealism is at odds with realism than it is for him to show that such idealism does not commit us to a total ban on warfare. Are we not most deeply moved by the dream of a non-violent world order in which interstate disputes are resolved peacefully, through negotiation or judicial processes? We now realize just how much weight the concept of 'the best interpretation' bears in Walzer's world-view. Walzer's main objection to realism is that it is insufficiently descriptive of our deepest values. We remain committed to morality even in the midst of war. But, he insists, these moral rules do not commit us to pacifism. Why not? Walzer responds that pacifism's idealism is excessively optimistic. In other words, pacifism lacks realism. More precisely, the ideals contained in our shared discourse on war presuppose that the non-violent world imagined by the pacifist is not actually attainable, at least for the foreseeable future. Since 'ought implies can', the set of 'oughts' we are committed to must express a moral outlook on war less utopian in nature. While we are committed to morality in wartime, we are forced to concede that, sometimes in the real world, resorting to war can be morally justified.[20]

This familiar objection to pacifism is by no means the only one employed by just war theorists. Another is that pacifism should be rejected because, by failing to resist international aggression with effective means, it ends up rewarding aggression and failing to protect people who need it. Walzer appears to agree with this, suggesting obliquely that pacifists 'have to recognize and accept the nonpacific results of trying to accommodate states like Saddam Hussein's Iraq'.[21] Pacifists reply to these just war arguments by contending that we do not need to resort to war in order to protect people and punish aggression effectively. In the event of an armed invasion by an aggressor state, an organized and committed campaign of non-violent civil disobedience – perhaps combined with international diplomatic and economic sanctions – would be just as effective as war in expelling the aggressor, with much less destruction of lives and property. After all, the pacifist might say, no invader could possibly maintain its grip on the conquered nation in light of such systematic isolation, non-cooperation and non-violent resistance. How could it work the factories, harvest the fields, or run the stores, when everyone would be striking? How could it maintain the will to keep the country in the face of crippling economic sanctions and diplomatic censure from the international community? And so on.[22]

Though one cannot exactly disprove this pacifist proposition – since it is a counter-factual thesis – there are powerful reasons to agree with John Rawls that such is 'an unworldly view' to hold. For, as Walzer points out, the effectiveness of this campaign of civil disobedience relies on the scruples of the invading aggressor. But what if the aggressor is brutal, ruthless? What if, faced with civil disobedience, the invader 'cleanses' the area of the native population, and then imports its own people from back home? What if, faced with economic sanctions and diplomatic censure from a neighbouring country, the invader decides to invade *it*, too? We have some indication from history, particularly that of Nazi Germany, that such pitiless tactics are effective at breaking the will of people to resist. The defence of our lives and rights may well, against such invaders, require the use of political violence. Under such conditions, Walzer says, adherence to pacifism would amount to a 'disguised form of surrender'.[23]

Pacifists respond to this accusation of 'unworldliness' by citing what they believe are real-world examples of effective non-violent resistance to aggression. Examples mentioned include Mahatma Ghandi's campaign to drive the British imperial regime out of India in the late 1940s and Martin Luther King Jr's civil rights crusade in the 1960s on behalf of African-Americans. Walzer replies curtly that there is no evidence that non-violent resistance has ever, of itself, succeeded. This may be rash on his part, though it is clear that Britain's own exhaustion after the Second World War, for example, had much to do with the evaporation of its empire. Walzer's main counter-argument against these pacifist counter-examples is that they only underline his main point: that effective non-violent resistance depends upon the scruples of those it is aimed against. It was only because the British and the Americans had some scruples, and were moved by the determined idealism of the non-violent protesters, that they acquiesced in their demands. But aggressors will not always be so moved. A tyrant like Hitler, for example, might interpret non-violent resistance as weakness, deserving contemptuous crushing. 'Non-violent defense', Walzer suggests, 'is no defense at all against tyrants or conquerors ready to adopt such measures.' The idea of an effective 'war without weapons', much less a world without war, is for Walzer a 'messianic dream'. For the foreseeable future, and in the real world we all inhabit, the best interpretation of our shared discourse on the ethics of war and peace is that of just war theory, which is committed to an effective yet principled use of defensive armed force in the face of aggression. The constraints on violence established by just war theory are, in fact, the necessary conditions for the more peaceful world which pacifists mistakenly believe is already within sight. 'The restraint of war', Walzer declares, 'is the beginning of peace.'[24]

Sensible as Walzer's remarks are, they remain quite narrow, by no means constituting an all-things-considered refutation of pacifism. Generally, there are two kinds of modern secular pacifism to consider: (1) a more consequentialist form of pacifism (or CP), which maintains that the benefits accruing from war can never outweigh the costs of fighting it; and (2) a more deontological form of pacifism (or DP), which contends that the very activity of war is intrinsically wrong, since it violates the foremost duties of justice, such as not killing human beings. Most common amongst contemporary secular pacifists, such as Robert Holmes, is a doctrine which attempts to combine both CP and DP. Walzer fails to make this distinction, much less offer sustained arguments against both branches. All his energies are spent on the single issue of the effectiveness of non-violent resistance to aggression.[25]

What arguments might a just war theorist, on behalf of Walzer, employ to overcome CP and DP? A just war theorist might, for a start, focus on the relationship in CP between consequentialism and the denial of killing. Pacifism in either form places overriding value on respecting human life, notably through its injunction against killing. But this value seems to rest uneasily with consequentialism, for there is nothing inherent to consequentialism which bans killing as such. There is no absolute rule, or side-constraint, that one ought never to kill another person, or that nations ought never to deploy lethal armed force in war. With consequentialism, it is always a matter of considering the latest costs and benefits, of choosing the best option amongst feasible alternatives. Consequentialism therefore leaves conceptual space open to the claim that under *these* conditions, at *this* time and place, and given *these* alternatives, killing and/or war appears permissible. After all, what if killing x people (say, soldiers in an aggressive army) appears the best option if we are to save the lives of $x + n$ people (say, fellow citizens who would perish under the brutal heel of an unchecked aggressor)? It is at least conceivable that a quick and decisive resort to war could prevent even greater killing and devastation in the future. So it seems problematic for the *consequentialist* pacifist, whose principles exhibit a profound abhorrence for killing people, to be willing in such a scenario to allow an even greater number of people to be killed by acquiescing in the violence of others less scrupulous. These are two telling points: CP does not, of itself, ground the categorical rejection of killing and war which is the essence of pacifism; and CP is open to counter-examples which question whether consequentialism would reject killing and war at all under certain conditions. Consequentialism might even, in a particular case, go so far as to recommend war under certain conditions.[26]

Casting doubt on DP is a complicated procedure, and one I have attempted more fully elsewhere.[27] Only a sketch of plausible just war arguments can here be offered on Walzer's behalf. The first question to ask is: which foremost duty does DP understand as being violated by warfare? If the DP response is the duty not to kill another human being, then the contention can be made that this is by no means uncontroversial. Consider the most obvious counter-example: aggressor A attacks B for no defensible reason, posing a serious threat to B's life. Some would suggest, in good faith, that B is not duty-bound not to kill A if that seems necessary to stop A's aggression. Indeed, they would argue that B may kill A in legitimate self-defence. The DP pacifist, however, might reply that extending to B moral permission to kill A, even in self-defence, violates the human rights of A. He might contend that just war theory merely compounds the wrongness of the situation by paradoxically permitting lethal force to stop lethal force.

One just war rejoinder to this DP contention is this: B does no wrong whatsoever – violates no human rights – by responding to A's aggression with lethal force if required. Why does B do nothing wrong? First, it is A who is responsible for forcing B to choose between her own life and rights and those of A. We can hardly blame B for choosing her own. For if she does not choose her own, she loses an enormous amount, perhaps everything. And it is patently unreasonable to expect creatures like us to suffer catastrophic loss by default. Consider also the issue of fairness: if B is not allowed to use lethal force, if necessary, against A in the event of A's aggression, then B loses everything while A loses nothing. Indeed, A gains whatever object he desired in violating or killing B. Such would seem an unfair reward of awful behaviour. Finally, B's having rights at all provides her with an implicit entitlement to use those means necessary to secure her rights, including the use of force in the face of a serious physical threat. These powerful considerations of responsibility, reasonableness, fairness and implicit entitlement come together in support of the just war claims that: B may respond with needed lethal force to A's initial aggression; B does no wrong in doing so; it would be wrong to prohibit B's doing so; and A bears all of the blame for the situation.[28]

DP pacifists are not, at this point, out of options. Holmes, for example, suggests that the foremost duty of justice violated by war is *not* the duty not to kill aggressors, but rather the duty not to kill innocent, non-aggressive human beings. To be innocent here means to have done nothing which would justify being harmed or killed; in particular, it means not constituting a serious threat to the lives and rights of other people. It is this sense of innocence that just war theory invokes when it claims that civilians should not be directly attacked during wartime. Even if civilians support the war effort politically, or even in terms of their personal attitudes towards the war, they clearly do not pose serious threats to others. Only armed forces, and the political-industrial-technological complexes which guide them, constitute serious threats against which threatened communities may respond in kind. Civilian populations, just war theory surmises, are morally off-limits as targets. Holmes contends that this just war rule of non-combatant immunity can never be satisfied. For all possible wars in this world – given the nature of military technology and tactics, the heat of battle, and the limits of human knowledge and self-discipline – involve the killing of innocents, thus defined. We know this to be true from history and have no good reason for expecting otherwise in the future. But the killing of innocents, Holmes says, is always unjust. So no war can ever be fought justly, regardless of the nature of the goal sought after, such as national defence from an aggressor's attack. The very activities needed to fight wars are intrinsically corrupt, and cannot be redeemed by the putative justice of the ends they are aimed at. How is a just war theorist to respond to this DP challenge?[29]

Some respond by casting doubt on the concept of innocence in wartime. But a just war theorist subscribing to the rule of non-combatant immunity will neither want, nor logically be at liberty, to argue in this fashion. Despite all the ambiguities regarding who exactly is 'innocent' during wartime, Walzer seems correct to maintain this concept. It is hard to see, for example, how infants could be anything other than innocent during a war, and as such entitled not to be made the object of direct and intentional attack. It is only those who, in Walzer's phrase, are 'involved in harming us' – i.e. those who pose serious threats to our lives and rights – that we can justly target in a direct and intentional fashion during wartime.[30]

The more appropriate just war response invokes, alongside Walzer, the doctrine of double effect (or DDE). The DDE, invented by Aquinas, is a complex idea which will be fully examined during chapter 5's look at *jus in bello*. For now, we note Walzer's observation that, in spite of its apparent technicality, the DDE is 'closely related to our ordinary ways of thinking about moral life'. The DDE assumes the following scenario: agent X is considering performing an action T, which X foresees will produce both good/moral/just effects J and bad/immoral/unjust effects U. The DDE permits X to perform T *only if*: (1) T is otherwise permissible; (2) X only intends J and not U; (3) U is not a means to J; and (4) the goodness of J is worth, or is proportionately greater than, the badness of U. Assume now that X is a country and T is war. The government of X, contemplating war in response to an attack by aggressor country Y, foresees that, should it embark on war to defend itself, civilian casualties will result, probably in both X and Y. The DDE stipulates that X may launch into this defensive (and thus otherwise permissible) war only if: (1) X does not intend the resulting civilian casualties but rather aims only at defending itself and its people; (2) such casualties are not themselves the means whereby X's end is achieved; and (3) the importance of X's defending itself and its people from Y's aggression is proportionately greater than the badness of the resulting civilian casualties. The DDE, in Walzer's mind, refers to common shared principles regarding the moral importance of intent, of appealing to better expected consequences, and insisting that bad should not be done so that good may follow.[31]

Just war theorists claim that civilians are not entitled to absolute immunity from attack during wartime. Civilians are owed neither more nor less than what Walzer calls 'due care' from the belligerent governments that they are not made casualties of the war action in question. 'Due care', we will see, involves fighting only in certain ways, applying limited force to specific targets. But does this just war claim simply beg the question against the latest DP principle? DPs insist on absolute immunity for civilians, which in our world would result in banning warfare, whereas just war theorists, acknowledging the threat, seem to dodge it by redefining the immunity to which civilians are entitled, demoting it to mere 'due care'. Despite appearances, it is not question-begging but principled disagreement which roots the difference. Just war theorists will argue that civilians cannot be entitled to absolute immunity because that would outlaw all warfare. But outlawing all warfare would ignore both the responsibility for interstate aggression and the implicit entitlement of a state to use necessary means (including armed force) to secure the lives and rights of its citizens from serious and standard threats to them. In the real world, it is neither reasonable nor fair to require a political community not to avail itself of the most effective means available for resisting an aggressive invasion which threatens the lives and rights of its citizens. It is simply not reasonable to require a state to stand down while the aggression of another state wreaks havoc – murder and mayhem – upon its people.[32]

This is not a complete defeat for DP, merely a suggestion of how such defeat might be sought. In my view, DP constitutes the most formidable *moral* challenge to just war theory, including Walzer's.

Further consideration of these concepts, however, is best saved for our forthcoming discussion of Walzer's theory of right conduct during wartime. Suffice it for now to say that the DDE is the principle most frequently employed to defeat the DP pacifist's assertion that it is always wrong to kill innocent human beings. Just war theorists prefer to substitute, for this DP claim, the following proposition: what is always wrong, both in peace and war, is to kill innocent human beings *intentionally and deliberately*. Unintended, collateral civilian casualties can be excused during the prosecution of an otherwise just war, wherein the end is the repulsion of aggression and the means are aimed at legitimate military targets.

Utilitarianism's challenge

Walzer's just war work presupposes not only a rejection of both realism and pacifism but also a particular conception of justice. Emphatically and repeatedly, Walzer declares that this conception is non-utilitarian. His entire conception of wartime justice is an extended contrast between what he calls a utility-based account and a rights-based account.[33] Walzer suggests that

> the arguments we make about war are most fully understood (though other understandings are possible) as efforts to recognize and respect the rights of individual and associated men and women. The morality I shall expound is in its philosophical form a doctrine of human rights . . .

Though 'considerations of utility play into the structure at many points . . . they cannot account for it as a whole. Their part is secondary to that of rights; it is constrained by rights.' 'At every point', he concludes, 'the judgments we make [about war] are best accounted for if we regard life and liberty as something like absolute values.'[34]

While Walzer admits that he does not offer a complete account of human rights, he comments extensively on how a rights-based account of justice differs from a utility-based conception. Rights are side-constraints; they serve not as goals of action but, rather, as constraints on action during wartime. Rights block or ban wartime actions which utilitarianism might otherwise recommend. Walzer offers the following example. During the Second World War, the Free

French forces enlisted the support of Moroccan mercenaries and, in return for the latter's assistance during the Italian campaign, agreed among other things not to interfere with the Moroccans should they decide to rape some Italian women. Many women were raped as a result. Walzer contends that 'the argument for giving soldiers privileges of this sort is a utilitarian one'. The French were focused on securing their overall goal, which was driving the Nazis out of France. They mistakenly allowed the end to justify the means, and committed an injustice by making this deal with the Moroccan mercenaries. Walzer concludes:

> Rape is a crime, in war as in peace, because it violates the rights of the woman who is attacked. To offer her as bait to a mercenary soldier is to treat her as if she were not a person at all but a mere object, a prize or trophy of war. It is the recognition of her personality that shapes our judgment.[35]

Rights, Walzer observes, are 'a palpable feature of the moral world', deep-rooted in a universally shared conception of the human person. Rights 'cannot simply be set aside; nor can they be balanced, in utilitarian fashion, against this or that desirable outcome'. Indeed, when we are '[c]onfronted by those rights, we are not to calculate consequences, or figure relative risks, or compute probable casualties, but simply to stop short and turn aside'. Most clearly: 'rights and rules are intended to bar utilitarian calculation.' Though he never says so explicitly, we can infer that, for Walzer, human rights serve as firm, universal rules which instruct us on how we ought to treat the human person. 'Treatment' here refers to both commission and omission in action: both to what we should do, and what we should avoid doing, if we are to treat human beings in a minimally just fashion. Thus, for Walzer to say that we all have human rights to life and liberty is to say that the human person is owed, as a matter of minimal justice, treatment from others which does not violate either his physical security or his free space of personal choice. Since they are 'something like absolute', human rights remain intact *unless* the rights-holder violates the rights of others.[36]

Utilitarianism, by contrast, is about the maximization of utility in the world: the greatest happiness for the greatest number, as Bentham famously put it. Justice is about making the world as well-off, as pleasant, as possible. We must note that, by utilitarianism, Walzer really means classical utilitarianism: Bentham's unconstrained felicific calculus, constructed to enable legislators to govern so that they maximize the amount of net sensory pleasure in the world. Though this is hardly the only kind of utilitarianism, the opposition between it and a rights-based account of justice is crystal-clear. Rights stick in the gears of Bentham's hedonistic calculus; they stop the machine designed to produce the greatest happiness for the greatest number. Rights are deliberately structured to do so, in order to protect individual persons from threats like what Alexis de Tocqueville first labelled 'the tyranny of the majority'. Rights entitle individuals to a protected sphere of free action in which what they do does not have to be justified by its contribution to the world's overall happiness. Our ideas of personhood, Walzer suggests, mandate such a space of pure individual discretion and liberty, subject of course to reciprocity. But Bentham frowned upon any political proposal not demonstrably linked with the generation of the greatest possible amount of net sensory pleasure in the world. It was for this, and related, reasons that Bentham thought the idea of human rights not simply 'nonsense' but 'nonsense upon stilts'.[37]

Walzer sees things the other way round, casting doubt on utilitarianism's conception of wartime justice. A major flaw he discerns is that 'utilitarian calculations have indeed required the "punishing" of innocent people', whereas just war theory is designed so that deliberate violence against innocent people is always ruled out. Since classical utilitarianism has as its goal the greatest happiness for the greatest number, it may on occasion permit, or even recommend, actions which violate the rights of individual persons. Utilitarianism may call for extreme personal sacrifices for the sake of maximizing overall public utility. It may permit violent or punitive measures against persons who have done nothing to deserve such rough treatment. Walzer offers the controversial example of the atomic bombing of Japan in 1945.

Walzer believes the decision to drop the atomic bomb was unjust, and the product of utilitarian thinking. Truman reasoned that an American invasion of Japan to end the Pacific War would cost about a million American lives (he apparently did not figure Japanese lives into the mix, as Bentham would have insisted). To avoid such slaughter, Truman deployed atomic weapons against Hiroshima and Nagasaki to force an unconditional surrender upon Japan. Though there were some military targets within both cities, everyone knew that the civilian populations were much larger.[38] So Truman's reasoning was utilitarian: better that these comparatively few innocents die than to risk a broader slaughter, even if that were to involve only legitimate targets, like soldiers. The innocent few must pay the price for the greater good of ending the war more quickly, with fewer overall casualties. Walzer's criticism is scathing: 'To kill 278,966 civilians (the number is made up) in order to avoid the deaths of an unknown but probably larger number of civilians and soldiers is surely a fantastic, godlike, frightening and horrendous act.' Utilitarianism 'encourages . . . [this kind of] bizarre accounting'. It is only 'the acknowledgement of rights that puts a stop to such calculations and forces us to realize that the [deliberate] destruction of the innocent, whatever its purposes, is a kind of blasphemy against our deepest moral commitments'. We remain firmly committed to the ideal that the morally innocent ought never to be deliberately harmed, punished or killed. 'There is no right', Walzer concludes, 'to commit crimes in order to shorten the war.'[39]

Not only does utilitarianism permit or recommend actions which are unjust; its very presuppositions are something Walzer doubts. Utilitarianism confronts related problems of excess contingency and fantastical calculation. The problem of excess contingency is this: since it is always a matter of selecting the most utile option amongst competing alternatives, and since the flow of time, information and circumstance is always changing the expected utility pay-offs for each, utilitarianism fails to provide the clear-cut, firm and universal rules of conduct which are most needed in wartime. For example, will it be better to appease an aggressor in order to avoid a destructive conflict, running the risk that appeasement may only whet its appetite for more? Or will it be better to resort to war now, running the risk of losing it and ending up in a worse position than if one had appeased in the first place? Walzer suggests that

> there is no practical way of making out that position – deciding when to fight and when not – on utilitarian principles. Think of what one would have to know to perform the calculations, of the experiments one would have to conduct, the wars one would have to fight – and leave unfought!

In short, the calculations required for sound utilitarian judgement during wartime are simply too fantastical to be serviceable to statesmen and soldiers on the ground. Walzer's point harks back to Kant's oft-cited comment:

Reason is not sufficiently enlightened to discover the whole series of predetermining causes which would allow it to predict accurately the happy or unhappy consequences of human activities . . . [b]ut reason at all times shows us clearly enough what we have to do in order to remain in the paths of duty.[40]

While he lands these fierce and powerful blows upon it, Walzer also believes that utilitarianism 'will, in general, endorse limited wars', much like a rights-based just war theory. These limits, though, will be grounded not on rights but rather upon concerns for mini-mizing suffering, for deterring future wars in general and, in the particular case, for easing the transition from war back to peace. Generally, it is most utile to fight only limited battles, aimed at modest and achievable goals. We will see subsequently that Walzer also endorses, though with reservations, consequentialist appeals to last resort, probability of success and proportionality of costs to benefits when it comes to justifying the resort to war. Finally, Walzer suggests that

[u]tilitarianism is most effective when it points to outcomes about which we have (relatively) clear ideas. For that reason, it is more likely to tell us that the rules of war should be overridden in this or that case than it is to tell us what the rules are.

Walzer believes – notoriously – that there are rare situations during wartime in which rights may be ignored for the sake of what he thinks is utility. These situations he labels 'supreme emergencies'. When 'the very existence of a community is at stake', then 'the restraint on utilitarian calculation must be lifted.' Only in such an emergency can 'an utilitarianism of extremity' be defended. This is a fascinating, and very problematic, claim for Walzer to make. It seems to fit awkwardly with the rest of his rights-based just war theory, and appears almost dangerous in portent. That is why it will be dissected in detail in the forthcoming chapter on Walzer's account of *jus in bello*. Suffice it for now to say that, although he makes room for appeals to utility at certain points in his theory, on the whole Walzer rejects utilitarianism as the all-things-considered best interpretation of the ethics of war and peace. Utilitarianism is too contingent in its recommendations, too fantastical in its accounting requirements, too difficult to apply, and too much at odds with how we currently struc-ture the moral world. The baseline structure of this normative sphere,

Walzer insists, is in terms of rights: rights to engage in war; rights to be immune from attack; rights with regard to the terms of the peace.[41]

Before we reconstruct and evaluate Walzer's rights-based just war theory in its own right, one final topic must here be considered. This topic, hinted at above, concerns the fact that classical utilitarianism is by no means the only form of utilitarianism on offer. Might a rule-utilitarian conception of wartime justice survive Walzer's ferocious accusations? Rule-utilitarianism was probably invented by John Stuart Mill. It seeks to combine the most attractive elements within both deontology and consequentialism in a coherent normative structure. The canonical form of rule-utilitarianism runs like this: we do not have to run incredibly difficult, and excessively demanding, utility calculations for every option we are considering. All we have to do, in terms of our conduct (whether in war or peace), is to adhere to a firm set of action-guiding rules, exactly as a rights-based or deontological account would have us do. These rules, however, must themselves be ultimately grounded not on vague Walzerian references to 'our ideas about personality and moral agency'[42] but more concretely on their material contribution to the world's overall utility. Gifted legislators, versed in utilitarianism, will formulate these general rules – which can even be phrased in terms of universal rights and duties, as Mill does – so as to maximize everyone's happiness and eventual flourishing. Rule-utilitarianism thus offers us firm rules and familiar ways of thinking about moral issues without foregoing the hard-headed appeal to best expected consequences as the litmus test for permissible action.[43]

The main thing to note, when considering how a rights theorist like Walzer might respond, is that rule-utilitarianism has come under withering fire for its very structure. It is often suggested that rule-utilitarianism is an ambitious but doomed attempt to square the circle. While it appeals to liberal sensibilities, keen on having it all, or at least on moderating between extremes, rule-utilitarianism runs afoul of the following difficulty: what if, in a hard case, the rule enjoins one to do something one believes will not further overall utility? An example would be a prohibition on torturing a captured soldier to get information on where and when his comrades are going to attack tomorrow. Some rule-utilitarians respond to this query by urging blind obedience to the rule. They cite the greater fallibility of the individual chooser compared with the gifted utilitarian legislators or theorists who designed the rule. Alternatively, they refer to the greater long-term utility which comes from adhering to the rules even if, in hard cases, the rules may get it wrong in the short term. Other rule-utilitarians respond to the query by urging a violation of the rule, provided one has the compelling evidence needed about which is in fact the most utile option. In this latter case, the assumption is that the rules cannot be absolute and so have to be framed, right from the start, with precisely these kinds of overriding clauses for securing the greater good.

A non-utilitarian like Walzer will not be impressed with these defences of rule-utilitarianism. For the first defence, supportive of obeying the rule in the hard case, rests on one of two questionable empirical assumptions. The first involves comparative fallibility and raises the question: could we not as readily assume that the individual actually involved in the choice situation to be better informed than remote legislators, or armchair theorists? The second controversial assumption is that obeying the rules will in fact generate larger long-term utility than occasional, well-meaning violation of them. The second defence of rule-utilitarianism, which favours violating the rule in the hard case, seems the most honest in utilitarian spirit. But this second defence reveals that, when push comes to shove, the rules will be put aside for the sake of overall utility. The rights-like concern with firm prohibitions on certain forms of conduct will, in the end, give way to precisely the kinds of unconstrained, fantastical calculations derided by Walzer. Indeed, *they must give way*, since utility-maximization remains the ultimate point and justification for the system. Rule-utilitarianism is thus thought by many rights theorists to be far from an ideal compromise between deontology and consequentialism: it seems radically unstable, perhaps even incoherent in the final analysis.[44]

We perceive these flaws when we consider one of the most influential and recent attempts to construct a form of wartime rule-utilitarianism. R. B. Brandt suggests that rule-utilitarianism can specify wartime laws which are 'absolutely binding', the violation of which is 'morally out of bounds absolutely and no matter what the circumstances'. These are rules which rational states would impartially choose, structured as they are to 'maximize expectable utility for nations at war'. What rules are these? Brandt includes categorical prohibitions on 'wanton murder', rape, 'ill treatment' of captured soldiers, 'ill treatment' of civilian populations, and even 'plunder of private property'. How can Brandt claim that such rules serve as categorical side-constraints on military action during wartime, yet simultaneously suggest that these rules have utilitarian rationale, which always appeals to contingent consequences? His answer is empirical: these rules are absolute, yet grounded by consequentialist appeal, because they rule out actions which 'are of negligible utility' in wartime. They rule out actions which do not, in fact, contribute to the end of victory and exact enormous costs on people. The utility calculus, Brandt assures us, will always give such tactics a very low ranking.[45]

Walzer's response to Brandt's suggestion here would be, or should be, that it is a questionable generalization at best and, at worst, is appallingly naïve. If only the world were really so structured that rape, murder and plunder of private property did not sometimes serve the pursuit of military victory. In contrast to Brandt's embarrassing comment that '[t]here is no military advantage, at least for an affluent nation, in the plunder of private or public property', Walzer could point to the obvious fact that (*ceteris paribus*) the more resources an army has, the better off it is. An invading army can make great service of plundered food, money, weapons, cars, trucks, livestock, etc. And this is leaving unsaid the truism that secure possession of property, or territory, is one of the main goals in war. A similar response can be offered to Brandt's claim that 'the rape of women or the ill-treatment of populations of occupied countries serves no military purpose'. Walzer would applaud the principle but question whether it can be grounded adequately on consequentialist appeal to utility alone. What if, for example, the military purpose of an aggressor nation is to cleanse a territory of its native population, take it over, and then repopulate the area with its own citizens? Under such conditions – recently experienced in the Bosnian civil war[46] – rape and ill treatment of the citizenry in the target area may well assist the aggressor in driving out the native population. Terror tactics no doubt arouse 'hatred and resentment', as Brandt points out, but from that it does not follow that such hatred and resentment always suffice to keep the victimized people in their own territory. Brandt can arrive at his conclusions only by abstracting from reality with empirical generalizations, seeing uniformity of consequences when variety and diversity seem more evident.[47]

This abstraction from reality is graphically revealed in Brandt's general principle, applicable to all types of war: a military action (e.g. a bombing raid) is permissible only if the utility . . . of victory to all concerned, multiplied by the increase in its probability if the action is executed, on the evidence (when the evidence is reasonably solid, considering the stakes) is greater than the possible disutility of the action to both sides multiplied by its probability.[48]

Reflection on this truly remarkable rule would lead just war theorists like Walzer to a number of conclusions. First, it shows how the framing of general rules does not exempt rule-utilitarianism from the criticism that it still implies fantastical – albeit higher-order – calculations. Does Brandt's all-purpose rule, as stated, make substantive sense at all, loaded as it is with generalities, qualifications, conditions, probabilities, possibilities and awkward mathematical operations? What constitutes 'reasonably solid' evidence? What roles do 'the stakes' play: do they change the weighting of values? By how much? Do they presuppose another multiplication operation? How does this rule escape the charge of excess contingency? Above all: how on earth are officers and soldiers supposed to make practical service of this rule during the heat of battle? Brandt himself, in a devastating admission, observes that his rule appears 'far too imprecise to be of practical utility'.[49] It is ironic indeed that this rule, though rooted in a theory which fancies itself more concrete and applicable, seems much more abstract than the just war rules which form the main object of the next three chapters.

Perhaps the most serious accusation Brandt faces is that his account still runs afoul of one of the most important just war principles, namely, that it is always wrong deliberately to violate the rights of innocent non-combatants. By his own admission, while rape and property plundering are ruled out by generalizing on their disutility, 'maximizing utility permits obliteration bombing', though only 'as a measure of deterrence or deterrent reprisal'. It is precisely actions like this which a rights-based just war theory rules out categorically as unjust. After all, obliteration bombing deliberately targets innocent non-combatants with death. Some just war theorists might even label such an act 'wanton murder', which Brandt previously assured us he ruled out 'absolutely'. His appeal to deterrent effects as justifying grounds for obliteration bombing is not a piece of rights-bound justice; it is a piece of unconstrained classical expected utility maximization. We witness once more the serious pressures rule-utilitarianism faces in terms of collapsing into its unconstrained and flawed progenitor. Whereas Walzer asserts that shortening war through the commission of crimes is unjust, Brandt suggests that 'widespread civilian bombing might be defended by arguing that a significant deterioration in civilian morale could bring an end to a war by producing internal revolution'. He admits: '[o]ur principle does not exclude the possibility of such reasoning.'[50] Our task now is to turn to Walzer's just war theory to understand how, and why, it *does* exclude the possibility of such reasoning. Can Walzer offer an account which improves on each of these three alternatives to his brand of just war theory?

Summary

Walzer's just war theory is at odds with such competing doctrines as realism, pacifism and utilitarianism. The first two rival doctrines doubt just war theory's core proposition, namely, that sometimes war can be morally justified. Walzer's criticism of descriptive realism is potent; however, his response to prescriptive realism is all but non-existent. His response to pacifism is similar: forceful and telling, but only with regard to a narrow range of points. Broader engagement was sought with both realism and pacifism, and suggestion made as to how a just war theorist might respond more fully to their claims. Utilitarianism suffers the brunt of Walzer's critical attack, and he subjects its classical form to a painful and sustained lashing. His principles can also be used to call its rule-based form into disrepute, though we shall see that Walzer cannot distance himself so utterly from consequentialism, or from some of the very criticisms he levels at it.

4 • Aggression and Defence: Walzer's Theory of *Jus ad Bellum*

The wrong the aggressor commits is to force men and women to risk their lives for the sake of their rights.[1]

Walzer

Meaning and the war convention

Jus ad bellum is a Latin term, referring to the justice of resorting to war. Walzer says the rules of *jus ad bellum* are addressed, first and foremost, to heads of state. Since political leaders are the ones who inaugurate wars, setting their armed forces in motion, they are to be held accountable to *jus ad bellum* principles. If they fail in that responsibility, then they commit war crimes. In the language of the Nuremberg prosecutors, aggressive leaders who launch unjust wars commit 'crimes against peace'. What constitutes a just or unjust resort to armed force is disclosed to us by something Walzer calls 'the war convention'. Walzer defines this war convention as 'the set of articulated norms, customs, professional codes, legal precepts, religious and philosophical principles, and reciprocal arrangements that shape our judgement . . .' of the ethics of war and peace. The shared war convention provides the raw material from which we construct the best interpretation of our universal, thin yet intense discourse surrounding wartime commitments. Walzer believes that this interpretation establishes a set of firm rules to guide the conduct of persons and states. He refers to this set as the rules of just war theory.[2]

The just war tradition

The most influential reading of the war convention probably belongs to the just war tradition. This tradition refers to a group of like-minded thinkers who employed similar concepts and values to construct a moral code regarding wartime behaviour. The tradition has enjoyed a long and distinguished pedigree, including such notables as Augustine, Aquinas, Grotius, Suarez, Vattel and Vitoria. Hugo Grotius probably deserves credit for being the most comprehensive and formidable member of the tradition. Many of the rules developed by the just war tradition have since been codified into contemporary international laws governing armed conflict. The tradition has thus been doubly influential, dominating both moral and legal discourse surrounding war.[3]

Walzer's understanding of just war theory has been shaped considerably by the works of the just war tradition. It follows that one profitable and instructive way to interpret Walzer's theory of *jus ad bellum* would be to compare and contrast it with the account of *jus ad bellum* offered by the just war tradition. The tradition contends that, for the resort to war to be justified, a state must fulfil each and every one of the following six requirements:

Just cause. A state may launch a war only for the right reason. The just causes most frequently mentioned include: self-defence from external attack; the protection of innocents; and punishment for wrongdoing. Vitoria suggested that all of the proffered just causes be subsumed under the one category of 'a wrong received'.[4]

Right intention. A state must intend to fight the war only for the sake of a just cause. Having the right reason for launching a war is not enough: the actual motivation behind the resort to war must also be morally appropriate.

Proper authority and public declaration. A state may go to war only if the decision has been made by the appropriate authorities, according to the proper process, and made public, notably to its own citizens and to the enemy state(s).

Last Resort. A state may resort to war only if it has exhausted all plausible, peaceful alternatives to resolving the conflict in question, in particular diplomatic negotiation.

Probability of Success. A state may not resort to war if it can foresee that doing so will have no measurable impact on the situation. The aim here is to block mass violence which is going to be futile.

(Macro-)Proportionality. A state must, prior to initiating a war, weigh the universal goods expected to result from it, such as securing the just cause, against the universal evils expected to result, notably casualties. Only if the benefits are proportional to, or 'worth', the costs may the war action proceed.

The criteria for a just resort to force which Walzer defends are strikingly similar to, though at times importantly different from, these six traditional norms. Walzer's omissions, amendments, explanations and justifications result in his own unique and substantive contribution to the tradition and, through it, to our shared war convention itself.

Just cause

For Walzer, the only just cause for resorting to war is to resist aggression. Other things being equal, wars of economic conquest, territorial expansion, religious crusade, revolutionary conversion or ethnic hatred are not just, and thus subject to criticism, resistance and punishment. But what, exactly, constitutes aggression? Walzer defines aggression as 'every violation of the territorial integrity and political sovereignty of an independent state'. A state Walzer defines as a political association of people, on a given piece of land, composed of both the governed and the government.[5]

The right of territorial integrity is the right of an independent state not to be invaded by another state: '[T]he right of a nation not to be invaded derives from the common life its members have made on this piece of land.' There is a very close connection between territory and community, much as there is a very close connection between house and home. Developing and perpetuating a shared way of life in a defined space grounds an entitlement to that space. The grounding is at least threefold: first, in terms of securing the material wherewithal to sustain the community's survival; second, in terms of acknowledging the very value of shared ways of life; and third in terms of the historical rootedness of this particular community in this exact physical space. 'It is the coming together of a people that establishes the integrity of a territory', Walzer claims; '[o]nly then can a boundary be drawn the crossing of which is plausibly called aggression.' Walzer quickly adds two caveats. The first is that not every boundary dispute is a just cause for war. But the deliberate breach of a national boundary by an invading army, for example, would clearly be such a cause. In general, Walzer's view of aggression 'focuses narrowly on actual ... invasions and physical assaults. Otherwise, it is feared, the notion of resistance to aggression would have no determinate meaning.' The second caveat is that Walzer concedes that the current set of boundaries is historically arbitrary. In spite of this, he asserts that '[n]evertheless, these lines establish a habitable world. Within that world, men and women ... are safe from attack; once the lines are crossed, safety is gone.'[6]

The right of political sovereignty is the right of a state to shape its domestic policies within its own borders, free of foreign coercion or control. It is the right of a political community to seek its own domestic destiny, to select the means required to achieve it, as well as to assume the risks attending the journey. It is the right of people freely associated together to determine those domestic choices – about citizenship, representation, taxation, production, distribution, exchange, regulation, and so on – which shape their lives and frame their future.[7]

The violation of either of these two primary state rights is aggression, 'the crime of war'. Aggression is both 'morally and physically coercive', forcing men and women to fight for their lives and their rights for no good reason. Aggression is behind all unjust wars. It is wrong to begin an unjust war, because 'war is hell'. War, Walzer suggests, is a form of tyranny: it violates important boundaries, imposing enormous costs and outrageous sufferings on people without their consent. So to cause such an experience – to expose so many people to such serious danger – without sufficient reason is the height of international injustice. Indeed, to do so is to violate 'rights to which we attach enormous importance ... rights that are worth dying for'.[8]

Why, exactly, are state rights to territorial integrity and political sovereignty worth dying for? Why are they portrayed as the foremost values of the international system, the violation of which constitutes 'the only crime that states can commit against other states'? Why should we believe that collective associations, like states, can have rights at all? Is Walzer's stance the product of sloppy thinking, a series of false generalizations at odds with the sobering strictures of methodological individualism? Is he advocating what some of his critics have lambasted as 'a romance of the nation-state', even 'a statism without foundations'?[9]

Walzer responds by arguing that these state rights 'derive ultimately from the rights of individuals, and from them they take their force'. Walzer does not believe that states are 'organic wholes', nor are they 'mystical unions'. A state is nothing more or less than a political association, in a given territory, composed of both the people and their government. 'The deepest purpose of the state', he submits, 'is . . . defense.' This sense of defence, for Walzer, is twofold: the defence of one's own personal life and liberty; and the defence of the common life one shares with other members of the state. 'State rights', Walzer declares, 'are simply . . . [the] collective form' of individual human rights.[10]

Individual human rights are rights to life and liberty, entitlements we all have and which we are to treat as 'something like absolute values'. Human rights, we have seen, are at the foundation of that interpretation of wartime morality Walzer offers as the most authoritative: 'Individual rights (to life and liberty) underlie the most important judgements we make about war.' About the foundation of these human rights themselves, Walzer by his own admission has little to say. 'It is enough', for his purposes, 'to say that they are somehow entailed by our sense of what it means to be a human being. If they are not natural, then we have invented them, but natural or invented, they are a palpable feature of our moral world.' 'I shall say here nothing', he concedes, 'of the ideas of personality, action and intention that this doctrine [of human rights] probably presupposes.'[11]

It is ironic that so much weight is put upon human rights in Walzer's just war theory yet so little is said either about their nature or justification. Walzer excuses himself on grounds that such an endeavour would involve him in so many, and such deep, philosophical perplexities that it would distract him from his main goal, which is to offer a practical just war theory. No doubt it would. No doubt, too, his writings commit him to the idea that human rights are fundamental values inherent in the thin theory of morality shared by all thick moralities. Human rights to life and liberty must, then, correlate with those universal and mainly negative prohibitions against murder, torture, gross cruelty, oppression, tyranny and deception that we discussed previously. Human rights, in the final analysis, are 'something like absolute' entitlements which we all have *not to be subjected to such treatments*. We know we have these entitlements not by appealing to the objective facts of human nature, nor by putting ourselves through some hypothetical rational-choice procedure, but rather by reflecting on how we – here and now, both at home and abroad – interpret the moral world. Walzer's contention is that, at its deepest level, the best current interpretation of the moral world will feature bedrock commitments to respecting everyone's life and liberty.[12]

How, exactly, is it that state rights are 'ultimately derived' from individual human rights, thus outlined? Walzer offers two answers. The first is that individual human rights cannot, in our world, be realized outside a secure social context, like that which the state can offer. So, if we want individual human rights to be realized, then we must be willing to authorize states to claim those elements they need to provide us with the substance of our human rights. Those elements, not implausibly, include access to material resources and a secured space allowing for free political choice. 'Rights in the world have value', Walzer observes, 'only if they have dimension.'[13]

His second answer to the question of derivation is more complex. He admits that 'the process of collectivization is a complex one' but 'is best understood ... in terms of social contract theory'. This contract, however, is not an explicit, deliberate bargain between self-interested rational choosers. 'The rights of states [do indeed] rest on the consent of their members. But this consent is of a special sort.' It is 'a process of association and mutuality'. Through 'shared experiences and cooperative activity', people in a given territory come over time to 'shape a common life'.[14] This common life is something we all consent to in the sense that we participate in it and come through interpretation to recognize ourselves in its context. We are both its creators and its creatures, this shared life we forge together in a common space. 'The social contract', Walzer says, 'is an agreement to reach decisions together about what goods are necessary to our common life, and then to provide those goods for one another.' It is 'a moral bond ... creating a union that transcends all differences of interest, drawing its strength from history, culture, religion, language and so on'.[15] 'Contract', he writes, 'is a metaphor' referring to a relation, 'Burkeian in character', between 'the living, the dead and those who are yet to be born'. It is a metaphor referring to the fact that people have always banded together, both for self-protection and for the enjoyment of those goods that they could not enjoy at all were they not members of a community, surrounded by the protection afforded by a state. Indeed, Walzer contends that membership in a political community is 'the primary good', the means by which all other goods – notably the social goods discussed in chapter 2 – get produced, distributed, defended, interpreted and enjoyed.[16]

It is crucial to note that, for Walzer, the moral standing of a state *is contingent upon* its protection of its members, both individually and collectively. A state's legitimacy 'depends upon the reality of the common life it protects and the extent to which the sacrifices required by that protection are willingly accepted and thought worthwhile'. 'If no common life exists', he says, 'or if the state doesn't defend the common life that does exist, its own defense may have no moral justification.' Thus, a state riven by serious ethnic division faces deep questions about its legitimacy. Likewise for a state in which the government turns against its own people and engages in 'terrible human rights violations', such as 'massacre or enslavement'. Such a state violates the thin and universal moral code contained within all thick moralities, and so can only be judged an outlaw regime with no entitlement to non-interference on the part of other states. But a state wherein the people enjoy 'a genuine contract' – offering both Hobbesian self-protection and a Burkeian 'community of character' – is a state entitled to territorial integrity and political sovereignty.[17]

So for Walzer any violation of either of these state rights is unjust, constituting aggression. Any invasive boundary-crossing into the territory of a legitimate, 'genuine contract' state counts as aggression, as does any grievous coercion of its domestic political choices. While Walzer does focus on acts of aggression which involve invasion and attack, it is not strictly speaking true to say that, for him, aggression necessarily involves physical assault, the deployment of armed force. Though he suggests that such is a useful, conservative presumption to have about aggression, we shall see that he does allow for exceptional cases of anticipatory attack. He also offers a helpful, albeit partial, list of actual instances of aggression in the twentieth century: Germany against Belgium in 1914; Italy against Ethiopia, and Japan against China, in the mid-1930s; Germany against Czechoslovakia and Poland in the late 1930s; and against Denmark, Belgium and Holland in 1940; Russia against Hungary in 1956 and against Czechoslovakia in 1968.[18]

Victims of aggression, thus conceived, 'are always justified in fighting' and, in most cases, 'fighting is the morally preferred response'. Why is this so, especially when Walzer admits that most cases of aggression involve a large and powerful state deploying its armed force to coerce a less powerful state to make unjust concessions? Isn't appeasement of the aggressor a defensible response from the victim? Isn't neutrality by third parties a legitimate choice? Walzer stresses that, ultimately, the decision to resist aggression, whether by the victim or by third-party vindicators, can only be a free choice of the state in question. This follows from the right of political sovereignty. But he clearly articulates his preference in favour of resistance, especially by the victim. For resistance 'confirms and enhances ... our common values [including] national pride, self-respect, freedom in policy-making' whereas appeasement 'diminishes those values and leaves us all impoverished'. Sometimes both appeasement and neutrality constitute 'a failure to resist evil in the world'. The unchallenged triumph of aggression, Walzer asserts, is 'a greater evil' than war.[19]

So the only just cause for resorting to war, as Walzer sees it, is in response to aggression. The response may be twofold: a war of self-defence on the part of the state victimized by aggression; and a war of other-defence, or 'law enforcement', on the part of any other state coming to aid the victim. We might note how Walzer's just cause doctrine is echoed in international law. Article 51 of the United Nations Charter, for example, says that '[n]othing in the present Charter shall impair the inherent right of individual or collective self-defence if an armed attack occurs'.[20]

Walzer is adamant that there is no such thing as a war just on both sides. All things considered, he believes, the evidence can point in only one of two directions: *either* that, in a given war, one side is the unjust aggressor, the other the justified defender, *or* that the war is unjust on both sides. This is to say that Walzer rejects a criterion of comparative justice, present in some accounts of the just war tradition, according to which both sides can have some quantum of justice.[21] His grounds for rejecting this criterion are persuasive: there seems to be logical tension in morally permitting both of the opposing sides to go to war against each other; and sometimes, it seems, comparative justice simply does not ring true. Sometimes, the world is confronted with a case of blatant aggression – for instance, Nazi Germany moving into Poland in 1939 – in which appeal to comparative justice fails, on any plausible ground, to persuade. In such cases, we want to say that the aggressor had no justice whatsoever on its side, whereas the victim was fully and not merely comparatively justified in responding to the aggression with armed force. In those cases where the evidence is more conflictual, the task is to gather further evidence, not simply permit both sides to fight. And in those cases where it seems that, after all evidence has been gathered, neither side has justice, then they are both to be denied and not permitted appeal to its grounds.

Right intention

With regard to this second rule of *jus ad bellum*, Walzer observes that 'a pure good will [is] . . . a political illusion'. He also notes a lack of clarity in the just war tradition with regard to whether this rule can be fulfilled only if there is purity of intention with regard to just cause, or whether it is possible to meet it, provided only that right intention is present amongst the ordinary mix of motives which animates state behaviour. Walzer himself opts for the latter course: he believes it is possible, and meaningful, to criticize some of the non-moral motives that states can have in going to war while still endorsing the moral motive. But that motive must be present: Walzer concurs that the right orientation towards just cause is a necessary aspect of the justice of resorting to war.[22]

A related question Walzer does not answer is this: must the moral motivation merely be present in the mix of motives, or need it be the main animating force in the mix? Consider, for example, the mix of motives that the Allied coalition, led by the United States, might have had in 1991 for launching the Persian Gulf War against Iraq: the repulsion of Iraq from Kuwait; the punishment of Iraqi aggression; the desire to secure the oil supply of the Persian Gulf region; the desire by the United States to prove its unsurpassed superiority following the end of the Cold War with the Soviet Union; and the drive of the American military to test out its latest weaponry in real battlefield conditions. While we might expect Walzer to endorse the requirement that the moral motive be dominant in the mix, there are serious difficulties involved in discerning which one dominates, as we can see here with regard to the Gulf War. This might make it more plausible, though less interesting, to conclude that the moral motive need only be real and present amongst the various non-moral motives for this criterion to be fulfilled.[23]

One interesting aspect of right intention which Walzer fails to consider is whether it should be part of the justice of the resort to war that a state commit itself both publicly and in advance, as a matter of right intention, to adhering to the other rules of war, contained in *jus in bello* and *jus post bellum*. The idea here, first proposed by Kant, is that a state should commit itself to certain rules of conduct, and appropriate war termination, as part of its original decision to begin the war. If it cannot so commit, it ought never to start the process. Such would seem an important and forward-looking way in which one could run a normative thread through each of the three just war categories, tying them into a coherent whole. This Kantian addition is compelling not only because of the moral import of an agent's intent but, moreover, to ensure consistency of just behaviour throughout all three phases of a military engagement.[24]

A frequent criticism of the right intention criterion is that it is impossible to know whether a state has fulfilled its requirements, given the vagueness of intent. But it should be noted, as Walzer does, that this criticism is easily exaggerated. Intentions can be, and ought to be, discerned through a reasoned examination of publicly accessible evidence, relying on behaviour, consideration of incentives, and explicit avowals of intent. Intentions are neither infinitely redescribable nor irreducibly private: they are connected to patterns of evidence, as well as constrained by norms of logical coherence. Right intention is not a vacuous criterion for moral judgement during war. Though difficult, it is possible to tell whether a state is prosecuting a war out of ethnic hatred, for example, as opposed to vindicating its right of self-defence. That kind of dark motivation produces distinctive and noticeable results, such as torture, massacres, mass rape campaigns, and large-scale displacements. We have the very recent civil wars in the former Yugoslavia to offer as historical evidence.[25]

Perhaps a deeper critical question will be raised in connection with right intention: can collective agents like states have intentions at all? Implicit in all of Walzer's reasoning thus far is a systematic analogy between the behaviour of states and the behaviour of individual persons. Does it make sense to speak of state 'rights' and 'intentions'? To refer to 'crimes' that states commit against each other, like aggression, which can be responded to and 'punished'? Of states acting for the right reasons, out of the proper motives? Walzer is the first to admit his reliance on what is now called 'the domestic analogy'.[26] This analogy implies that one of the most useful ways we have to understand how states behave *vis-à-vis* each other is to liken such behaviour to the way in which individuals behave *vis-à-vis* each other. It is important to note that this analogy need not, and for Walzer does not, involve any kind of mystical conception of the state. The domestic analogy, rather, draws its vitality from the sheer difficulty of speaking about the behaviour of complex entities like states without employing simplifying assumptions, such as that they have a discernible identity, have intentions, face choices between alternatives, are thus responsible, and so on. It should also be emphasized that the domestic analogy is merely that: it is only generally persuasive and neither precludes the existence of important disanalogies nor commits us to a monolithic and homogeneous conception of the state. The main point here, as Walzer sees it, is interpretative: we have always employed the domestic analogy in our moral discourse about the ethics of war and peace. It is inherent in the deepest structure of our talk about war, and we all understand what is meant by it. Thus, any account which purports to be the best interpretation of that discourse must itself make use of the domestic analogy.

Public declaration of war by a proper authority

Walzer makes substantive use of the traditional *jus ad bellum* criteria of just cause and right intention. But what of the others? Walzer makes next to no mention of the criterion of public declaration of war by a proper authority. This seems an oversight on his part. For once we get beyond its apparent quaintness, we see how it represents an important constraint on the power of heads of state, and state mechanisms in general, to risk the lives and liberties of their citizen members in such a dangerous enterprise as war. If state prerogatives in times of war are to be kept in line with the human rights of their member citizens – which purportedly ground such state rights in the first place – then we cannot lose sight of this just war criterion. The people must, in some public procedure, meaningfully consent to the launching of a war on their behalf.

This public consent requirement need not preclude a rapid and effective response to some 'blitzkrieg' instance of aggression. Usually, there are defensible constitutional procedures designed to deal with such scenarios. (One such procedure would be authorizing the executive branch of government to deal militarily with such scenarios as it deems fit and then, should it seem as though a more lengthy response to the aggression is required, that such be authorized through a more deliberative process, for instance in the legislature.) Furthermore, the enemy state and its member citizens are entitled to receive a public declaration of war so that there is no duplicitous manoeuvring; so that, in short, they are apprised that they are facing war, and all it entails, as a result of their aggressive actions. Entitlement to such public notification is codified in the Hague Convention, an aspect of our shared war convention which Walzer has here overlooked. The case of the Vietnam War is also relevant for suggesting why Walzer should not overlook this criterion. Many critics of US President Lyndon Johnson blasted him, at the time and since, for escalating the war through a series of executive orders, as opposed to submitting the matter for more representative debate in the US Congress. Infuriated by what it saw as an abuse, with devastating consequences, of the short-term presidential war-power, Congress passed the War Powers Resolution in 1973.[27]

It is to be wondered at why Walzer does not enshrine a norm of proper authority/public declaration even on his own terms, since he is concerned with ensuring that the prerogatives heads of state enjoy during wartime do not detach from their normative moorings in the human rights of the people. He displayed this concern clearly in his early work, *Obligations*. There, he focused on the potential threat to individual human rights posed by a state policy of military conscription. He concluded that a just society ought to abide by the good-faith claims of conscientious objectors to be exempt from military service. A just state in the midst of a serious and justified war may, however, reasonably ask for some kind of assistance from conscientious objectors, such as clerical or administrative work, in return for respecting their personal beliefs that they ought not to kill, much less be forced to kill, for political reasons. He concluded that such a state ought to meet its military needs through voluntary enlistment, where possible. There are many incentives which armed forces can, and do, employ to keep enlistments at the desired levels. As most military experts agree, very rarely is there a credible military case for universal conscription. It would seem defensible perhaps only in those so-called 'supreme emergencies' wherein the entire state in question is credibly threatened with destruction and genocide. More will be said about Walzer's controversial view of supreme emergencies in the next chapter.[28]

Last resort

'It is obvious', Walzer says, 'that measures short of war are preferable to war itself.' Of course, '[o]ne always wants to see diplomacy tried before the resort to war, so that we are sure that war is the last-resort.' In spite of this endorsement of the traditional last-resort criterion, Walzer is quick with some caveats. First, he points out that, strictly speaking, there is no such thing as a last resort. No matter how fearful the situation has become, there is always something else that can be tried – yet another round of diplomatic negotiations, for instance – prior to the resort to war. So it would be absurd, in this literal sense, to say that states may turn to war only as a last resort. Literal lastness never comes; thus, it is only normative lastness which we can require. States must have explored all *reasonable and plausible* avenues prior to launching armed force.[29] A second caveat concerns the fact that negotiations, threats and economic sanctions are frequently offered as more compelling means of international problem-solving than the use of force. At face value, this claim is indisputable: if a reasonable resolution to the crisis in question can be had through a credible and permissible threat, or through a negotiating session, or perhaps through sanctions, then surely that is preferable to running the sizeable risks of war. Upon closer inspection, however, much depends on the nature of the particular act of aggression and the nature of the aggressive regime itself. Sometimes threats, diplomacy and sanctions will not work. Walzer cites the incidents leading up to the Persian Gulf War as a case in point. Care must be taken that appeals to last resort do not end up rewarding aggression.[30] Finally, theorists like Albert Pierce and Lori Damrosch have pointed out that the levelling of systematic economic sanctions often violates the *jus in bello* principle of non-combatant immunity, since it is most often innocent civilians (often the poorest and most vulnerable) who bear the brunt of economic embargoes. In the absence of force directed against them, outlaw regimes always seem to find a way, within their own borders, to take care of themselves. The Hussein regime in Iraq, once more, is a very instructive case study.[31]

It seems much more plausible to contend *not* that war must be the literal last resort after all other means have been exhausted but, rather, that states ought not to be hasty in their resort to force. There ought to be a strong presumption against the resort to armed force.[32] But beyond this general principle, so much here depends on the concrete details of the actual situation in question. It is critically important, for example, when the aggressor is mounting a swift and brutal invasion, to respond effectively before all is lost. It is also relevant to consider the nature of the territory of the victim of aggression; if it is a tiny country, like Israel, the need for a speedy and effective response against aggression will probably be much greater than that required by a country the size and strength of the United

States. The response of the international community is likewise relevant. But attention must always be focused on the nature and severity of the aggressor and its actions, for often the international community is sluggish in mounting an effective response to aggression. The key question this criterion demands always to be asked, and then answered in the affirmative, is this: is the proposed use of force reasonable, given the situation and the nature of the aggression?

Probability of success

Probability of success is another *jus ad bellum* rule for which only general principles can be convincingly conveyed. Its prudential flavour explains this: probability of success is always a matter of circumstance, of taking reasonable options within the constraints and opportunities presented by the world. The traditional aim of this criterion is to bar lethal violence which is going to be futile. As such, the principle is laudable and necessary for any comprehensive just war theory. Walzer himself endorses consideration of 'reasonable expectations of success'.[33] Great care, however, needs to be exercised that this criterion, like last resort, does not amount to rewarding aggression, and especially by larger and more powerful nations. This is so because smaller and weaker nations will face a comparatively harder task when it comes to fulfilling this criterion. Walzer concurs, contending that we ought not to acquiesce in a grave crime such as aggression. And the calculation of expected probability of success for resorting to war, after all, is incredibly difficult. The vicissitudes of war are, as we know from history, among the most difficult phenomena to predict. Even when the odds have seemed incredibly long, remarkable successes have sometimes, somehow, been achieved. Such are the stuff of military legend. One example, from ancient history, would be the victory of Alexander the Great over Darius of Persia at Issus in 333 BC. Walzer himself cites the initial successes of the Finnish resistance to the Soviet invasion of 1939–40. The lack of predictability, though, does not always turn out for the better. A notorious example is that the armies of Europe expected, in September 1914, to be home to celebrate Christmas.[34] Walzer also suggests that there are considerations of self-respect here, according to which victims of aggression ought to be permitted at least some resistance, should they decide on it, as an expression of their strong objection to the aggression and as an affirmation of their rights. It seems reasonable to agree with Walzer that, given an act of aggression and given that the other *jus ad bellum* criteria are met, there is a presumption in favour of permitting some kind of armed response, even when the odds of military success (however defined) seem long. At the same time, this rule is not dormant: it remains important that communities contemplating war in response to aggression still consider whether such an extreme measure has any reasonable probability of success. That is the least, we might say, that they owe themselves.

(Macro-)proportionality

(Macro-)proportionality is one of the most contentious and challenging *jus ad bellum* criteria. It mandates that a state considering launching a just war must weigh the expected universal benefits of doing so against the expected universal costs. Only if the projected benefits, in terms of securing the just cause, are at least equal to, and preferably greater than, such costs as casualties may the war action proceed. Walzer wrestles at length with the difficulties presented by this rule. On the one hand, the unchecked triumph of aggression is for him 'a greater evil' than war. He also comments that '... prudence can be, and has to be, accommodated within the argument for justice'. His endorsement of such criteria as last resort and probability of success shows him making such accommodations. On the other hand, Walzer comments on 'the terrible presumption' behind the cost–benefit comparisons implicit in appeals to proportionality. He declares that 'we have no way that even mimics mathematics' of making such proportionality judgements. He asks rhetorically: 'How do we measure the value of a country's independence against the value of defeating an aggressive regime?' How can we pretend to measure, on the same scale of value, the benefits of defeating aggression against the body count needed to achieve it?[35]

The challenges of proportional calculation explode, in both number and complexity, as soon as one puts the least thought to the question. What count as costs and benefits in wartime? Only elements we can quantify, like the body count? But usually we also want to appeal to qualitative elements, like sovereignty. Is there a distinction between explicit and implicit costs? Short-term and long-term benefits? Is it only the costs and benefits of prudence that matter, or do those of morality count as well? How to weigh the 'universal' costs and benefits against each other when, usually during war, those who pay the costs are not the same group as those who enjoy the benefits, such as when soldiers pay the present price for the future independence of their fellow countrymen? The manifest, and manifold, difficulties involved in proportionality calculations cause vexation for Walzer. We saw in the last chapter that he cites such difficulties as evidence against the utilitarian understanding of the rules of war. The calculations needed are simply too complex and wide-ranging. It is wildly improbable that we could ever devise a completely satisfying set of cost–benefit formulae with regard to wartime action. Far better, Walzer suggests, to stick to a firm set of clear and universal rules to guide conduct.

Walzer's final judgement on this issue seems to be that there is some '... truth in the proportionality maxim'. But he insists that 'it is a gross truth' that can only point to obvious considerations of prudence and utility as limiting conditions on the pursuit of rights-respecting justice in wartime. Proportionality, at best, provides some checks and balances, some outside constraints, on the drive to secure a just cause. For example, he says that, even though justice may have permitted otherwise, it was appropriate on grounds of proportionality that the United States did not go to war against the Soviet Union after the latter invaded Hungary in 1956, or Czechoslovakia in 1968.[36]

The Second World War as an example of a just war

One of Walzer's most fervent, and frequently repeated, beliefs is that the Second World War, on the part of the Allies, was a just war. Not only was Nazi Germany a multiple aggressor, violating state rights through numerous invasions in the 1930s, Nazism itself was

an ultimate threat to everything decent in our lives, an ideology and a practice of political domination so murderous, so degrading even to those who might survive, that the consequences of its final victory in World War II were literally beyond calculation, immeasurably awful. We see it ... as evil objectified in the world, and in a form so potent and apparent that there never could have been anything to do but fight against it.

This very tight, and emotionally expressive, passage refers to nearly all his *jus ad bellum* norms: that the Nazis had, through their multiple aggressions, given just cause to the Allies to respond with war; that there was no choice, in the last resort, but for the Allies to fight; and that the (macro-)proportionality condition was fulfilled by the Allies because succumbing to Nazi aggression would have been 'immeasurably awful'. He also could have mentioned that the Allies did seem to have the proper, Nazi-smashing motivation, that they enjoyed a measure of probability of success right from the start and that their resort to force was publicly declared by their legitimate national governments.[37]

Revisions to the general account of *jus ad bellum*

One obvious question to ask here is: are these the only kinds of conflict to which Walzer's just war theory applies? Paradigmatic cases of interstate war, with a nefarious aggressor on the one side, and the defenders of truth and justice on the other? If so, then Walzer's theory seems severely dated, for many of the world's most recent and pressing conflicts have to do with the launching of anticipatory attacks, with intervening in non-aggressive states on grounds of humanitarianism, and with civil war between rival groups within a single state. Relevant examples include the civil wars in Somalia (1993), Bosnia (1992–5) and Rwanda (1994–5), as well as the massive armed intervention by NATO in the Kosovo province of Serbia in 1999.[38]

Walzer admits that there need to be at least three revisions to 'the legalist paradigm' of *jus ad bellum* that he has thus far developed. We must crucially add that these revisions all have to do with just cause. He presupposes, without mention, that all the other criteria – right intention, proportionality, etc. – for a justified resort to force still hold for the three revisions which follow. The amendments are all in terms of expanding the just cause for resorting to armed force beyond the current ambit of responding to interstate aggression.

The first such revision deals with anticipatory attack. Here, Walzer walks a fine line between two extremes: denying that anticipatory attack by one state on another is ever justified; and supporting the doctrine of preventive war. A preventive war, as he sees it, is a war prosecuted in the present for the sake of maintaining the future balance of power, itself thought necessary for long-term peace and security. Such wars used to be very frequent in Europe, especially in the eighteenth century. The grounds most frequently offered for preventive war are utilitarian, and Walzer relishes his familiar contention that the calculations required to ground preventive war are too fantastical to be plausible. Furthermore, the danger to which preventive war is intended to respond is too distant and speculative. If anticipatory attack is to be grounded at all, the danger it is aimed at must be imminent, not distant; it must be a threat which is concrete, not merely abstract.[39]

A sufficient threat for justifying an anticipatory attack, Walzer suggests, is composed of three elements. The first is 'a manifest intent to injure', revealed *either* through a bitter history of conflict between the communities in question, like the Arab–Israeli struggle, *or* through recent and explicit threats. Walzer suggests that the object of a justified anticipatory attack can only be 'a determined enemy', one demonstrably committed to doing harm to one's own political community. The second element of sufficient threat is 'a degree of active preparation that makes the intent a positive danger'. Mere malign intent, even given a conflictual history and/or recent hostile declarations, is not enough to ground anticipatory strikes. There must also be a measurable military preparation on the part of the proposed object of the attack, such as its build-up of offensive forces along the border. Finally, the situation must be one 'in which waiting, or doing anything other than fighting, greatly magnifies the risk [of being attacked]'. Only under all three conditions is an anticipatory attack justified. Walzer's favourite example is Israel's first strike during the Six Day War of 1967.[40]

In general, 'states may use military force in the face of threats of war, whenever the failure to do so would seriously risk their territorial integrity or political independence.' Indeed, he goes so far as to contend that, should State X be faced with these three conditions involving Bellicose State Y, then Y has already committed aggression against X and thus X at least has just cause to launch an attack. We now see how, for Walzer, the actual deployment of force is not a necessary condition for aggression to have occurred. It is no less a violation of state rights to pose 'a serious risk' to the political sovereignty and territorial integrity of a legitimate state than it is to launch an armed invasion against it. Though there are obvious and serious concerns to be raised here, with regard to loosening the conception of aggression, Walzer himself stresses that anticipatory attack can only be truly exceptional, and a very burdensome weight of justification is borne by the attacker to prove, with evidence, that the three general criteria really do hold in its case.[41]

Lest one get the impression that Walzer is far too partial, in his just war judgements, to those communities he is personally connected to, like America and Israel, it should be noted that, for him, America's armed intervention in Vietnam was unjust.[42] Indeed, the entire subtext of historical application in *Just and Unjust Wars* is devoted to showing that the Second World War exemplifies just, whereas Vietnam exemplifies unjust, wars. Armed intervention, Walzer says, 'can sometimes be justified' and it 'always has to be justified'. The burden of proof regarding justification is always on the side of the intervenor and is 'especially heavy', owing to the value of non-intervention, which is corollary to political sovereignty. 'The members of a political community', other things being equal, 'must seek their own freedom, just as the individual must cultivate his own virtue.'[43] It is only if other things are *not* equal that intervention can be grounded. When does that occur? Walzer cites three cases.

The first case is one where the state in question contains many nations – diverse political communities – and one of them is already engaged in an internal war for secession from the central government, which in turn is fighting to keep it down. Walzer stresses that a justified intervention from an outside party cannot merely be in support of some garden-variety disenchanted minority group. Outside support may be forthcoming only if the leaders of that disenchanted minority group clearly articulate its communal will, have mobilized their people on a significant basis, and have already launched an internal struggle against the central government. In a sense, such a secessionist movement has to win what international lawyers often call 'belligerent rights' to external recognition and assistance. They have to prove themselves worthy, so to speak, of armed intervention on their behalf: by proving their representativeness; by taking clear action in favour of their own cause; by their overwhelming investment in their own future independence.[44]

The second case justifying intervention for Walzer is counter-intervention, designed to offset the influence of another foreign power who has already intervened unjustly, often in a civil war context. The goal of counter-intervention, as Walzer sees it, is not to win the war but rather to enable genuine self-determination. The ideal is to offset the imbalance injected into the local struggle by the first foreign intervention, and then let local forces prevail. This is a rather precious and artificial way of putting it, and one recalls Walzer's own scepticism about our ability to measure accurately such probabilities. In practical terms, how is an army to know the difference between when it has merely offset the foreign interference and when it has actually tipped the scales in favour of its own side, presumably undermining 'genuine' self-determination at the local level? Though he offers no clear answer to this important question, Walzer does stress that counter-intervention may only be on behalf of a legitimate regime, one that possesses the required 'fit' of contractual consent between the governed and their governors, and which has passed the self-help test.[45]

It is under this rubric that Walzer contends America's intervention in Vietnam in the 1960s–1970s was unjustified. American intervention in Vietnam was most frequently justified, at the time, as an overt counter-intervention in South Vietnam to offset the prior covert intervention of communist North Vietnam. Walzer does not deny that the North was actively involved in weakening the regime of the South. But his contention is that the South Vietnam regime was illegitimate by the time the US intervened in any event. Not only did the regime betray its pledge to participate in Vietnam-wide elections in 1956;[46] its very weakness and instability was radical enough to undermine its claims of representing its people. There were, for example, nine separate administrations in South Vietnam in the two years between 1963 and 1965. The weakness of the government of the South was a reality induced not merely by covert tinkering from the North, but moreover by the southern regime's own lack of legitimacy amongst its people. '[T]he continuing dependence of the new regime on the U.S. [was] damning evidence against it ... a government that receives economic and technical aid, military supply, strategic and tactical advice, and is still unable to reduce its subjects to obedience, is clearly an illegitimate government.' And counter-intervention on behalf of an illegitimate government is not counter-intervention at all. It is aggressive intervention in a civil war, and thus unjust.[47]

The third and final revision to Walzer's canonical account of *jus ad bellum* concerns humanitarian intervention. Humanitarian intervention seems at first to pose a special problem for Walzer's aggression-based paradigm, since it involves armed intrusion in a country which has not committed aggression against another state. Moreover, such intervention is animated by moral and political ideals which may seem to lack universal endorsement, and thus raise the ugly spectre of violent paternalism on the global stage: treat your people the way we believe you should, or be subject to the threat of armed punishment.

The only kind of armed humanitarian intervention which Walzer accepts is intervention designed to rescue citizens of a state from 'acts that shock the moral conscience of mankind'. He is willing to countenance armed humanitarian intervention only in cases where the state in question is engaging in widespread human rights violations. He is keen to stress the degree to which the human rights violations must be 'massive' and 'terrible', such as incidents of 'massacre and enslavement', to ground armed intervention by a foreign power.[48] Walzer has come under critical fire for this, and has fired back. Critics like Charles Beitz, David Luban and Gerald Doppelt have suggested that regimes which fail to respect human rights, and yet do not go so far as to massacre or enslave their citizenry, have lost their legitimacy as readily (though not as dramatically) as those monstrous few which resort to bloody massacre. Why should foreign states, which themselves respect human rights, be barred in principle from intervening in such illegitimate regimes?[49]

Walzer offers a manifold response. First, his own conception of human rights, we have seen, is minimalist and thin, focused on those basic claims to life and liberty which correlate with universal prohibitions against murder, torture and enslavement. So he might argue about which kinds of government misdeed actually count as human rights violations. The regimes that Beitz, Doppelt and Luban cite might well, under Walzer's conception, not qualify as human rights violators at all. Walzer's preferred response, however, is to insist on the principle of national self-determination, of communal autonomy. Faced with what we might call 'run-of-the-mill' government hostility to human rights claims, citizens need to take it upon themselves to begin the kind of political activism and struggle needed to win such freedoms and benefits. Self-help is the order of the day. This coheres with Walzer's general understanding of a political community as one in which people band together not only for self-protection but also to shape a common way of life, 'to express their inherited culture through political forms worked out among themselves'.[50] Such political communities 'cannot be set free, as he [i.e. an individual] cannot be made virtuous, by any external force'. 'It is not true', for Walzer, 'that intervention is justified whenever revolution is; for revolutionary activity is an exercise in self-determination, while foreign interference denies to a people those political capacities that only such exercise can bring.' Thus, it is only those 'terrible human rights violations' that 'make talk of community or self-determination . . . seem cynical and irrelevant' which justify armed humanitarian intervention by a foreign power. In these extreme cases, it is precisely the incapacity for self-determination that draws foreigners in. The domestic citizenry is not only desperate but doomed without international armed rescue. Walzer actually believes that such humanitarian intervention is obligatory, whereas intervention in a secessionist struggle, or in a civil war, is merely permissible. This sense of obligation is displayed when he avers: 'People who initiate massacres lose their right to participate in the normal . . . processes of domestic self-government. Their military defeat is morally necessary.'[51]

Walzer's critics argue that he is himself guilty of a kind of cynicism with regard to human rights violations. For if human rights constitute the moral basis of his doctrine, how is it that some human rights violations are allowed to go unchallenged, on grounds of communal self-determination? Why must we attend only to the most horrific and obvious cases of massacre, cases in which there is near-unanimity on the need to intervene? Walzer's two examples are India's 1971 humanitarian intervention in Bangladesh and NATO's 1999 intervention in Serbia on behalf of the Kosovars.[52] Walzer responds, intriguingly, by urging that he does not rule out all attempts to exercise foreign influence in a country which violates human rights yet does not engage in massacres. What he does rule out, in such cases, is war.[53] But Beitz wonders why Walzer can tolerate non-violent interference with these countries and yet balk at violent interference. What is the difference in principle here – the difference in just cause, so to speak – as opposed to the admitted difference in proportionality considerations? Beitz's pointed question is designed to flesh out a tension he sees in Walzer's work, namely, that between the explicit grounding of the just war theory in human rights protection, and an implicit sense that, when push comes to shove, it is really the communal prerogatives of sovereign states which enjoy pride of place. This tension will appear again when we reflect on Walzer's supreme emergency doctrine in the next chapter.

Walzer responds to this forceful challenge by stressing, first, that there is a difference of degree so large between violent and non-violent interference that it all but constitutes a difference in kind. For violent intervention involves a state of killing and being killed, an unleashing of danger so serious and far-reaching that it seems non-comparable to diplomatic protest, non-cooperation and censure. Secondly, Walzer believes that Beitz's challenge, as stated, relies on a dichotomy between individual human rights and the rights of legitimate states which is overdrawn. Individuals need state protection for their own effective and reliable self-protection. Moreover, the individual right to liberty implies some entitlement to participate in a shared way of life, free of foreign coercion or control. It would be paternalistic, he suggests, to deny people those capacities for self-determination that are implied in political activity, opposition and struggle. Indeed, a war on their behalf could end up being violently paternalistic. Walzer admits that self-help is a 'stern doctrine' but nevertheless one to which we are most deeply committed. The unleashing of international armed force for humanitarian purposes is grounded only in those very rare cases where there is no hope of self-determination, when commonplace callousness by a government has been replaced by a 'savage turn' on its people, resulting in massacre or enslavement. The fact that we must, morally, wait until there is near-unanimity on the need to intervene in a particular case is for Walzer not a weakness but a strength, cohering completely with his conventionalist convictions.[54]

Summary

In this chapter, we have come to understand Walzer's interpretation of the rules of *jus ad bellum* which inhere in our shared war convention. This interpretation includes just cause, right intention, last resort, probability of success and (macro-)proportionality as criteria which must all be fulfilled before a state may resort to war. And while this interpretation is most readily applied to classic instances of interstate aggression and resistance, he does offer some revisions to it which can allow, as matters of exception, anticipatory attacks, counter-interventions in civil wars, and humanitarian interventions. Critical questions were raised most sharply about the nature of human rights, the relationship between human rights and state rights and the relation between prudence and justice. The contention was also made that Walzer's account should include certain other criteria – like public declaration by a proper authority – currently absent.

5 • Innocence and Emergency: Walzer's Theory of *Jus in Bello*

[T]he structure of rights stands independently of political allegiance; it establishes obligations that are owed, so to speak, to humanity itself . . .

There is no right to commit crimes in order to shorten a war.

Walzer[1]

'*Jus in bello*' is the Latin term just war theorists use to refer to justice in war, to right conduct in the midst of battle. Walzer insists that *jus in bello* is a category separate from *jus ad bellum*. He reasons that we have not finished our normative labour once we have determined whether a state has resorted to war justly, using the principles developed in the last chapter. For even if a state has resorted to war justly, it may be prosecuting that war in an unjustified manner. It may be deploying decrepit means in pursuit of its otherwise justified end. Just war theory insists on a fundamental moral consistency between means and ends with regard to wartime behaviour. Since Walzer views just war theory as the best interpretation of our shared discourse on the ethics of war and peace, it follows for him that we must likewise be committed to this core consistency: justified ends may only be pursued through justified means.

Concern with consistency, however, is not the only, or even the main, reason behind our endorsement of separate rules regulating wartime conduct. Such rules are also required to limit warfare, to prevent it from spilling over into an ever-escalating, and increasingly destructive, experiment in total warfare. If just wars are limited wars, designed to secure their just causes with only proportionate force, the need for rules on wartime restraint is clear. Even though modern warfare has displayed a disturbing tendency towards totality – particularly during the two world wars – it does not follow that the death of old-time military chivalry marks the end of moral judgement. As Walzer proclaims, '[w]e still hold soldiers to certain standards.'[2]

Walzer claims that our shared war convention commits us to respecting three standards, or rules, of *jus in bello*. The first is one of discrimination: armies are to discriminate or distinguish between military and civilian targets, and aim their lethal force only at legitimate military, and military supply, targets. The second standard commits armies to launch only proportionate force at these legitimate targets. Finally, armies are not to employ methods which are intrinsically heinous; they may not commit actions which 'shock the moral conscience of mankind'. Walzer is emphatic that we hold *all* soldiers to all three of these standards. Unlike our *jus ad bellum* judgements, which tend to be binary – condemning one side and justifying the other for resorting to war – our judgements about right conduct apply across the board during wartime. Since *jus in bello* and *jus ad bellum* are separate, it is an error to link the justice of conduct to the justice of cause: soldiers fighting for a just cause can run afoul of *jus in bello* as readily as those prosecuting an unjust war. We expect no more, no less, from soldiers of all sides than that they adhere to the three standards of right conduct.[3]

Before examining Walzer's understanding of the content of these three standards, it is worth stressing how responsibility for fulfilling *jus in bello* differs from the responsibility inhering in *jus ad bellum*. Responsibility for the justice of resorting to war, we saw, rests on those key members of the governing party most centrally involved in the decision to go to war, particularly the head of state. Responsibility for the conduct of war, by contrast, rests on the state's armed forces. In particular, responsibility for right conduct rests with those commanders, officers and soldiers who command and control the lethal force set in motion by the political hierarchy. In general, anyone involved in formulating and executing military strategy during wartime bears responsibility for any violation of the *jus in bello* standards. In most cases, such violation will constitute a war crime. Detailed discussion of war crimes trials will be reserved for the next chapter on justice after war.

Discrimination and non-combatant immunity

Walzer insists repeatedly that the requirement of discrimination is the most important *jus in bello* rule. Soldiers charged with the deployment of armed force may not do so indiscriminately; rather, they must exert effort to discriminate between legitimate and illegitimate targets. How are soldiers to know which is which? Walzer answers:

a legitimate target in wartime is anyone or anything 'engaged in harming'. All non-harming persons or institutions are thus immune from direct and intentional attack by soldiers. Since the soldiers of the enemy nation, for instance, are clearly 'engaged in harming', they may be directly targeted, as may their equipment, their supply routes and even some of their civilian suppliers. Civilians not engaged in the military effort of their nation may not be targeted with lethal force. In general, Walzer asserts that '[a] legitimate act of war is one that does not violate the rights of the people against whom it is directed'.[4] In response, one might ask: how is it that armed force directed against soldiers does not violate their rights, whereas that directed against civilians violates theirs? In the chaos of wartime, what exactly marks the difference?

One of the murkiest areas of Walzer's just war theory concerns the moral status of ordinary soldiers. His references to them exhibit, on the one hand, a humane sympathy for their 'shared servitude' as 'the pawns of war'. On the other, his references occasionally display a glib callousness, as when he concurs with Napoleon's (in)famous remark that 'soldiers are made to be killed'.[5] How can soldiers be made to be killed when, as human beings, they enjoy human rights to life and liberty? If it is our shared ideas about human personality which (somehow) justify human rights, how can Walzer claim that these possessors of personality may be directly, intentionally targeted with lethal force? The answer must be that soldiers do something which causes them to forfeit their rights, much as an outlaw country forfeits its state rights to non-interference when it commits aggression. This is indeed the case for Walzer: '[N]o one can be forced to fight or to risk his life, no one can be threatened with war or warred against unless through some act of his own he has surrendered or lost his rights.' One could be forgiven for inferring from this principle that only soldiers of an aggressor nation forfeit their rights, since they are the only ones engaged in the kind of rights-violative harm which grounds a violent, punitive response. Interestingly, and perhaps problematically, Walzer denies this. He believes that *all* soldiers forfeit their right not to be targeted with lethal force, whether they be of just or unjust nations, whether they be tools of aggression or instruments of defence.[6]

Walzer's concept here is of 'the moral equality of soldiers'. The first 'war right' of soldiers is to kill enemy soldiers. We do not, and should not, make soldiers pay the price for the injustice of the wars they may be ordered – perhaps even conscripted – to fight. That is the logically and morally separate issue of *jus ad bellum*, for which Walzer has already elaborated a theory of justice, focusing on the responsibilities of political leaders. But lawyers like the chief British prosecutor during the Nuremberg trials, and philosophers like Thomas Pogge, ask: why should we not hold soldiers responsible for the justice of the wars they fight? If we held soldiers responsible in this regard, would that not constitute an additional bar against aggressive war? Would that not account for the fact that, even though the war was set in motion by others, soldiers remain its essential executors? Would that not impose and highlight an important responsibility for soldiers, namely, to refuse to participate in the prosecution of aggressive war?[7]

Walzer experiences difficulty answering this argument fully. As an opening gambit, he contends that soldiers 'are most likely to believe that their wars are just'. But this alone cannot justify their actions, since their beliefs may not be well grounded, especially considering the incentive they have to believe such justification in the first place. Walzer also says that soldiers rarely fail to fight, owing to '[t]heir routine habits of law-abidingess, their fear, their patriotism [and] their moral investment in the state'.[8] But the fact that soldiers rarely fail to fight does not demonstrate that they are always justified in fighting, especially if the cause is unjust. Walzer next suggests that knowledge about the justice of the wars soldiers fight is 'hard to come by'. This is a surprising claim from a just war theorist devoted to making that knowledge more accessible and comprehensible. Perhaps, then, this is a reference to the soldier's general lack of education, as well as to government tendencies towards secrecy. Fair enough, but ignorance at best constitutes an excuse, and not a justification, for wilfully fighting in an unjust war: it seems a stretch to assert that such ignorance can morally ground a 'war right' to kill enemy soldiers. Walzer's subsequent move appeals to the authority of Vitoria, who suggested that if soldiers were allowed to pick and choose the wars they were willing to fight in, the result would be 'grave peril' for their country. But this empirical generalization is speculative: why wouldn't the result actually be the preferred one, namely, that states would be seriously hampered only in their efforts to prosecute an aggressive war which they could not justify to their soldiery?[9]

Walzer turns to his conventionalist methodology for assistance in this regard: as a matter of fact, he suggests, we do not blame soldiers for killing other soldiers. We blame soldiers only when they deliberately kill either civilians or enemy soldiers kept by them as disarmed prisoners of war. We extend to all soldiers caught in the midst of battle the right to deploy armed force on behalf of their own country.[10] This is a true legal contention, and not an implausible moral one, but the latter is not so obvious as Walzer suggests. Do we really believe that those soldiers who fought for Hitler, for example, were utterly blameless for their bit part in the execution of his mad aggression? No doubt, we tend to exonerate conscripts like the Hitler Youth in the closing days of the war, presuming they were far too young, gullible and propagandized to have made a free choice. But what about those mature German soldiers who invaded Poland, or France, at the war's outset? It is not so clear to me that, as a matter of fact, we do not blame them for fighting on behalf of their country.

Walzer stresses more generally the pervasive socialization of soldiers of *any* nation, their relative youth, their frequent conscription, and their usual background as members of underprivileged classes as grounds for not holding soldiers responsible for the wars they fight. While soldiers 'are not ... entirely without volition', '[t]heir will is independent and effective only within a limited sphere.' This sphere contains only those tactics and manœuvres soldiers are engaged in. It would thus constitute unfair 'class legislation' for us to hold soldiers like these responsible for the justice of the wars they fight. We should focus on those most to blame, the leaders who set the war in motion.[11] But from the fact that political leaders are *mostly* to blame for the crime of aggression, does it follow that they are *solely* to blame, as Walzer here insists? Perhaps a compelling alternative would be to suggest that, for reasons Walzer mentions, there should be a presumption against holding soldiers responsible for the crime of violating *jus ad bellum*. But this presumption does not preclude us from concluding, in particular cases based on public evidence, that some soldiers of a particular aggressor state either did know, or really should have known, about the injustice of the war they were fighting, that they could have refused to participate in it, and thus that they may be held responsible, albeit with lesser penalties than the head of state. Such soldiers would be like minor accomplices to a major crime. Walzer's belief about the absolute separateness of *jus ad bellum* from *jus in bello* cannot, I suggest, be sustained in light of these considerations.

Walzer, in a tantalizing footnote, appears to flirt with a similar linkage between the two traditional just war categories. With specific reference to the soldiers of a democratic country engaged in aggressive war (such as America during Vietnam), Walzer stipulates that, as citizens, the soldiers should vote against the war but, as soldiers, 'they fight as members of the political community, the collective decision having already been made, subject to all the moral and material pressures ...' referred to in the preceding paragraphs, like their mediocre education, etc. Walzer says that any soldier with courage enough to refuse to fight such a war does 'act very well' and should be not only tolerated but honoured by a just society. 'That doesn't mean, however, that the others [i.e. the soldiers who still fight] can be called criminals.' Why not? Walzer's limp reply is to reiterate the socialization of most soldiers and to comment that '[p]atriotism ... is the ordinary refuge of ordinary men and women, and it requires of us another sort of toleration'. What precise sort Walzer fails to specify, yet it would seem a rather dangerous kind, as it weakens our condemnation and deterrence of the very kind of aggressive war Walzer so strongly rejects.[12]

Even if we agree with the anti-Walzer proposal that some soldiers may be held responsible for *jus ad bellum* violations, can we still concur with Walzer's idea that all soldiers generally remain legitimate targets during wartime? After several false starts, Walzer offers us a compelling reason to do so: soldiers, whether just or unjust, are 'engaged in harm'.[13] They bear arms effectively, are trained to kill for political reasons and are 'dangerous men': they pose serious threats to the lives and interests of those they are deployed against, whether for a just cause or no. Walzer suggests that an armed man trying to kill me 'alienates himself from me ... and from our common humanity' and in so doing he forfeits his right to life. This establishes, I believe, a strong *prima facie* case that, for soldiers, targeting other soldiers with lethal force is justified. Soldiers, whether for just or unjust reasons, remain among the most serious and standard external threats to life and vital interests. Only public, compelling and accessible knowledge about the injustice of the cause of his own country can undermine a soldier's entitlement, in the face of such a threat, to respond in kind.[14]

The converse of this general principle, of course, is that those who are not 'engaged in harm' cannot be legitimate targets during wartime. Walzer suggests that this is the most plausible, and publicly accessible, sense of 'innocence' in wartime. Its first application has to do with soldiers themselves: when soldiers no longer pose serious external threats – notably by laying down their weapons and surrendering – they may no longer be targeted and should, in fact, be extended benevolent quarantine for the duration of the war. He squares this with his remarks about forfeiture thus: '[T]he alienation [of the right to life] is temporary, the humanity immanent.' Thus, ceasing to pose an external threat ceases the forfeiture, and the soldier's human rights spring forth intact.[15]

The second application of Walzer's harm principle deals with civilians. Even though some civilians may inwardly approve, or even have voted in favour of, an unjust war effort, they nevertheless remain externally non-threatening. They do not bear arms effectively, nor have they been trained to kill, nor have they been deployed against the lives and vital interests of the opposing side. Civilians are not in any material sense 'dangerous men'. Thus, 'they have done nothing, and are doing nothing, that entails the loss of their rights.' So they may not be made the direct and intentional objects of military attack.[16] This is clearly controversial. Some thinkers argue that the fact that civilian taxes fund the military renders null and void any pretence of their being 'innocent'. Civilians are causally involved in financing the harm soldiers do. Others view nationality as shared destiny, or suggest that modern warfare is totalizing anyway and so wonder what the point of discrimination really is in our age. These are not trivial arguments, especially the first regarding taxation, but they fail to persuade. It is hard to see, for example, how infants could be anything other than innocent during wartime. Only the most dogmatic believer in collective responsibility could deny this, and then at the cost of his credibility. There is, moreover, little evidence that modern warfare is intrinsically totalizing: the Persian Gulf War, for instance, did not escalate into an indiscriminate slaughter. No doubt there are searching questions about the exact specification of 'innocents' in wartime but I follow Walzer in believing that it remains an important just war category, needed not only to restrain violence but also to express our strong moral commitment to punish only those who deserve it. In the midst of 'the fog of war', one of the most concrete and verifiable ways to determine such desert is to define it in terms of external engagement in serious harm.[17]

Owing to these contentions, civilians should be thought of as 'innocent' of the war, and thus entitled not to be made the objects of

direct, intentional attack. That this norm of non-combatant immunity is, as Walzer claims, the subject of very widespread, cross-
cultural concurrence is revealed by the fact that it is the most
frequently and stridently codified rule in the international laws of
armed conflict, especially the Hague and Geneva Conventions. 'Non-
combatants', Walzer emphasizes, 'cannot be attacked at any time.
They can never be the objects or targets of military activity.'[18]
Difficulties arise, of course, when we consider those people who
seem, simultaneously, to be both civilians and engaged in harming,
such as civilian suppliers of military hardware. What is the status of
such people? Walzer suggests that 'the relevant distinction is . . .
between those who make what the soldiers need to fight and those
who make what they need to live like all the rest of us'. So targeting
farms, schools and hospitals is illegitimate, whereas targeting munitions factories is legitimate. Walzer stresses, however, that civilians
engaged in the military supply effort are legitimate targets *only* when
they are engaged in that effort; to target them while at home in residential areas would be illegitimate: 'Rights to life are forfeit only
when particular men and women are actually engaged in war-making
or national defence.' Walzer agrees with Thomas Nagel's eloquent
explanation that 'hostile treatment of any person must be justified in
terms of something *about that person* [his italics] which makes the
treatment appropriate'. We distinguish combatants from non-
combatants 'on the basis of their immediate threat or harmfulness'.
And our response to such threats and harms must be governed by
relations of directness and relevance.[19]

Walzer's overall judgement on targeting is this: soldiers may target
other soldiers, their equipment, their barracks and training areas,
their supply and communications lines and the industrial sites which
produce their supply. Presumably, core political and bureaucratic
institutions are also legitimate objects of attack, in particular things
like the Defence Ministry. Illegitimate targets include residential
areas, schools, hospitals, farms, churches, cultural institutions and
non-military industrial sites. In general, anyone or anything not
demonstrably engaged in military supply is immune from direct
attack. Walzer is especially critical of targeting basic infrastructure,
particularly food, water, medical and power supplies. He criticizes
American conduct during the Persian Gulf War on this basis, since
very heavy damage was inflicted on Iraq's water treatment system,
and presumably would also frown upon NATO's targeting the

Serbian electric power grid during its 1999 armed intervention on behalf of the ethnic Albanian Kosovars. While soldiers cannot fight well without food, water, medicine and electricity, those are things they – and everyone else in their society – require as human beings and not more narrowly as externally threatening instruments of war. Thus, the moral need for a direct and relevant response only to the source of serious harm renders these things immune from attack.[20]

Another serious perplexity about targeting concerns the close real-world proximity of illegitimate civilian targets to legitimate military and political ones: munitions factories, after all, are often side-by-side with non-military factories, and at times just around the corner from schools and residential areas. This returns us to the complex issue of the Doctrine of Double Effect (DDE). It will be recalled, from our chapter 3 discussion of pacifism, that the core moral problem is this: even if soldiers intentionally aim only at legitimate targets, they can foresee that taking out some of these targets will involve collateral civilian casualties. And if civilians do nothing to lose their human rights to life and liberty, does it not follow that such acts will be unjust? Furthermore, since such acts are constitutive of warfare – the very stuff and substance of the conduct of war in our world – doesn't it follow that war itself can never be fought justly, and thus should never be resorted to, as the pacifist concludes?

Though Walzer is initially suspicious of the DDE, in the end he endorses one version of it as a plausible method for 'reconciling the absolute prohibition against attacking noncombatants with the legitimate conduct of military activity'. The DDE, we saw, stipulates that an agent A may perform an action X, even though A foresees that X will result in both good (G) and bad (B) effects, provided all of the following criteria are met: (1) X is otherwise permissible; (2) A only intends G and not B; (3) B is not a means to G; and (4) the goodness of G is worth, or is proportionately greater than, the badness of B. Assume now that A is an army and X is an otherwise permissible act of war, like taking aim at a military target. The good effect G would be destroying the target, the bad effect the collateral civilian casualties. The DDE stipulates that A may do X, provided that A only intends to destroy the military target and not to kill civilians; that A is not using the civilian casualties as means to the end of destroying the military target; and that the importance of hitting the target is 'worth' the collateral dead.[21]

The first serious objection raised against the DDE concerns its controversial distinction between intending Z's death and 'merely foreseeing' that one's actions will result in Z's death. Many have contended that the DDE is so elastic as to justify anything: all an agent has to do, to employ its protective moral cloak, is to assert: 'Well, I didn't intend *that*; my aim, rather, was this . . .' On Walzer's behalf, it is clear that intentions are neither infinitely redescribable, nor irreducibly private, as this criticism seems to imply. Agents are not free to claim whatever laudable intention they want in order to justify their actions, however heinous. Intentions must meet minimal criteria of coherence and, moreover, must be connected to patterns of action which are publicly accessible. The criminal justice system of most countries is predicated on these ideas: for such serious crimes as murder, the case must be made by the prosecution that the accused had *mens rea*, or the intent to kill. This is done by offering third-person, publicly accessible evidence tied to the accused's actions, behaviour and assertions leading up to the time of the murder, as well as considering whether he had both incentive and motive to commit the crime. Juries, as reasonable and experienced persons, are then invited to infer the accused's state of mind. The plausibility of this procedure undermines the popular academic claim that the DDE can be used to justify any heinous action, whether in war or peace. Walzer agrees, suggesting that we know the intentions of agents through their actions: '[T]he surest sign of good intentions in war is restraint in its conduct.' In other words, when armies fight in strict adherence to *jus in bello* – taking aim only at legitimate targets, using only proportionate force, not employing intrinsically heinous means – they cannot meaningfully be said to intend the deaths of civilians killed collaterally. Their actions, focusing on military targets and taking due care that civilians are not killed, reveals their intentions.[22]

What exactly constitutes 'due care' by armies that civilians are not killed during the prosecution of otherwise legitimate military campaigns? For Walzer, it involves soldiers accepting more risks to themselves to ensure that they hit only the proper targets: 'We draw a circle of rights around civilians, and soldiers are supposed to accept (some) risks in order to save civilian lives.' This principle might, for instance, entail that soldiers use only certain kinds of weapons (e.g. 'smart' bombs, laser-guided cruise missiles), move in more closely on the targets (e.g. flying lower on a bombing raid), gather and analyse intelligence on the precise nature of suspected targets, perhaps provide some kind of advance warning to nearby civilians, and certainly plan the tactic in advance with an eye towards minimizing civilian casualties. Walzer suggests we locate the limits of additional risk-taking that soldiers can and should shoulder on behalf of those civilians they endanger at that point where 'any further risk-taking would almost certainly doom the military venture or make it so costly that it could not be repeated'.[23]

Walzer maintains that civilians are not entitled to some implausible kind of fail-safe immunity from attack; rather, they are owed neither more nor less than this 'due care' from belligerent armies. Providing due care is equivalent to 'recognizing their rights as best we can within the context of war'. Interestingly, Walzer concedes that the requirements of due care – in particular, to formulate strategies designed to minimize civilian casualties – reveal that, in some respects, 'utilitarian arguments and rights arguments ... are not wholly distinct'. We should note that a deontological pacifist would disagree, and insist that real respect for rights – as Walzer himself seemed previously to suggest – involves rejecting this kind of aggregative thought about due care constituting full respect for them. Civilians, the pacifist would conclude, *are* entitled to fail-safe immunity and, since it cannot be provided to them, war must forever remain unjust.[24]

What about the second criterion of Walzer's DDE? Can it ever be met to our satisfaction in the real world? On Walzer's behalf, it seems possible to discern whether a belligerent, such as country C, is employing civilian casualties as a means both to its immediate end of hitting the legitimate target and to its final end of victory over rival country D. If there were greater civilian than military casualties in D, for example, it would be clear which group of people was bearing the brunt of C's attack. Relatedly, if there were systemic patterns – as opposed to unavoidable, isolated cases – of civilian bombardment by C on the civilians of D, it would also be compelling to conclude that C was directly targeting the civilian population of D. Conversely, if the systemic pattern of C's war-fighting indicates its targeting of D's military capabilities, with only incidental civilian casualties resulting, then it would be reasonable to infer that C was not trying to use civilian casualties as a pressure tactic to force D to retreat and admit defeat.

The truly difficult aspect of Walzer's DDE is the third criterion: contending that the goodness of hitting the legitimate military target is 'worth', or proportional to, the badness of the collateral civilian casualties. A pacifist, for example, will always deny this. Is the need to hit a source of harm sufficient to justify killing people who Walzer admits have done nothing to deserve death? Does the source of harm have to pass some threshold of threat before one can speak of the need for its destruction outweighing civilian claims? If so, how to locate that threshold? More sharply, can one refer to the ultimate 'worth' of hitting the target to justify collateral civilian casualties without referring to the substantive justice of one's involvement in the war to begin with?

Walzer does not confront these potent queries directly, though one gains the impression from his work that the 'worth' in question refers simply to the target forwarding the war aims of the country in question. Provided only that hitting the legitimate target will contribute (how much?) to victory, the collateral civilian casualties will be 'worth' it. I do not believe that such an agnostic attitude with regard to war aims will here suffice. I fail to grasp how it can be morally justified foreseeably to kill innocent civilians in order to hit a target that only serves the final end of an aggressive war. The only justification sufficient, in my mind, for the collateral civilian casualties would be that the target is materially connected to victory in an otherwise just war. This suggests that aggressors not only violate *jus ad bellum*, but in so doing face grave difficulties meeting the requirements of *jus in bello* as well. To be as clear as possible: to satisfy the *jus in bello* requirement of discrimination, a country when fighting must satisfy all elements of the DDE. But it seems that only a country fighting a just war can fulfil the proportionality requirement in the DDE. Thus, an aggressor nation fighting an unjust war may, for that very reason, also violate the rules of right conduct. Here too we see that Walzer's insistence on the separateness of *jus ad bellum* and *jus in bello* may not be sustainable. Kant may well have been more correct when he insisted on the need for a consistent normative thread to be run though conduct during all three phases of war: beginning, middle and end.[25]

(Micro-)proportionality

The *jus in bello* version of proportionality mandates that soldiers deploy only proportionate force against legitimate targets. Walzer is as uncertain about this requirement as he was about its *jus ad bellum* cousin. He notes that while the rule is designed to prohibit 'excessive harm' and 'purposeless or wanton violence' during war, 'there is no ready way to establish an independent or stable view of the values' against which we can definitively measure the costs and benefits of a tactic. One case where he talks about, and endorses, a form of (micro-)proportionality involves the Persian Gulf War. During the war's final days, there was a headlong retreat of Iraqi troops from Kuwait along a road, subsequently dubbed the 'Highway of Death'. So congested did that highway become that, when American forces descended upon it, it was a bloodbath whose aftermath was much photographed and publicized. Although the Iraqi soldiers did not surrender, and thus remained legitimate targets, Walzer suggests that the killing was 'too easy'. The battle degenerated into a 'turkey shoot', and thus the force deployed was disproportionate. Perhaps another example, from the other side of the same war, would be Saddam Hussein's very damaging use of oil spills and oil fires as putative means of defence against an amphibious invasion of Kuwait by the Allies.[26]

Walzer insists that the 'chief concern' in wartime is the question of who may be targeted with lethal force. The question of what means may be employed in the targeting is 'circumstantial'. He suggests that the elaborate legal rules defining what means may, and what others may not, be employed during war is beside the point. These rules – such as those prohibiting the use of chemical weapons on the battle-field – may be desirable, he says, but are not morally obligatory. After all, if solders may be killed, how much can it matter by what means they are killed? While that is a persuasive way of putting the matter, Walzer should not be flippant about setting these rules aside, or assigning them second-place status in *jus in bello*, behind discrimination. For the robust and elaborate set of legal rules banning the use of certain weapons in wartime is, at the very least, an important piece of evidence for any account of wartime ethics which purports to be conventionalist. There is a vast number of relevant conventions on this issue, aside from the canonical Hague and Geneva Conventions, such as those banning the use of chemical (1925 and second protocol 1996), biological (1972) and 'excessively injurious weapons' (1980). Also relevant are the conventions against genocide (1948) and against methods of warfare which alter the natural environment (1977).[27]

In addition to the thickly textured legal conventions, one might suggest that there is a widely shared moral convention which stipu-lates that even though soldiers may be targeted with lethal force, some kinds of lethal force – such as burning them to death with flame-throwers, or asphyxiating them with nerve gas – inflict so much suffering and express such cruelty that they are properly condemned. Moreover, the reasoning which distinguishes between legitimate and illegitimate weapons is very similar to the reasoning which generates the combatant/non-combatant distinction. For example, there is a legal ban on using bullets which contain glass shards. These shards are essentially impossible to detect. If the soldier survives the shot, and the bullet is removed by surgery, the odds are that the glass shards will remain in his body. These shards can produce massive internal injuries, long after the soldier has ceased being 'a dangerous man' to the other side. Parallel reasoning was behind the 1999 passing into law of the international treaty banning land mines: land mines, too frequently, remain weapons of destruc-tion long after the conflict is over. Finally, restrictions on weapons can play a causal role in reducing destruction and suffering in wartime, something which *jus in bello* as a whole is designed to secure. Walzer does not even explicitly object to particular weapons on the grounds that they are more likely than not to have serious spill-over effects on civilians, and thus run afoul of discrimination. Biological weapons would fall under this category, as would many land mines. Such a stance would be consistent with other judgements one might expect, but does not hear, from him, such as criticizing America's extensive use of napalm and Agent Orange in Vietnam, which inflicted long-term damage to Vietnamese agriculture. Walzer is curiously unreflective about these considerations.[28]

Walzer recovers his reflectiveness about weaponry only when he considers nuclear arms, which for a number of reasons have not been declared illegal by ratified international treaty. 'Nuclear weapons explode the theory of just war', Walzer famously declares.[29] This is a graphic but unfortunate formulation, for it seems to endorse the popular academic view that just war theory is out of date in the post-Hiroshima era. But Walzer cannot believe this, for he has already explained to us, using just war concepts, how the atomic bombing of Japan was unjust. Thus, what his dramatic declaration must really mean is that nuclear weapons can never be employed justly. Why not? First, and most crucially for Walzer, they are radically indis-criminate weapons. Perhaps only a handful of the most volatile biological weapons are more uncontrollable in their effects. Second, nuclear weapons are unimaginably destructive, not just in terms of short-term obliteration but also long-term radiation poisoning and climate change, so that their use will always run afoul of proportionality. Finally, there is the hint in Walzer that, owing to these two factors combined, deliberate use of nuclear weapons – and emphatically an all-out nuclear war – is an act evil in itself.

No means *mala in se*

The most general rule of *jus in bello* which Walzer endorses is that armies may never employ acts or weapons which 'shock the moral conscience of mankind'. This seems to be Walzer's equivalent of the traditional ban on 'means *mala in se*', or methods evil in themselves. The imprecise yet interesting idea here is that some weapons and means of war are forbidden not so much because of the badness of the consequences they result in but, more importantly, because they themselves are intrinsically awful. Is this anything more than rhetorical heightening, an especially emphatic banning of indiscriminate and/or disproportionate targeting? Walzer believes so. Perhaps the most fruitful way to determine his concept of an intrinsically corrupt means is to define it as being rights-violative in itself. Using rape as a tool of warfare is a clear example. Rape is ruled out not so much because of all the pain it produces, or because it is aimed at civilians, but because the act itself is rights-violative, a disgusting disregard for the humanity of the woman raped, a coercive violation of her bodily integrity and her entitlement to choose her own sex partner(s).[30] We might infer for similar reasons that, for Walzer, methods like campaigns of genocide and ethnic cleansing probably also fall under this category. We do not have to do a cost–benefit analysis to determine whether such are impermissible in warfare; we already judge such acts to be heinous crimes. The intentional destruction, and/or forcible displacement, of whole peoples, as Walzer suggests, is something we find 'literally unbearable'. Indeed, the international community passed a convention in 1948 banning genocide. Nuclear weapons may also fall under this category for Walzer because use of them implies deliberate killing of the innocent, and on a wildly destructive scale. There cannot be much doubt that nuclear weapons have indeed 'shocked mankind' and are the objects of widespread fear and loathing.[31]

Reprisals

Walzer allows for reprisals in his just war theory. This is in spite of his acknowledgment that '[n]o part of the war convention is so open to abuse, is so openly abused, as the doctrine of reprisals'. Such a doctrine permits a violation of *jus in bello* rules but only in response to a prior violation by the opposing side. To his credit, Walzer refuses to condone any violation of the rule of discrimination as part of reprisal: 'we must condemn all reprisals against innocent people.' What of (micro-)proportionality and no means *mala in se*? While he does not explicitly say so, one supposes Walzer cannot countenance a violation of the latter rule for mere reprisal purposes. His single example of a justified reprisal focuses on proportionality and prohibited weapons. He claims that Winston Churchill was 'entirely justified when he warned the German government early in World War II that the use of [poison] gas by its army would bring an immediate Allied reprisal'. Such threats by heads of state have apparently become rather commonplace, since American President George Bush warned Iraq in 1991 that, should it deploy chemical weapons on the battlefield, America would reserve the right to deploy other weapons of mass destruction, up to and including nuclear armaments. It is important to note here that, presumably, Walzer means that not only the threat but also the threatened action are grounded by his doctrine of reprisal.[32]

Walzer justifies his permission for retaliations on the need to enforce the rules of the war convention during battle: '[i]t is the explicit purpose of reprisals ... to stop the wrongdoing *here* [his italics] with this final act' of *jus in bello* violation. Reprisals are designed to make the enemy stop its own *jus in bello* transgressions: state S violates proportionality, say, and state T responds in kind so as to punish S and hopefully prevent future violations.[33] Can we come up with relevant modern examples here? Walzer might, on these grounds, commend America's 1986 bombing of Libya as retaliation for the latter's involvement in terrorist strikes, or America's 1998 bombing of suspected terrorist sites in Sudan and Afghanistan as reprisals for presumed involvement in American embassy bombings throughout Africa. After all, with the important exception of the Lockerbie jet bombing in 1988, Libya has seemed to stop being a major state sponsor of terrorism since the American attack. And failure to respond to the embassy bombings in Africa would have only invited further violence by anti-American extremists.

Walzer's reprisal doctrine is worrisome. It apparently ignores the serious likelihood that reprisals, far from chastening the state which originally violated *jus in bello*, will actually spur further violations. To put it in just war terms, reprisals have dubious probability of success. After all, what government is likely just to sit there and suffer a violation of *jus in bello*? If it is the government that committed the first, unbidden, violation, why would it hesitate to commit a second one in response? If it is the government that received the first violation, then it will, not implausibly, fear that a failure to respond in kind will only whet its opponent's appetite for more destruction. Reprisal, in short, is a recipe for escalation, at its extreme risking the onset of total war, a phenomenon just war theory utterly rejects.

Walzer might contend that a certain kind of reprisal may well succeed in stopping escalation. Of course it *may*, but what kind of reprisal is that likely to be? Realistically, it seems, only a very severe, disproportionate one. And while Walzer extends his reprisal permissions solely in terms of relaxing proportionality (and not, thankfully, in terms of relaxing discrimination), we can still ask: how much is too much relaxation? Or is there too much relaxation at all when it comes to reprisals? Might Walzer, for example, condone the Gulf War 'turkey shoot' incident on the Highway of Death if it were in reprisal, say for Iraq setting Kuwait's oil wells on fire? Or if state T were to lose one brigade of its soldiers to nerve gas unleashed unbidden by state S, does that mean for Walzer that, to ensure an effective enforcement of the rules, T should now gas two, three, four brigades of S's soldiers in response? Or perhaps deploy a tactical nuclear device against S's battlefield positions? For me, these are rhetorical questions. They also underline the very precarious position of the ordinary soldier in Walzer's just war theory, subject as he is to all of these measures.[34]

Reprisal is a very tempting option in warfare, especially when one notes that, given its nature, the aggressor nation will most likely be the one which first violates *jus in bello*. And while relaxing proportionality against legitimate targets may feel like a fitting response to prior violations of a principle as important as discrimination – for instance, gassing enemy soldiers who engaged in civilian massacre – it is unlikely to achieve its more reasoned goal of deterring future violations. As deterrence, reprisal is dubious. As retribution, reprisal may seem elemental, yet it is unlikely to achieve more than a modest, temporary satisfaction of popular outrage. It would thus seem far better to adhere to the following policy on reprisals, adopted from a familiar phrase: winning well is the best revenge. But what if, Walzer would ask, one cannot put the first two together: what if winning cannot be had, in the real world, by fighting well and by resisting the sinful pleasures of revenge? What if, ultimately, violating *jus in bello* seems the only way to stave off devastating loss?

Supreme emergencies

Walzer notes that, when it comes to war, 'we want to have it both ways: moral decency in battle and victory in war; constitutionalism in hell and ourselves outside'.[35] We are therefore confronted with a grave dilemma when it looks as though we can win the war only by setting aside the rules of right conduct. Walzer, to his credit, refuses to indulge the fantasy that such situations cannot actually happen. His way out of this dark dilemma, however, is one of the most difficult and controversial aspects of his just war theory. It is his doctrine of supreme emergency and it permits not merely violation of (micro-)proportionality against enemy soldiers but even violation of discrimination against enemy civilians. It is something like the ultimate, no-holds-barred reprisal against the ultimate threat. How does Walzer pose, and then respond to, the problem?

Walzer stipulates that soldiers cannot appeal to military necessity to set aside the three rules of right conduct, as elaborated above, because these laws have already been structured with military necessity in mind: 'Belligerent armies are entitled to try to win their wars, but they are not entitled to do anything that is or seems to them necessary to win.'[36] Furthermore, the threat of suffering run-of-the-mill military defeat in wartime is not sufficient for a country to set aside *jus in bello*:

[T]he rules of war may at some point become a hindrance to the victory of one side or another. If they could then be set aside . . . they would have no value at all. It is precisely then that the restraints they impose are most important.

But sometimes a country at war is faced with something much more dangerous than run-of-the-mill military defeat. A country can sometimes suffer what Churchill called a 'supreme emergency'. Walzer suggests that when 'the very existence of a community may be at stake', 'the restraint on utilitarian calculation must be lifted. Even if we are inclined to lift it, however, we cannot forget that the rights violated for the sake of victory are genuine rights, deeply founded and in principle inviolable.'[37]

There is more than a mere taste of powerful paradox in this doctrine of supreme emergency. Its full flavour is captured by Churchill himself: '[W]e have a right, indeed are bound in duty, to abrogate for a space some of the conventions of the very laws we seek to consolidate and reaffirm.' Why did Churchill believe that the British enjoyed such a remarkably permissive right during the Second World War? He suggested that the British were 'fighting to re-establish the reign of law and to protect the liberties of small countries. Our defeat would mean an age of barbaric violence and would be fatal, not only to ourselves, but to the independent life of every small country in Europe.' 'It would not be right', Churchill averred, 'that the aggressive power should gain one set of advantages by tearing up all laws, and another set by sheltering behind the innate respect for law of its opponent. Humanity, rather than legality, must be our guide.'[38] Walzer's supreme emergency doctrine has affinities with Churchill's. Walzer stresses that, since appeals to emergency and crisis are inherent in the overheated wartime atmosphere, any appeal to supreme emergency must be subjected to the most rigorous public scrutiny. A supreme emergency exists only when there is proof of a serious threat which is not only close and imminent but also 'unusual and horrifying'. There is an important ambiguity with regard to what Walzer means by 'unusual and horrifying'. On the one hand, he suggests that the 'ultimate horror' in question is a serious threat to a people's 'survival as an independent nation', to 'the survival and freedom of political communities'. The emphasis, in other words, is on the grievous threat to the *sovereignty* of the community in question. On the other hand, the 'ultimate crisis of collective survival' denoted by supreme emergency refers to 'entire peoples being enslaved and massacred', that is, the emphasis is not merely on losing sovereignty but more on being subject to a further set of appalling measures, like widespread murder, by an unjust conquering regime.[39] Walzer's only example of a real-world supreme emergency conflates both senses. It is Churchill's Britain between mid-1940 and late 1941. Walzer argues that Britain was justified during this period in engaging in deliberate saturation bombing of residential areas in Germany, even though this violated non-combatant immunity. For Germany's blitzkrieg had left it triumphant throughout western Europe and the controversial Molotov–Ribbentrop Pact for the time secured peace with the Soviet Union in eastern Europe. America, of course, had not yet entered the European war during this time. Ignoring the massive assistance Britain was receiving from its Commonwealth, Walzer concludes that the UK stood alone against the Nazi menace. And it was a menace in both senses: to the sovereignty of the British people collectively and to the individual human rights of many if not all Britishers, should the Nazis conquer their island nation. He asks: '[C]an one do *anything* [his italics], violating the rights of the innocent, in order to defeat Nazism?' He answers yes, and justifies himself thus:

> Nazism was an ultimate threat to everything decent in our lives, an ideology and a practice of domination so murderous, so degrading even to those who might survive, that the consequences of its final victory were literally beyond calculation, immeasurably awful. We see it – and I don't use the phrase lightly – as evil objectified in the world.[40]

Is Walzer implying that both senses must be met for the close and imminent threat to be truly 'unusual and horrifying'? He never says so explicitly but is not inclined, as we have seen, to make sharp distinctions between a people's collective right to political sovereignty and individual rights to personal security, believing that the two bear close causal connections in the real world. This indeed seems the most comprehensive reading of Walzer: a supreme emergency exists only when there is proof of a close, potent and imminent threat of losing sovereignty and integrity and then being subjected to widespread massacre or enslavement. One crucial consequence of Walzer's conception here is that only just states may avail themselves of the supreme emergency escape clause; only those who have met *jus ad bellum* may invoke supreme emergency. This for at least two reasons. The first is explicit textual references to 'a nation fighting a just war' invoking supreme emergency, and as a result committing murder, 'though for a just cause'.[41] The second, unstated by Walzer, is that both by fact and definition a just state would not put another in a condition of supreme emergency; only a brutal, aggressive, rights-violative regime would do that. Though he resists it, and leaves it unstated, it seems that Walzer has no choice but to acknowledge some kind of ultimate link between *jus ad bellum* and *jus in bello*.

Since Britain in 1940–1 was confronted by the Nazis with both the loss of its sovereignty and the serious risk of being subjected to massacre or enslavement, it was appropriate for it to use its RAF bombers to lash out against the civilian population of Nazi Germany, in the hope that this might have some quelling effect on the Nazi war machine. Walzer stresses, however, that these conditions of supreme emergency evaporated by 1942, since by then both the USA and USSR had joined the battle, turning the tide against Hitler. This may be a bit strict, on his own terms, with regard to the dating: the war's outcome was arguably still in contention throughout 1942 and even early 1943. It is clear, though, that by mid-1944 the Allies could have expected eventual victory. In any event, Walzer concludes that continued Allied bombing of German residential centres – most graphically the razing of Dresden in 1945 – was unjust, since it targeted civilians and supreme emergency conditions no longer applied.[42]

Consider the quandaries regarding Walzer's doctrine of supreme emergency. What exactly is the status of this supreme emergency 'loop-hole' Walzer discerns in the war convention? Is it a *moral* loop-hole, suggesting that it is just for a nation to set aside the rules of justice for the sake of 'a greater good', like collective sovereignty or a world without genocide? If so, then how can Walzer appeal at the last moment to an aggregative, consequentialist concept like 'a greater good', when all along he has been resisting the appeal of an aggregative, consequentialist conception of wartime morality, in particular utilitarianism? How can he, at the last moment, suggest that the need for fundamental consistency between means and ends be put aside? Furthermore, how can Walzer rely on the domestic analogy throughout his just war theory and yet, in this case, endorse something which we would not commonly endorse in the interpersonal case? Walzer himself, after all, admits that we do not think it morally justified when person P, to prevent his own death at the hands of murderous attacker R, reaches out and drags innocent person S into the fray, using S as a shield between him and R. Walzer has trouble squaring our condemnation of the interpersonal case with our purported condoning of the interstate case:

> [C]ommunities, in emergencies, seem to have different and larger prerogatives. I am not sure I can account for the difference, without ascribing to communal life a kind of transcendence that I don't believe it to have. Perhaps it is only a matter of arithmetic . . . [perhaps rather] it is possible to live in a world where individuals are sometimes murdered, but a world where entire peoples are enslaved or massacred is literally unbearable.[43]

The reference to arithmetic is startling, and makes us mindful of the utilitarianism Walzer is otherwise at pains to criticize. His supreme emergency doctrine bears a striking similarity to the rule-utilitarianism discussed in chapter 3: during ordinary conditions of war, we are to adhere absolutely to the rules of *jus in bello*. However, when confronted with the very hardest case, we are to set aside these rules and do what we must to prevail. The fact that rights protections can ultimately be set aside in this fashion may reveal what, for Walzer, is really the primary political commitment. He puts it thus: '[T]he survival and freedom of political communities – whose members share a way of life, developed by their ancestors, to be passed on to their children – are the highest values of international society.' Perhaps what supreme emergency reveals about Walzer's theory, like rule-utilitarianism confronted with a hard case, is that individual human rights are not as fundamental for him as shared ways of life. Though we have shown that he is certainly not a simple 'statist' or 'communitarian' in the pejorative senses employed by cosmopolitans, Walzer may well be under the spell of some kind of Hegelian 'romance of the nation-state'. The seriousness of this is that Walzer may be faced with the same kinds of searing questions faced by rule-utilitarianism: if the rules can be put aside here, why not elsewhere? If in the end the triumph of the independent just state is what matters most, then why have separate rules of *jus in bello* at all? Why not let the just state avail itself of any means to crush the unjust aggressor right from the start?[44]

Walzer, in some sense, feels the sharpness of these questions. He admits that they force him into a paradoxical position: it is moral to set aside the rules of morality during a supreme emergency. '[I]n supreme emergencies', he says, our judgments are doubled, reflecting the dualist character of the theory of war and the deeper complexities of our moral realism; we say yes *and* no, right *and* wrong [his italics]. That dualism makes us uneasy; the world is not a fully comprehensible, let alone a morally satisfactory place.

The deliberate killing of innocents, though murder, can nevertheless be justified in a supreme emergency: it is simultaneously right and wrong. At the same time, with respect to the same action, we say yes and no. Bomb the residential areas deliberately – murder those civilians – but do so only because you are 'a nation fighting a just war [which] is desperate and survival itself is at risk'. Walzer even suggests that soldiers and statesmen really have no other choice but to opt for the collective survival of their own communities. They have no choice but to get their hands dirty, availing themselves of brutal, rights-violative measures for the sake of the long-term survival and rights-satisfaction of their own people.[45]

Calling this paradoxical position a 'utilitarianism of extremity', though, is most unhelpful on Walzer's part. For utilitarianism implies a commitment to an overall greatest good, for instance, to a conviction that it is better to ensure long-term freedom and survival than to avoid the serious stain of committing murder in the short term. Walzer talks like this when he stresses that rights are 'overridden' in a supreme emergency, presumably by the 'highest values' of a just and independent shared communal existence. Moreover, the utilitarian reference denies what Walzer previously insisted on: the total separation and equal importance of *jus ad bellum* and *jus in bello*. When push comes to shove, it is better to 'wager this determinate crime (the killing of innocent people) against that immeasurable evil (a Nazi triumph)'.[46] *Jus in bello*, in a supreme emergency, is of lesser import than *jus ad bellum*. The conduct may thus be put aside for the sake of the cause. But if this is true, then how is it wrong to violate *jus in bello* during a supreme emergency? In other words, Walzer's reference to utilitarianism does not fit together with his reference to paradox: utilitarianism is designed to avoid paradox by offering up a coherent ranking of the alternatives based on the goal of maximizing best overall consequences.

It seems to me, on the basis of these considerations, that Walzer's doctrine of supreme emergency is muddled in conception and dangerous in consequence. Sorting out the fragmented remarks, we come to the conclusion that Walzer's doctrine here is one of two forms: it is either a form of consequentialism, not unlike rule-utilitarianism, or it is a form of moral paradox. If it is a form of consequentialism, mandating the long-term survival of just political communities no matter what it takes in the short term, then it is at odds with either: (1) his own emphasis on the inviolability of rights; (2) our conventional condemnation of the same kind of action in the interpersonal case; or (3) his insistence on *jus in bello* and *jus ad bellum* being totally separate. If, on the other hand, the doctrine is a form of paradox, then it runs afoul of Walzer's own insistence that the best interpretation of our political commitments must at least be logically coherent.

Supreme emergencies, I believe, are not instances of genuine paradox. They are, rather, cases of moral tragedy. A moral tragedy occurs when, all things considered, every viable option one is confronted with involves a serious moral violation. In a supreme emergency, this is clear: if one violates *jus in bello*, one commits murder and perhaps other crimes. On the other hand, if one does not violate *jus in bello,* one's omissions may result in the death and devastation of one's people at the hands of a brutal, rights-violative aggressor. While the aggressor, of course, would bear the biggest burden of blame for this, I think we would still criticize a regime that stood by and did nothing for the sake of principle while such destruction was meted out to its people.[47] Thus, in a supreme emergency we are not truly confronted with options that are both right and wrong; rather, we are confronted with options *all of which are wrong.* It is a moral blind alley: there is nowhere to turn and still be morally justified.[48] In other words, I suggest we understand supreme emergency as a case where we exit the moral realm and enter the harsh Hobbesian realm of pure survival, where brutal, 'do-or-die' measures will be taken and may accordingly be excused but never morally justified. Supreme emergency is the only realm of true necessity in wartime. The suggested alternative, then, is this: in a supreme emergency, a just state will commit actions which are morally wrong in order to save itself and its people. While wrong, such actions may nevertheless be excused on grounds of the most extreme duress.[49]

Summary

Walzer defends three rules of right conduct during wartime: discrimination and non-combatant immunity; (micro-)proportionality; and a ban on means *mala in se*. His defence of non-combatant immunity is eloquent and formidable, but his insistence on it leads him to underestimate the question of prohibited weaponry. His allowance for reprisals and supreme emergency strikes which violate right conduct rules are very interesting yet deeply problematic. They are the darkest and most dangerous aspects of his just war work, in my mind far too permissive of actions which, at best, can be excused on grounds of severe duress and, at worst, constitute some of the most appalling crimes which can ever be committed. An underlying theoretical point throughout this chapter has been whether Walzer can sustain his separation between *jus ad bellum* and *jus in bello*. Reasons were provided for doubting this, reasons which will be returned to in our discussion of justice during the third and final phase of war termination.

6 • Terms of Peace: Walzer's Theory of *Jus post Bellum*

There can be no justice in war if there are not, ultimately, responsible men and women.

Walzer[1]

Jus post bellum refers to justice after war. It concerns the propriety of conduct during the termination phase of war: the lead-up to, and immediate aftermath of, signing a peace treaty which brings the war in question to an end. This is a neglected, yet important, issue in just war theory. Its import seems only to have grown in recent years, as any reflection on the difficult termination phases during the Persian Gulf War, the Bosnian civil war, and NATO's Kosovo intervention will disclose. To his credit, Walzer does not ignore this topic, as far too many just war theorists do. While he does contribute to the sparse *jus post bellum* literature, there is no denying that his account remains short, spotty and unsatisfying.[2]

Just as Walzer's 'refutation' of pacifism is limited to a mere six pages, focusing on a single argument, *jus post bellum* gets short shrift in his work. He writes but fourteen pages on the topic, and conceptualizes it as a mere adjunct to the topic of *jus ad bellum*. He reasons that since *jus ad bellum* concerns the ends for which states may fight, any discussion of *jus post bellum* must take into account such ends. While that is undeniable, it hardly constitutes a full account of *jus post bellum*. Walzer fails to grasp how *jus post bellum* deserves recognition as a distinct third phase of war, and how it does so for the same reason he gives for carving a distinction (though in his account an excessively sharp one) between *jus ad bellum* and *jus in bello*. Just as a war may be begun justly, but then fought unjustly, it stands to reason that a war may be begun justly, and fought justly, but then end with a set of unjust settlement terms. To block this, a set of *jus post bellum* norms ought to be constructed, using the core principles of just war theory as the foundation.

What I propose to do in this chapter, then, is to fashion one such set of *jus post bellum* norms, drawing on Walzer's work. Since his account of *jus post bellum* – with the important exception of war crimes trials[3] – is so fragmented and underdeveloped, this seems the most fruitful way to contribute to the state of the art. We see this underdevelopment in Walzer's writings, where he breezily refers to the need for 'defeat, demobilization and (partial) disarmament' of the aggressor nation during the termination phase. Whenever he talks about *jus post bellum*, he displays a curious tendency simply to list what he thinks the norms of conduct should be. He mentions 'resistance, restoration, reasonable prevention'; he enumerates 'disengagement, demilitarization, arms control, external arbitration'. He also, in a footnote, throws out the claim that 'the temporary occupation of enemy territory' may be involved. These listings clearly require more than a mere mention, for here as elsewhere in just war theory we look for substantive explanation and justification. We should try to put some meat on these bones.[4]

The ends of a just war

The first step, as Walzer indicates, is to answer the question: what may a state rightly aim at with regard to a just war? Before responding to this, it must be noted that the large assumption is being made here that the state which has won the war has also fought a just war.[5] Another underlying assumption here is that, as Kant claims, the raw fact of victory in war does not of itself confer rights upon the victor, nor duties upon the vanquished. It is only when the victorious regime has fought a just and lawful war that we can speak meaningfully of rights and duties of victor and vanquished at the conclusion of armed conflict.[6]

It is often contended, to return to Walzer's question, that the just goal of a just war is the proverbial *status quo ante bellum*: the victorious just regime ought simply to re-establish the state of affairs which obtained before the war broke out. However, as Walzer points out, such an assertion makes no sense at all: one ought not to want the literal restoration of the *status quo ante bellum* because that situation was precisely what led to war in the first place. Also, given the sheer destructiveness of war, any such literal restoration is empirically impossible. War simply changes too much. So the just goal of a just war, once won, must be a more secure and more just state of affairs than existed prior to the war. This condition Walzer refers to as one of 'restoration plus'.[7] What might such a condition be?

The general answer seems to be a more secure possession of our rights, both individual and collective. More precisely, the answer to the question 'What should a just state aim at with regard to the ends of a just war?' is one we have already encountered, in the form of the just cause criterion of *jus ad bellum*: a just state may aim at the vindication of those rights which have been violated by an aggressor regime. The aim of a just and lawful war is the vindication of the fundamental rights of political communities, ultimately on behalf of the human rights of their individual citizens. The overall aim is, in Walzer's words, 'to reaffirm our own deepest values' with regard to justice, both domestic and international. It is not implausible to follow John Rawls in claiming that, in our era, no deeper political values exist than those human rights which justify a reasonable political life and set of social institutions as such.[8]

From this general principle, that the proper aim of a just war is the vindication of those rights whose violation grounded the resort to war in the first place, more detailed commentary needs to be offered. For what does such 'vindication' of rights amount to: what does it include; what does it permit; and what does it forbid? The last aspect of the question seems the easiest to answer, at least in abstract terms: the principle of rights vindication forbids the continuation of the war after the relevant rights have, in fact, been vindicated. To go beyond that limit would itself be akin to aggression: men and women would die for no just cause. This bedrock limit to the justified continuance of a just war seems required in order to prevent a just war from spilling over into something like a crusade, which demands the utter destruction of the demonized enemy. This reaffirms Walzer's general view that the very essence of justice of, in, and after war is about there being firm moral limits, or side-constraints, upon its aims and conduct.[9]

This emphasis upon the maintenance of limits in wartime has the important consequence that there can be no such thing as a (morally mandated) unconditional surrender. This is so because, as Walzer observes, 'conditions inhere in the very idea of international relations, as they do in the idea of human relations'. The principles vindicated successfully by the just state themselves impose outside constraints on what can be done to an aggressor following its defeat. This line of reasoning might spark resistance from those who view favourably the Allied insistence on unconditional surrender during the closing days of the Second World War. But we need to distinguish here between rhetoric and reality. The policy of unconditional surrender followed by the Allies at the end of the war was not genuinely unconditional; there was never any insistence that the Allies should be able to do whatever they wanted with the defeated nations. Churchill himself, for example, said that 'we are bound by our own consciences to civilization . . . [we are not] entitled to behave in a barbarous manner.' At the very most, the policy which the Allies pursued was genuinely unconditional only *vis-à-vis* the governing regimes of the Axis powers, but not *vis-à-vis* the civilian populations in those nations. Such a more discriminating policy on surrender may be defensible in extreme cases, involving truly abhorrent regimes, but is generally impermissible. For insistence on unconditional surrender is disproportionate and will prolong fighting as the defeated aggressor refuses to cave in, fearing the consequences of doing so. Walzer believes this was the case during the Pacific War, owing to America's insistence on Japan's unconditional surrender. It is thus the responsibility of the victor to communicate clearly to the losing aggressor its intentions for post-war settlement, intentions which must be consistent with the other *jus post bellum* principles developed in this chapter.[10]

What does the just aim of a just war – namely, rights vindication, constrained by a proportionate policy on surrender – precisely include or mandate? The following seems to be a plausible list of propositions (P), consistent with Walzer's world-view, regarding what would be at least permissible with regard to a just settlement of a just war:

(P1) The aggression needs, where possible and proportional, to be rolled back, which is to say that the unjust gains from aggression must be eliminated. If, for example, the aggression has involved invasion and the unjust taking of land L, then justice requires that the invader be driven out of L and secure borders re-established. The equally crucial corollary to this principle is that the victim of the aggression is to be re-established as an independent political community, enjoying political sovereignty and territorial integrity.

(P2) The commission of aggression, as a serious international crime, requires punishment, in two forms: (1) compensation to the victim for at least some of the costs incurred during the fight for its rights; and (2) war crimes trials for the initiators of aggression, for the crime of violating *jus ad bellum*.

(P3) The aggressor state might also require some demilitarization and political rehabilitation, depending on the nature and severity of the aggression it committed and the threat it would continue to pose in the absence of such measures.

As these propositions make clear, a just ending to a just war involves: rolling back aggression and re-establishing the integrity of the victim of aggression as a rights-bearing political community; punishing the aggressor; and in some sense deterring future aggression, notably with regard to the actual aggressor but, in so doing (and at least to some degree), other would-be aggressors. 'One can', Walzer avers, 'legitimately aim not merely at a successful resistance [to aggression] but also at some reasonable security against future attack.'[11] Metaphorically, one might say that a just war, justly prosecuted, is something like radical surgery: an extreme yet necessary measure to be taken in defence of fundamental values, like human rights, against serious, lethal threats to them, such as violent aggression. And if just war, justly prosecuted, is like radical surgery, then the justified conclusion to such a war can only be akin to the rehabilitation and therapy required after the surgery, in order to ensure that the original intent is effectively secured – defeating the threat, protecting the rights – and that the patient is materially better off than prior to the exercise. And the 'patient' in this case can only be the entire society of states.[12] Comment has already been offered on what proposition P1 requires and why: aggression, as a crime which justifies war, needs to be rolled back and have its gains eliminated as far as possible and/or proportional; and the victim of aggression needs to have the objects of its state rights restored to itself. This principle seems quite straightforward, one of justice as rectification. But what of P2 and P3? What of compensation, 'political rehabilitation' and war crimes trials?

Compensation

Consider first the issue of compensation. Because aggression is a crime which violates critically important rights and causes much damage, it seems reasonable to contend that the aggressor nation, 'Aggressor', owes some duty of compensation to the victim of the aggression, 'Victim'. This is the case because, in the absence of aggression, Victim would not have to reconstruct itself following the war, nor would it have had to fight for its rights in the first place, with all the death and destruction that implies. Putting it bluntly, Aggressor has cost Victim a considerable amount, and so at least some compensation for that cost seems due. The critical questions seem to be: *how much* and *from whom* in Aggressor is the compensation to be paid out?

The 'how much' question, clearly, will be relative to the nature and severity of the act of aggression itself, alongside considerations of what Aggressor can reasonably be expected to pay. Care needs to be taken not to bankrupt Aggressor's resources, if only for the reason that the civilians of Aggressor still, as always, retain their claims to human rights fulfilment, and the objects of such rights require that resources be devoted to them.[13] There needs, in short, to be an application of the principle of proportionality here. The compensation required may not be draconian in nature; indeed, perhaps it need only be a token amount of purely symbolic significance, should Victim feel that would suffice for respect of the principle.

This reference to the needs of the civilians in Aggressor gives rise to considerations of discrimination with regard to answering the 'from whom' question: when it comes to establishing terms of compensation, care needs to be taken by the victorious Victim, and/or any third-party Vindicators on behalf of Victim, not to penalize unduly the civilian population of Aggressor for the aggression carried out by their regime. This entails, for example, that any monetary compensation due to Victim ought to come, first and foremost, from the personal wealth of those political and military élites in Aggressor who were most responsible for the crime of aggression. Walzer suggests that such a discriminating policy 'can hardly' raise the needed amount for compensation, and so ignores the fact that, historically, those who launch aggressive war externally have often used their power internally to raise considerable personal fortunes. In light of this supposed shortfall, Walzer argues that, since '[r]eparations are surely due the victims of aggressive war', they should be paid from the taxation system of the defeated Aggressor. There ought to be a kind of post-war poll tax on the population of Aggressor, with the proceeds forwarded to Victim. In this sense, he says, 'citizenship is a common destiny.' I believe, however, that this fails to respect the discrimination principle during war termination. Though Walzer insists that '[t]he distribution of costs is not the distribution of guilt',[14] it is difficult to see what that is supposed to mean here: why not respond by asking why civilians should be forced, through

their tax system, to pay for the damage if they are not responsible for
it? Respect for discrimination entails taking a reasonable amount of
compensation only from those sources who both can afford it and
were materially linked to the aggression. If such reparations 'can
hardly' pay for the destruction Aggressor meted out on Victim, then
that fiscal deficiency does not somehow translate into Victim's moral
entitlement to tax everyone in Aggressor. The resources for reconstruction simply have to be found elsewhere.

Rehabilitation

In terms of demilitarization and political rehabilitation, the notion is
that Aggressor may be required to demilitarize, at least to the extent
that it will not pose a serious threat to Victim, and other members of
the international community, for the foreseeable future. The appropriate elements of such demilitarization will, obviously, vary with the
nature and severity of the act of aggression, along with the extent of
Aggressor's residual military capabilities, following its defeat. But
they may, and often do, involve: the creation of a demilitarized
'buffer zone' between Aggressor and Victim/Vindicator, whether on
land, sea or air; the capping of certain aspects of Aggressor's military
capability; and especially the destruction of Aggressor's weapons of
mass destruction. Once more, proportionality must be brought to
bear upon this general principle: Aggressor may not be so demilitarized as to jeopardize its ability to fulfil its function of maintaining
law and order within its own borders, and of protecting its people
from other countries who might be tempted to invade (for whatever
reason) if they perceive serious weakness in Aggressor. Another way
this requirement could be fulfilled would be for the victors to provide
reliable security guarantees to the people of Aggressor.

The imposition of some substantial requirement of political rehabilitation is perhaps the most serious and invasive measure permitted
to a just regime, following its justified victory over Aggressor. As
Walzer asserts, the 'outer limit' of any surrender by Aggressor to
Victim is the construction and maintenance of a new kind of domestic political regime within Aggressor, one more peaceable, orderly
and pro-human rights in nature. It is probably correct to agree with
him, however, when he cautions that, as a matter of proportionality,
such measures are in order only in the most extreme cases, such as

Nazi Germany and imperial Japan at the close of the Second World War. Though Walzer only refers to Nazi Germany here, I believe the same holds true for imperial Japan. Owing to his understandable animus against Nazi Germany, Walzer fails to recognize fully the ultra-aggressive nature of Japan's actions during the war. While it seems right to agree with him that imperial Japan was not quite so heinous as Nazi Germany, it is clear – and the people of China and Korea would surely concur – that the Japanese dictatorship was still abhorrent and rights-violative in the extreme.[15]

If the actions of Aggressor during the war were truly atrocious, or if the nature of the regime in Aggressor at the end of the war is still so heinous that its continued existence poses a serious threat to international justice and human rights, then – and only then – may such a regime be forcibly dismantled and a new, more defensible regime established in its stead.[16] But we should be quick to note, and emphasize, that such construction would seem to necessitate an additional commitment *on the part of Victim/Vindicators* to assist the new regime in Aggressor with this enormous task of political restructuring. This assistance would be composed of seeing such 'political therapy' through to a reasonably successful conclusion – for instance, until the new regime can 'stand on its own', as it were, and fulfil its core functions of providing domestic law and order, human rights fulfilment, and adherence to the basic norms of international law. The rehabilitations of the governing structures of both West Germany and Japan following the Second World War, largely by the United States, seem quite stellar and instructive examples in this regard. They also illustrate the profound and costly commitments that must be borne by any Victim/Vindicator seeking to impose such far-reaching and consequential terms on the relevant Aggressor following defeat.

One open question concerns whether we 'probably' should agree with Walzer that rehabilitation should be reserved only for the most grave cases of aggression, like Nazi Germany. Why should we not impose at least some rehabilitative measures on any aggressor? Given the serious nature of any act of aggression – so serious that, by Walzer's own lights, it justifies war – why should we avoid subsequent political reform within the defeated aggressor, unless its regime is morally unsalvageable? After all, the immediate post-war environment would seem the perfect opportunity to pursue such reform, and presumably it would contribute to a more peaceful world order in the long run. The reason why Walzer hesitates to affirm this view is because of the great value he attaches to political sovereignty, to shared ways of life and to free collective choice, even if they end up failing to express the degree of domestic human rights fulfilment that we in Western liberal democracies might prefer. He cautions against 'the terrible presumption' behind changing domestic political institutions, even in aggressors.[17]

Perhaps a compromise principle on this issue, which could still win Walzer's endorsement, is to suggest that there should be a presumption in favour of permitting rehabilitative measures in the domestic political structure of a defeated aggressor but that such rehabilitation itself needs be proportional to the degree of depravity inherent in the political structure itself. This way, complete dismantling and constitutional reconstruction – like the sea-change from totalitarian fascism to liberal democracy – will be reserved for the exceptional cases that Walzer cites. But comparatively minor renovations – like human rights education programmes, police and military training programmes, international observers verifying subsequent election results, perhaps even federative autonomy for contested regions, etc. – can be permitted in any defeated aggressor, subject to need and proportionality. It is interesting to observe that many of the most recent peace treaties – like that ending the Bosnian civil war – have included this more permissive principle in favour of political rehabilitation. Political activity here seems to be outpacing political theory. This may well indicate a deepening and extension of our shared war convention since Walzer last wrote about it.[18]

We might also expect, as part of such regular rehabilitation, a formal apology by Aggressor to Victim/Vindicator for its aggression. While it is right to agree with Walzer that 'official apologies somehow seem an inadequate, perhaps even a perfunctory, way' of atoning for aggression,[19] this of itself is no reason to rule such an apology out of the terms of the peace. For even though formal apologies cannot of themselves restore territory, revive casualties or rebuild infrastructure, it is obvious that they do mean something to us. If not, why do such formal apologies, and victims' campaigns to secure such apologies, generate considerable political and media attention? If not, why do informed people know that Germany has apologized profusely for its role in the Second World War whereas Japan has hardly apologized at all? A conventionalist like Walzer must concede that it is part of our continuing commitment to a moral world that we expect wrongdoers (eventually) to admit their wrong-doing and express their regret for it. We feel that victims of wrongdoing are owed that kind of respect and that aggressors must at least show recognition of the moral principles they violated. Apologies are a non-trivial aspect of a complete peace treaty.

War crimes trials

This leaves the vexed topic of war crimes trials, the one aspect of *jus post bellum* which Walzer does discuss in detail. The normative need for such trials follows from Walzer's dictum that: 'There can be no justice in war if there are not, ultimately, responsible men and women.'[20] Individuals who play a prominent role during wartime must be held accountable for their actions and what they bring about. There are, of course, two broad categories of war crimes: those which violate *jus ad bellum* and those which violate *jus in bello*.

Jus ad bellum war crimes have to do with 'planning, preparing, initiating and waging' aggressive war. Responsibility for the commission of such a crime falls on the shoulders of the political leader(s) of the aggressor regime. Such crimes, in the language of the Nuremberg prosecutors, are 'crimes against peace'.[21] What this principle entails is that, once more subject to proportionality, the leaders of Aggressor are to be brought to trial before a public and fair international tribunal and accorded full due process rights in their defence. Why subject this principle to proportionality constraints? Why concur with Walzer when he says that 'it isn't always true that their leaders ought to be punished for their crimes'?[22] The answer is that sometimes such leaders, in spite of their moral decrepitude, retain considerable popular legitimacy, and thus bringing them to trial could seriously destabilize the polity within Aggressor. The international community recently faced this situation twice. The first was in Somalia, in 1992/3, when attempt was made to arrest faction leader Mohammed Farah Aidid for war crimes, resulting in a serious escalation in the conflict, which ultimately backfired and resulted in the international force withdrawing from the country. The second time was in Bosnia, in 1994/5, when charges against Bosnian Serb leaders Ratko Mladic and Radovan Karadzic seriously increased tensions and delayed the onset of a not unreasonable peace agreement. Care needs to be taken, as always, that appeal to proportionality does not amount to rewarding aggressors, or to letting them run free and unscathed despite their grievous crimes. Yet this care does not vitiate the need to consider the destruction and suffering that might result from adhering totally to what the requirements of justice as retribution demand. One interesting and not unprincipled compromise position, with regard to Bosnia, has been not to move directly into Bosnian Serb lands to arrest Mladic and Karadzic – owing to the serious instability that would probably produce – but, rather, to pen the two of them into their narrow territory for the rest of their lives, by stipulating that, should they ever cross an international border, they will immediately be arrested and brought to trial. The two are, it is said, under a kind of house arrest.[23]

Should political leaders on trial for *jus ad bellum* violations be found guilty, through a public and fair proceeding, then the court is at liberty to determine a reasonable punishment, which will obviously depend upon the details of the relevant case. Perhaps the punishment will only consist of penalizing the leaders financially for the amount of compensation owed to Victim, as previously discussed. Or perhaps, should the need for political rehabilitation be invoked, such leaders will need to be stripped of power and barred from political participation, or perhaps even jailed. It is clear that it is not possible, *a priori*, to stipulate what exactly is required with regard to such personal punishments. The point here is simply that the principle itself, of calling those most responsible for the aggression to task for their crimes, must be respected as an essential aspect of justice after war. It is relevant to add that the actual enforcement of this principle might constitute a non-trivial deterrent to future acts of aggression on the part of ambitious heads of state. If such figures have good reason to believe that they will themselves, personally, pay a price for the aggression they instigate and order, then perhaps they will be less likely to undertake such misadventures in the first place. Important progress has recently been made on this front. First, the former prime minister of Rwanda in late 1998 was found guilty of war crimes and crimes against humanity in conjunction with the brutal civil war that consumed Rwanda in the summer of 1994. Moreover, Serbian President Slobodan Milosevic was formally indicted for committing war crimes in May 1999, the first time a sitting head of state has been charged with war crimes.[24]

Walzer stresses that a head of state cannot escape judgement at trial by appealing to the function of his office. The fact that he 'represents' his people on the world stage, and rationalizes his actions in terms of 'reasons of state', can provide no exoneration for the crime of launching an unjust war. Why not? 'Representative functions [far from exonerating representatives] are instead peculiarly risky . . . because statesmen . . . act for other people, and with wide-ranging effects.' Heads of state covet power, actively seek it, enjoy its exercise, and exert enormous influence. If they 'hope to be praised for the good they do, they cannot escape blame for the evil'. Heads of state are as subject to blame – both moral and legal – as the rest of us, perhaps even more so. Walzer suggests that, when fishing for *jus ad bellum* war crimes, we cast our net wider than the head of state. No doubt, we must first look to the head of state but then should move down the chain of authority to see if other individuals are also decisively implicated. There will probably be others, such as the heads of the various armed forces, the head of national security, the head of intelligence-gathering, the defence minister, certain top-level civil servants, and so on. It was also contended in the last chapter, against Walzer, that some soldiers might meaningfully be included in this chain of authority. The general principle we are to apply in this regard, Walzer suggests, is the following: the greater a person's influence on his country's actions, the greater his responsibility for them.[25]

Some of Walzer's most interesting reflections in this regard concern the collective responsibility that citizens of a democracy face when their country launches an unjust war, as Walzer believes America did during Vietnam.[26] Walzer suggests that we discern their responsibility by first considering what the responsibility of citizens in a perfect democracy would be. By such a 'perfect democracy', Walzer means something like Rousseau's ideal society: a small participatory, or direct, democracy, peopled by enthusiastic citizens animated by the general will, that is, a sincere regard for the common good of the community they are all equally members of. Walzer asserts that in the idealized case, even though 'it cannot be said that every citizen is the author of every state policy', it remains true that 'every one of them can rightly be called into account'. So who would be responsible for an aggressive war in this instance? '[A]ll those men and women who voted for it and who cooperated in planning, initiating and waging it . . . All of them are guilty of the crime of aggressive war, and of no lesser charge.' Those who voted against the war are not to blame, whereas those who did not even bother to vote 'are blameworthy, though they are not guilty of aggressive war'. Why is this the case? Walzer suggests that we recall the parable of the Good Samaritan, which illustrates our agreement that if it is possible for one to do good without great cost to oneself, then one ought to do good. Walzer says that when it comes to resisting aggressive war, 'the obligation is stronger' than in the Good Samaritan story, because 'it is not a question of doing good but of preventing serious harm, and harm that will be done in the name of my own political community – hence . . . in my own name'. An engaged citizen in a perfect democracy which is waging an aggressive war 'must do all he can, short of accepting frightening risks, to prevent or stop the war'. In general, 'the more one can do, the more one has to do.'[27]

Very few of us, however, live in a perfect democracy. How then does this idealized model of democratic responsibility translate under conditions of an actual, imperfect, contemporary democracy? Walzer believes it crucial to get the right description down. Such a democracy has a large, diverse and scattered population, and is 'governed at a great distance from its ordinary citizens by powerful and often arrogant officials'. While these officials are periodically endorsed through elections, 'at the time of the choice very little is known about their programs and commitments'. Active political participation is the rare exception rather than the regular rule, and knowledge about the justice of wars fought is 'occasional, intermittent . . . [and] partially controlled by these distant officials . . . which . . . allows for considerable distortions'.[28] Under these normal conditions in an advanced Western democracy, the bulk of the burden for waging aggressive war will still fall most heavily on the governing élites and intelligentsia – 'the new mandarins' – who support the war. We know this excuses those citizens who vote against the war and emphatically those who also protest against it, rally opposition to it, and so on. But does it completely excuse those citizens who support the unjust war effort? It does so, Walzer says, only if the information required to make a plausible judgement is seriously distorted by the élites, and correct information is exceedingly difficult for the citizenry to get its hands on. It does not excuse the citizenry if, with effort, they could come across this information and make principled judgements. If citizens choose not to seek out such information, preferring either to potter around in their gardens, or to endorse the war out of unreflective patriotism, then they are blameworthy, though not of the full charge of aggressive war. What they are guilty of, Walzer suggests, is 'bad faith as citizens'. The information about the war's injustice is available; it is critically important to do what one can to prevent serious harm (especially that being done in one's name); so failure to do so constitutes, at least, a failure to meet the moral requirements of decent democratic citizenship. Widespread bad faith, in Walzer's eyes, constitutes a searing indictment of the democracy in which it occurs.[29]

Jus ad bellum war crimes trials, we know, are not the only ones mandated by just war theory: attention must also, in the aftermath of conflict, be paid to trying those accused of *jus in bello* war crimes. Such crimes include: the deliberate use of indiscriminate and/or disproportionate force; failing to take due care to protect civilian populations from lethal violence; the employment of weapons which are themselves intrinsically indiscriminate and/or disproportionate, such as those of mass destruction; employing intrinsically heinous means, like rape campaigns; and treating surrendered prisoners of war in an inhumane fashion, such as torturing them. Walzer makes a compelling argument that primary responsibility for these war crimes must fall on the shoulders of those soldiers, officers and military commanders who were most actively involved in their commission.[30]

A critical aspect to note here is that, unlike *jus ad bellum* war crimes, *jus in bello* war crimes can be, and usually are, committed by all sides in the conflict. So care needs to be taken that Victim/Vindicator avoid the very tempting position of punishing only *jus ad bellum* war crimes. In order to avoid charges of asymmetry – or 'double-standard' – and revenge punishment, Victim/Vindicator, despite the justice of its cause in fighting, must also be willing to submit members of its military for the commission of *jus in bello* war crimes to an impartially constructed international tribunal.

This matter ties into one aspect of the longer-term international reform which will be dealt with in the next chapter: the need for the construction and maintenance of a permanent, competent and impartially constituted international court for war crimes trials, perhaps to be located at The Hague as part of a revamped International Court of Justice (ICJ). The members of the international community, in July 1998, voted in favour of a treaty establishing such a permanent court at The Hague. The treaty still requires the ratification of sixty countries, though, before the court will be legitimate and functioning. The idea is this: all war crimes, in all wars, ought to be seriously investigated and tried according to a set of fair procedures; and all sides to such conflicts ought to fall under scrutiny in this regard, and not simply those who happened to be on the losing side, even if they were the aggressors. Finally, the existence of a *permanent* international court for war crimes trials, and not merely those *ad hoc* courts currently in existence, would seem needed to build up the kind of consistent, coherent and morally defensible jurisprudence surrounding war crimes that seems essential to add further legitimacy and effectiveness to war crimes prosecution.[31]

The exact kind of punishment for *jus in bello* war crimes, as for *jus ad bellum* violations, cannot be specified philosophically in advance of considering the concrete details of the case in question. It may involve such things as disciplinary action within the service, expulsion from the armed forces, jail time, perhaps the paying of personal restitution, and so on.

Walzer takes some time considering the two defences, or excuses, soldiers most often employ in *jus in bello* war crimes cases: that of battle frenzy; and that of superior orders. The idea behind the first defence is that a particular battle, or even a whole war, is so intense, chaotic and brutalizing that, although it starts out measured and discriminating, it ends up escalating to the point where atrocities get committed. Walzer is very sceptical of this argument, contending that even in alleged cases of battle frenzy, other soldiers present at the scene retain their control and combat sense under exactly the same conditions as those who fly off the handle and commit atrocities, like slaughtering civilians. The only plausible case for this implausible defence, Walzer suggests, is when an officer actually encourages battle frenzy as a way of cementing the fighting spirit or unity of his troops. But this is at best a mitigating factor, not an excuse. Walzer comments that such an officer is not only stupid – since soldiers fight best when they are disciplined and controlled – but is issuing a blatantly immoral order, and the soldiers under him should not follow such an order.

This ties into the second defence most frequently offered by soldiers in defence of *jus in bello* war crimes charges: superior orders. Though such a defence strategy invokes savage scorn, almost reflexively, owing to its extensive use by the Nazis, Walzer does not indulge in such easy criticism. He is well aware of the fact that, from the first day of induction into the armed forces, a soldier is literally drilled into obeying the orders of his commanding officers. This is the case in both just and unjust states. Failure to obey always comes with punitive measures. The very point of military training is to habituate soldiers to follow orders under the most hellish conditions of war, so that they can retain fighting coherence and achieve their objectives. Even so, Walzer insists that ordinary soldiers, by their participation in our shared war convention, know when they are confronted with a blatantly immoral order (such as massacring civilians), and they are duty-bound not to follow it. If they do so, they should be charged with war crimes. The only excuse here is if the blatantly immoral order is coupled with a credible threat of execution for disobedience. Nazi officers, for example, would routinely shoot their own disobedient soldiers in front of their unit to enforce compliance. A soldier with a gun at his head, clearly, is a man acting under extreme duress and so cannot be held responsible for his actions. The person to be held responsible here would be the person who issued the immoral order, and coupled it with the grievous threat as a matter of policy. Walzer stresses that the excuse of superior orders will only hold if the penalty for disobedience is extremely severe, such as execution. He notes that there is always some penalty for disobedience, but does not allow any old penalty to suffice as an excuse. The threat of demotion in the ranks, for instance, is obviously not enough to excuse murder. It has to be something as grave as execution to count.[32]

Officers and commanders, for Walzer, carry a considerable moral burden during wartime. They are duty-bound not to issue orders which violate any aspect of the war convention, nor are they to threaten excessively severe penalties for failing to comply with an order. Furthermore, they must plan military campaigns so that foreseeable civilian casualties are minimized, and must teach and train their soldiers not only about combat but also about the rules of just war theory. But what about those officers and commanders who violate *jus in bello* during Walzer's supreme emergency? Should they be brought up on charges as well, following a presumed victory? Walzer says they ought not to face jail time, but they should still be blamed. For they committed unjust actions, though for a just cause. Walzer brings up the example of Arthur Harris, head of British Bomber Command during the Second World War. He suggests that it was proper that Harris, alone among senior British commanders, failed to receive commendation after the war, owing to his terror bombing of Germany. This 'dishonouring of Arthur Harris', Walzer suggests, illustrates the appropriate response here to vindicate the war convention for future generations.[33]

Listing of *jus post bellum* principles

Perhaps it would be helpful, based on the argumentation above, to list a coherent set of substantive principles for *jus post bellum*, in a manner similar to that for the two other just war categories. A just state, seeking to terminate its just war successfully, ought to be guided by all of the following rules:

Just cause for termination. A state has just cause to seek termination of the just war in question if there has been a reasonable vindication of those rights whose violation grounded the resort to war in the first place. Not only have most, if not all, unjust gains from aggression been eliminated and the objects of Victim's rights been reasonably restored, but Aggressor is now willing to accept terms of surrender which include not only the cessation of hostilities, a formal apology and its renouncing the gains of its aggression but also its submission to reasonable principles of punishment, including compensation, *jus ad bellum* and *jus in bello* war crimes trials, and perhaps rehabilitation.

Right intention. A state must intend to carry out the process of war termination only in terms of those principles contained in the other *jus post bellum* rules. Revenge is strictly ruled out as an animating force. Moreover, the just state in question must commit itself to symmetry and equal application with regard to the investigation and prosecution of any *jus in bello* war crimes.

Public declaration and legitimate authority. The terms of the peace must be publicly proclaimed by a legitimate authority, which is to say the national governments of Victim/Vindicator.

Discrimination. In setting the terms of the peace, the just and victorious state is to differentiate between the political and military leaders, the soldiers and the civilian population within Aggressor. Undue and unfair hardship is not to be brought upon the civilian population in particular; punitive measures are to be focused upon those élites most responsible for the aggression.

Proportionality. Any terms of peace must be proportional to the end of reasonable rights vindication. Absolutist crusades against, and/or draconian punishments for, aggression are especially to be avoided. The people of the defeated Aggressor never forfeit their human rights, and so are entitled not to be 'blotted out' from the community of nations. There is thus no such thing as a morally mandated unconditional surrender.

Any serious defection from these principles of *jus post bellum*, on the part either of Victim/Vindicators or Aggressor, is a violation of the rules of just war and so should be punished. At the very least, such violation of *jus post bellum* mandates a new round of good-faith diplomatic negotiations – perhaps even binding international arbitration – between the relevant parties to the dispute. At the very most, such violation gives the aggrieved party a just cause – *but no more than a just cause* – for resuming hostilities. Full recourse to the resumption of hostilities may be made only if all the other criteria of *jus ad bellum* are satisfied in addition to just cause.

Summary

Walzer offers a patchy yet broadly useful account of justice after war. Using his sketchy yet suggestive reflections as a base, this chapter offered a set of *jus post bellum* rules modelled after those of the two traditional just war categories, seeking to meet Kant's insistence that there should be consistent rules of conduct guiding state actors during the beginning, middle and end of war. The terms of the peace, for ending any particular war, should fulfil just cause for termination, right intention, public declaration by a proper authority, discrimination and proportionality.

7 • Considering Globalism, Proposing Pluralism: Walzer on International Justice in General

[T]he state is still the critical arena of political life. It has not been transcended ... as individuals need a home, so rights require a location.

Walzer[1]

Our task as philosophers requires that we try to imagine new, better political structures. Yes, we must be realistic, but not to the point of presenting ... the essentials of the status quo as unalterable facts.

Thomas Pogge[2]

Many, if not most, of Walzer's critics have accused him of being insufficiently critical of the status quo of international relations. They believe that his conventionalism is intrinsically conservative and that his just war theory, influential as it has been, merely serves as a kind of bandage over the real wound: the radical deficiencies of the current world structure. Instead of trying to develop and explain rules regulating warfare, they ask, why not work for a world in which war becomes a thing of the past? Instead of presupposing – some say fetishizing – the existence of the nation-state, why not work for a world which has moved beyond the nation-state and embraced more inclusive and progressive forms of global governance? Walzer does not ignore these criticisms, as some have suggested, but is quite dismissive of the theory and ideals behind them. While he does say that reforming the international system is 'a worthwhile task', he believes that such reform cannot, and ought not, to be carried out so far as advocates of world government would have it. The goal of this chapter is to examine and explain Walzer's reflections on international justice, more broadly conceived.[3]

Global Governance

(A) Walzer's case against

Walzer's dismissal of global governance is at times pejorative. A world without war is for him a 'messianic dream'. To defend world government is to 'adopt that posture of passivity that might be called waiting for the UN (waiting for the universal state, waiting for the messiah)'. A world state 'is like . . . the millennial kingdom or the end of time: we can imagine it in any way we please; it is an empty vision; it provides no practical guidance.' One can almost hear his contempt when he suggests that 'the only problem' which advocates of world government 'cannot solve is the political problem of creating, once and for all, this omnipotent source of solutions'. Even debating the precise meaning of the UN Charter – and the UN hardly counts as a full-blown world state – is something Walzer derides as 'utopian quibbling'. At best, he asserts, global associations like the UN have a 'political and educative role', reconfirming our universally shared, thin commitment to human rights and underlining our judgements as to particular acts of aggression and the need for resistance. Such associations do not make for global governance; Walzer contends that the UN merely pretends to be what it has barely started to become.[4]

Although his anti-world state vituperation sometimes gets the better of him, Walzer does have substantive objections to the global governance proposal. The main one concerns its lack of real-world promise. Genuine global governance, if it exists at all, is so far over the political horizon that it makes little sense for us, here and now, to devote finite resources, even conceptual ones, to the project. Global governance may be a kind of theoretical solution to pressing international problems but it is not the practical one at this historical moment. Right now what we need most, so to speak, are precisely the bandages, such as just war theory, for the wounds they cover up are real and sore. The science of statecraft has not yet progressed to the point where more radical surgery, more profound transformation, can occur. States and peoples are simply, and evidently, not yet ready to endorse global governance on the scale 'dreamt of by the reformers'. Walzer notes that the desire for a world state, or at least for the transcendence of political sovereignty, is most frequently expressed by citizens of mature, long-standing sovereign countries, in particular those of western Europe. In areas of the world where political independence is a newer phenomenon, we should expect and note that the desire of peoples to enjoy their own state shows no sign of diminishing and is, arguably, increasing. And this desire is not limited to the freshly minted states of eastern Europe: it extends to those of post-colonial Africa, Asia and even the Americas.[5] Walzer refers, in this regard, to the virtues of his conventionalism: the world state reformers are too far afield from what we are ready to endorse and so they violate, or perhaps are ignorant of, our considered consensus. He believes that this lack of respect for conventional commitments to the nation-state expresses a kind of conceptual aggression, or philosophical imperialism, that can readily translate into its physical counterpart. He blasts the 'covering law universalism', or pretence to objective truth, purportedly disclosed by the method of discovery in political theory. 'Covering-law universalism is a jealous God ... [and it] offers a way of explaining and justifying assimilation, integration and unification, within and across states and empires.' An actual global authority, at this historical moment and animated by such beliefs, would be 'no less threatening than an imperial state'. Indeed founding it would, for the foreseeable future, require precisely the kind of coercion and rights-violation we condemn in our war convention. And the threat posed by an actual world state, in Walzer's eyes, extends beyond political control into culture and economics:

> The very phrase, 'communal wealth', would lose its meaning if all resources and all products were globally common. Or, rather, there would be only one community, a world state, whose redistributive processes would tend over time to annul the historical particularity of the national clubs and families.[6]

The world state reformers, in essence, fail to grasp how 'the political community with its government, that is, the state, is still the critical arena of political life'. The state 'has not been transcended'. This is so because peoples rely on their states for protection from the ever-present risks, and frequent brutalities, of global politics and, moreover, because states best express political life as it is currently experienced. This expression, while thin, universal and protective of individual rights at its core, is nevertheless experienced in a thick and particularist way. Moral and political life confronts us first and foremost in its robust reality, rooted in particular communities of which we are members and participants, in which we recognize important aspects of ourselves. Political life as Walzer understands it is shaped by shared spaces, historical memories, cultural refinements, linguistic expressions and common institutions long experimented with. Politics, in other words, is about the community coming together in a defined space, agreeing to pursue certain social goals and accepting the risks needed to achieve them. But the globe itself does not yet form such a community.[7]

At best, the globe for Walzer is 'a community of nations, not of humanity, and the rights recognized within it have been minimal and largely negative'. These universal rights, of course, are real and important, and we remain committed to their realization. Yet we are also committed to the continued existence of our more local attachments and political identities. This is graphically revealed, Walzer believes, by the explosion in the number of nation-states over the past 200 years. The world state reformers, Walzer suggests, would have us choose between the two but in fact, at this moment, we want it both ways: universal respect for 'the minimal rights of all' on the one hand, yet the maintenance of communal difference and cultural pluralism on the other. Walzer believes we both can and should have it both ways. In fact, he argues that the two aims blend in together very smoothly. Just as, in liberal democratic states, all citizens enjoy the same bundle of rights that in part entitle them to live life as they best see fit (subject to reciprocity), so too the ideal internationally is for all nation-states to have the same set of rights that imply, among other things, some protected space for the expression of communal difference.[8]

(B) Beitz's case in favour

There are, however, global governance advocates who do not base their claims on the idea that humanity constitutes a full-blooded political community. Perhaps the most relevant contemporary work here has been done by Charles Beitz and Thomas Pogge. What grounds the need for global political institutions is not, they suggest, political desire, or a shared way of life, or even humanitarian sentiment but, rather, the normative need to regulate present and growing causal connections between the peoples of the world. Given that our actions can, and often do, have a real impact on other people around the globe, and given that these causal effects carry moral import, it follows that global governance is something to which we must turn our attention. Beitz and Pogge are here inspired by Kant, who pointed out that justice can only be said to obtain between peoples whose actions can impact on each other. Kant asserted that all those who *can* impact on each other, through their actions, *ought* to enter into relations of justice for the regulation of their external conduct. The point of such regulation for Kant was to allow for the greatest possible freedom of action for all, consistent with a like freedom for each.[9]

Beitz contends that conventionalists like Walzer fail to acknowledge the importance of Kant's claim that just institutions must be established between all those whose actions can affect each other. This failure is rooted in the fact that such theorists have come to accept, as an article of faith, the traditional understanding of international relations as a state of nature, with the primary protagonists being nation-states. Beitz devotes himself to blasting this conventional wisdom apart, and in so doing to underline the existence of substantial causal links across the globe. He has four chief points to make:

1. In the state of nature postulate, it is assumed that all state actors are selfish and fearful of each other and that this sensibility is so potent that it sets a firm framework for what it would be rational (or not) to do. In particular, it makes some kind of conflict between these fearful egoists, in a world of scarce resources, appear inevitable, if not intractable. However, as Beitz points out, in current international relations, there actually exist many ties and associations which straddle the divide between states, such as corporations, non-governmental organizations (NGOs), churches, family ties, and so on. Although one would never know it reading Walzer's work, states are not the only actors in relations between peoples; there exist sub- and supra-state associations and ties which can serve not only some kind of conflict-mediating role but also as possible grounds for more extensive political co-operation.

2. In the state of nature postulate, it is assumed that there is a rough equality of power and ability amongst the actors. This is what makes it rational, in the social contract tradition, for all to agree to the terms of the contract which establishes civil society. However, as Beitz points out, this assumption does not hold in the actual state of international relations. It is not at all clear, for instance, what the United States has to fear about the power of any of the nations of sub-Saharan Africa, or what China has to fear from the Caribbean island nations. This fact of a clear inequality of power between

nation-states goes some way to explaining how it is today, in spite of the causal links Beitz discerns, that there is little appreciable sense of international community. This is relevant for Walzer's theory because it provides another explanation for a reality he places considerable emphasis on: perhaps the lack of global communal feeling has less to do with how we experience the moral world in thick, particularist ways and more to do with the relative distribution of global power, which produces smug callousness on the one hand, and bitter resentment on the other. Perhaps, then, if global political arrangements were different, then there might be more of the kind of fellow feeling Walzer believes essential to ground common institutions.

3. In the state of nature postulate, not only are the relevant actors selfish and fearful, they are also thought to be isolated and independent. They have only their own resources and wits to draw upon in the war of everyman versus everyman. However, as Beitz notes, in the real world states are neither isolated nor independent. Even island nations like Japan, which might appear self-sufficient, are in fact heavily reliant on outside sources for imports of prerequisites, like foodstuffs, raw materials and energy supplies. The ties between states – of trade and commerce, of military and political alliance, of educational exchanges, and so on – have created a considerable degree of interdependence amongst nations.

4. Finally, in the state of nature postulate, it is assumed that there is no reliable way to enforce common rules and procedures. This fundamental lack of assurance makes self-help, including resort to armed force, the order of the day. Beitz contends, by contrast, that there are reliable ways in which nation-states try to enforce a set of customary rules and procedures, such as those embodied in positive international law. These ways include diplomatic censure, punitive tariffs, economic boycotts and sanctions and, ultimately, armed force itself, whether unilaterally or multilaterally. Even though we do lack the much greater assurance offered by a full-blown world government, we have a number of reasonably effective means for upholding and vindicating a number of core rules and procedures in relations between nations.[10]

While Walzer endorses some of Beitz's claims – for example, he clearly agrees with the fourth – he disagrees with those propositions most relevant to the present debate on globalism. While Walzer writes that 'international society is not anarchic', he swears that it is still 'a very weak regime', a 'very loose society of states'. His inter-

national focus is solely upon states: non-state actors, like corporations and NGOs, are all but absent from his writings. Moreover, he
denies the existence of the strong ties of interdependence that Beitz
discerns and which could ground Kant's call for a 'juridical condition' to be established globally. Walzer declares that while '[p]erfect
self-enclosure [of a nation-state] has probably never existed', 'relative
self-enclosure seems to me an evident truth'. Walzer refers explicitly
to island nations like Japan and expresses incredulity at Beitz's claim
that they are subject to substantial relations of interdependence.[11]

Walzer claims that anyone doubting the proposition that nation-
states remain 'relatively self-enclosed' would have to account, 'on
psychological grounds', why newly liberated peoples so strongly
desire nation-states of their own. Moreover, they would have to call
into question what Walzer takes as fact: that '[p]olitical power within
a particular community remains the critical factor in shaping the fate
of the members'.[12] Beitz could point out, in response, that Walzer has
made stronger arguments. For the first one fails to grasp the insight
into the nature of justice which Beitz, following Kant, is stressing.
Beitz would claim that it is morally irrelevant that newly liberated
peoples *want* their own nation-state: the proposition on the table is
whether or not such peoples are engaged in interactions with other
people around the world in ways that are morally salient. For
instance, do such interrelations have a deep impact on people's lives
and carry with them the potential to inflict harm? If so, then they
ought to enter into some kind of transnational relation of justice,
even if they retain out of communal desire some subsidiary form of
governance amongst themselves.

This is the global version of the earlier debate, discussed in the first
two chapters, about the nature of justice itself. Does justice have
more to do with shared meanings and their proper interpretation, or
with the fairness of how persons actually get treated by each other
and by institutions which affect them all? What is more important,
from the moral point of view: culture or causality? Ways of life or the
consequences of our interactions? If the former, then Walzer's
substantive approach to justice has the upper hand; if the latter,
proceduralists like Rawls, Kant and Beitz do. Is this an issue one can
'decide', or does it rather rest upon a foundational value commitment, an elemental split in conviction and perspective regarding the
essence of justice?

Walzer's shared-meaning approach has going for it respect for cultural diversity and the fact that it somehow feels more familiar. Proceduralism has going for it concern with fair treatment for all, especially with regard to ensuring a decent minimum for the worst-off in society. Which is more of the essence of justice itself? Walzer suggests that both can play a role, with the former being prior to the latter, i.e. with proceduralism mopping up the spills shared meaning cannot handle. Proceduralists see things the other way round, namely, that appeals to communal resonance and cultural diversity are allowed only after free and fair institutions have secured everyone's vital interests. Given that Walzer includes vital human interests within his 'thin' conception of justice as fidelity to shared meaning, need there be such a sharp distinction? Personally, I do not believe so; but Walzer seems to. Is this just a matter of methodological pride on his part? This is probably a large part of it, with both sides claiming justifications – first discussed in chapter 1 – that rub each other the wrong way, that reach too far and assert too much on their own behalf. Yet there seems a core difference of substance with regard to the degree of latitude allowed to communal resonance *as a matter of justice*. Walzer's Hegelian and Burkeian influences lead him to allow such appeal wider berth than proceduralists like Kant, Rawls and Beitz will countenance.

There remains, in short, a baseline dispute between the two views about the exact moral import of communal membership and identity. This is perhaps most graphically revealed in Walzer's doctrine of supreme emergency, which I suggested shows the dark edge of his communal concessions. Ditto for his earlier beliefs about accommodating caste systems, and refusal to specify baseline protections for the worst-off, an omission of some irony for a socialist. In my view, Walzer's subsequent accommodation of proceduralism, and discovery of a universal thin core of personal protections and human rights, marks moral progress. And while I believe that community attachment above and beyond that baseline threshold of rights protection is merely permissible, I can understand Walzer's conviction that it has greater resonance for many people than just that. But what of his factual claim that communities are 'relatively self-enclosed'?

Beitz would be most keen to deny Walzer's assertion that contemporary nation-states enjoy 'relative self-enclosure'. Whether domestic political power remains 'the critical factor' shaping the fate of a nation is an interesting and complex empirical claim which is by no means as obvious as Walzer's protestations would have us believe.

Even Walzer himself admits that national destiny 'is shaped within political and economic limits', imposed externally by terms of trade, foreign-policy stances and natural-resource endowments. He even concedes that 'there are some states with relatively little room for maneuver [sic]'.[13] Beitz might suggest that we consider the global economy in this regard. It is not merely that the interest-rate policy of the Federal Reserve Bank of America sets the tone for stock and bond markets worldwide; nor is it merely that the wealthy West can dictate favourable terms of trade to, or dump its waste on, or get cheap labour from, struggling states elsewhere; nor is it merely that a run on the baht in Thailand in 1998 can result in the devaluation of such far-away currencies as the Russian rouble and the Brazilian real. The salient reality is the widening and deepening of the fact that our free and uncoordinated economic choices – as we freely go about our lives, in our own political communities – are increasingly impacting across the world, benefiting some and harming others. It has even been said that the globalizing regime in world trade, for instance as regulated by the World Trade Organization (WTO), is eroding the power of even strong Walzerian states to block their citizens from the effects of these decisions about production, consumption, distribution and exchange. These effects can either be very profitable (for the richest few in the West) or severely harmful (for the poor majority, especially in underdeveloped countries). And this is leaving unsaid how other important spheres of activity – like pop culture, communications and marketing – are increasingly global in nature. It also leaves unstated the impact that deliberate and co-ordinated political strategies, by powerful national governments, can have on the lives of billions half-way across the globe. Recent examples would be the expansion of NATO into central and eastern Europe, and immigration and refugee policy choices by advanced Western democracies.[14]

In light of the depth of these global connections, can Walzer sustain his claim that 'what actually happens within a country is a function, above all, of local political processes'?[15] On the one hand, globalization is clearly an increasingly important reality which Walzer fails to acknowledge fully. His 'relative self-enclosure' thesis seems precious, even partisan, in the contemporary era. He appears almost wilfully blind to the forceful undercurrents of political and economic interconnection, evidenced most graphically by associations like the WTO, the European Union and the North American Free Trade Agreement. On the other hand, while globalists are more in tune with these recent developments, they often exaggerate their case, especially when they pronounce melodramatically on 'the death of the nation-state'. States, for all the current pressures on them,[16] remain the crucial determinants of the direction and calibre of international relations. Their clear and continuing advantage over such other contenders as corporations – in terms of their access to military power, their unrivalled revenue-generating capacities (through taxation) and their control over borders and membership – ensures that states must still be crucial factors in any theory of global justice which purports to be realistic and relevant to our age.

I hesitate to pronounce one way or the other, for globalists or against, since so much here depends on rich and complex empirical findings which do not commit false generalizations. Walzer suggests that, for every case of a nation-state being economically dependent on externally imposed terms of trade, we remind ourselves of cases like Iran and Cuba, which reveal that internal choices 'can turn a country around in a way no decision by another country, short of a decision to invade, can possibly do'.[17] Several comments suggest themselves. The first is to stress the empirical complexities: is Cuba's economic ruination the product 'above all' of its own domestic, pro-Castro choices or, rather, more the combined effect first of the American embargo and then the collapse of Soviet aid? The second is to stress that Walzer's claim here is compatible with Kant's. Whether local political decisions have *the most effect* is beside Kant's point that, given that international realities still have *some substantial effect* on the domestic scene, putatively separate nation-states ought to work towards some form of global governance. Furthermore, Walzer's examples here are of nation-states shooting themselves in the foot, so to speak, with bad domestic choices. One might respond: in light of trans-border ties, can nation-states expect to do well for themselves, and prevent externally imposed harm to their citizens, if they make good domestic choices? Local governments may still be able to mess things up, and impose considerable injustices of their own but, given international constraints, can they really make things right if they want to, and protect their citizens adequately from deprivations that may be imposed externally?

It may be worth observing that Walzer's own membership in the world's most powerful country may blind him somewhat to the effects that international factors can have on domestic political, and socio-economic, conditions. For America is much more on the active, rather than the passive, end of global interconnectedness. Walzer's other identification with Israel might also play some role in his insistence that nation-states remain 'relatively self-enclosed'. That country's unique history, and geo-political position, has led it to pursue quite aggressively and adroitly the very kind of 'relative self-enclosure' Walzer takes as fact for all other nations. We should also note that Walzer made these claims in 1982 and may have since changed his mind, owing to the enormous growth of globalization which has occurred since then. One would be interested in reading an update.

The closest thing to such an update was offered by Walzer in 1995. In a response to Beitz, Walzer eventually concedes that 'the tendency is clear' with regard to 'evolving patterns of global proximity, knowledge and interaction'. 'This', he admits, 'is the story that needs telling if the requirements of justice are to be expanded' from the nation to the globe, and perhaps even from the meaning of particular attachments to the development of fair procedures for universal interaction. Yet without further ado, Walzer pronounces that 'for now at least, ordinary moral principles regarding humane treatment and mutual aid do more work than any specific account of [global] distributive justice'. This remark, while clearly not a cave-in to the globalists, nevertheless suggests a widening of political horizons for Walzer. Gone is the narrowness of the local reference, and the myopia of the self-enclosure thesis, supplanted by norms for humane treatment and mutual aid *not only during wartime but in the regular conduct of international affairs.* Presumably he refers here to two standard principles of justice, arguably embedded firmly in our universally shared thin moral code: do not intentionally inflict harm without just cause (humane treatment); and, when one can do so at reasonable cost, one ought to extend aid and assistance to those who genuinely need it (mutual aid). While non-harming and mutual aid do represent significant and meaningful normative constraints upon nation-states, it is clear that, 'for now', Walzer refuses to endorse those more invasive constraints upon political communities that the advocates of global governance have in mind.[18]

'[F]ar-reaching redistributions of wealth and resources', on the global stage, are things Walzer will countenance only in causally clear-cut cases of colonial or imperial deprivation. '[T]hese unjust determinations [and their] deleterious social and economic consequences' call for reparations. British rule in India, Russia's in

Lithuania and America's impact on Vietnam 'morally require . . . remedial measures'. The reference to specific cases is very much intentional, and indicative of Walzer's general frame of mind. He is as yet unpersuaded of the existence of systemic deprivations in the global system, realities which if present might serve to ground the global governance he otherwise derides. He thus occupies a position midway between the extreme nationalist view that international deprivations are akin to natural disasters, for which no one can be held responsible, and the extreme globalist view that international deprivations are the foreseeable result of an international global ordering, for which someone can and should be held responsible. While there have been a few concrete cases of external agents causing specific deprivations that ought to be remedied, most deprivations can be accounted for locally through decrepit national governance.[19]

(C) Pogge's case in favour

Pogge gives grounds for doubting Walzer's compromise position, and tries to prove the extreme globalist understanding. Pogge is an original scholar who has written some of the most provocative contemporary material on this issue of international causal connections, and how they impact on the question of justice. He observes the existence of extreme and widespread deprivations in the world, especially socio-economic ones, and those disproportionately experienced in underdeveloped countries. 'Hundreds of millions', he writes, 'are born into abject poverty and remain poor, dependent and uneducated all their lives. These persons are so poor and so cut off from minimally adequate nutrition, hygiene and medicines that some 20 million of them die each year of starvation or easily curable diseases.' These socio-economic depravities, Pogge says, constitute human rights violations because the very point of human rights is to protect vital human needs from deprivation, and these deprivations need not occur, since they result from human choice and action.[20]

How is it, exactly, that such systemic socio-economic depravities need not occur? How is it not merely conceptually but empirically possible to rectify them, enabling the satisfaction of these vital human needs here and now? The key, Pogge contends, is to realize who or what is most causally responsible, or implicated, in these depravities. He contends that these depravities are either the established (direct and intentional), or at least the engendered (indirect yet predictable), result of what he calls, after Rawls, 'the global basic structure'.[21] This structure, which Pogge admits sounds 'forbiddingly abstract', refers in general to 'the largely constitutive ground-rules that shape society'. The basic structure is 'the terms of social interaction ... which significantly involve or at least affect all its participants'. The basic structure, in other words, is the set of the most important ground-rules which govern our conduct. Furthermore, 'these ground-rules define a society's central procedures, bodies and offices and they regulate the assignment of benefits and burdens (rights and duties, powers and immunities, goods and services) to participants in general and to the occupants of special roles.' Pogge contends that the effects of the basic structure are 'profound, pervasive, inescapable and present from birth' in the following way. Social institutions condition us from the moment we are born, shaping our values, our modes of thinking and our very options in life, fixing what Pogge calls our 'pay-off matrix'. This matrix is 'the schedule of incentives and disincentives' to kinds of behaviour, and ways of life, which we might be considering. This matrix 'determines (in a rough, statistical way)' the significant aggregate features of the social context within which we live our lives, such as the kinds of freedoms, rights and duties we can enjoy, the political influence we might have, the level of wealth, health care and education we might expect, the rate of crime and illness we have to face, the kinds of work and leisure available to us, our life expectancy, and so on.[22]

Basic structures, thus conceived, may well seem to be, in general terms, the factors which most influence the provision or deprivation of the kinds of vital freedoms and benefits that we imagine as the objects of our rights claims. In other words, Pogge would find Walzer's account of distributive justice – discussed in chapter 2 – to be deficient, since it starts off with the existence of various social goods as its first premise. These goods exist; they have various meanings; these meanings tell us how to distribute the goods; etc. Pogge would suggest that we need to dig deeper and consider the prior question of how these goods came into existence in the first place. If we did, Pogge believes we would hit upon the existence of the basic social structure. It is this structure which ought to be the first premise and concern of distributive justice, seeing that it exerts the greatest causal force regarding not only the production and distribution of social goods but also, through such processes, the calibre of treatment afforded to persons.

What specific kinds of institution count as part of the basic structure in our time? Domestically, we can see the powerful causal role
of the following: the mode of economic organization (in particular
concerning the use of money, the existence of markets, the kind of
tax system and the system of property entitlements); the political-
legal-bureaucratic procedures for making public policy choices; the
use of socially sanctioned armed force; the family; and the systems
for delivering health care and education. How a society decides to
shape such basic social institutions will have a great impact on the
lives of its members. Pogge invites us to consider, by way of example,
the recent wholesale regime changes in eastern Europe: 'These
changes have shown that institutional choices, such as that between
socialism and capitalism, can have a dramatic impact on the distribution of income and wealth, education and health care, rights and
liberties, and quality of life.'23

One of Pogge's burning passions is to show that, in addition to
these familiar domestic social institutions, there exists a global basic
structure which can, and almost always does, exert considerable
causal influence on the domestic basic structures of particular nation-
states. What counts as part of the global basic structure? Pogge
answers: the very fact that we have carved the world up into nation-
states at all, and have since deemed states to be the absolute
proprietors of all the natural resources within their respective terri-
tories; the terms of trade between nation-states; the use of diplomacy
and armed force between nation-states; and more unspecified yet
very familiar policy influences which one nation-state can exert on
another, owing to its relative supremacy. These international realities, Pogge submits, also exert a 'profound, pervasive and
inescapable influence' on human beings, and are present from birth.
Whether one is born a citizen of America as opposed to Bangladesh,
for example, matters deeply to one's future well-being in our era. We
ought not, Pogge insists, to make the mistake of believing this to be
mostly a matter of luck. That would be, to use one of Walzer's
favourite phrases, 'a piece of mystification'. These social institutions
are in fact substantially the product of human choice throughout
history, and thus are subject to intelligent redesign. The existence of
Bangladesh, or America, did not just happen as a matter of luck or
historical destiny. Likewise for the existence of the set of social institutions within each country, and for the enormous disparity in
power, wealth and quality of life between them.24

Pogge believes that powerful nation-states, over time, have either consciously or unconsciously shaped the ground-rules of the global system to benefit themselves disproportionately at the expense of poorer and weaker nation-states. The result has been the kind of widespread, rights-violating deprivation referred to previously. Pogge comments:

[T]he global poor live in a context of a worldwide system based on internationally recognized territorial domains, interconnected through a global network of market trade and diplomacy. Thanks to our vastly superior military and economic strength, we citizens of the developed countries enjoy a position of overwhelming political dominance in this system and, through this system, we also dramatically affect the circumstances of the global poor – via investments, loans, military aid, trade, sex tourism, cultural exports, and much else. Their very survival [for example] often depends decisively ... upon our demand behaviour, which may determine such things as whether local landowners will grow cash crops for export ... or food for local consumption.[25]

Since Pogge shares Rawls's presumption that the moral vantage point for assessing institutional structures is to consider how the worst-off fare under them, relative to alternative institutional schemes, Pogge concludes that the global basic structure is currently unjust. This is so because it inflicts severe and undeserved depravities on many – perhaps even the majority of – people in the underdeveloped countries, and thus violates the core moral commitment not to inflict serious yet preventable harm on the undeserving. Pogge believes there are alternative institutional structures which would result in less harm and that, to the extent to which we fail to switch over to them, we are guilty of grave injustice. These alternative structures involve, at the very least, 'significant growth in supranational institutions' which can effectively channel more resources towards the global poor. Pogge concludes, in contrast to Walzer's comfortable conventionalism: 'I have come to doubt the appealing moral proposition that there is nothing seriously wrong, morally speaking, with the lives we lead.'[26]

Pogge presents a considerable challenge, both to Walzer's belief in relative national self-enclosure and to his belief that global governance can only be grounded if there is an existing sentiment of human community. Is Pogge's 'the story that needs to be told' to expand the scope of international justice in Walzer's mind? Pogge has done empirical research on this interesting idea of a global basic structure, and he relies on familiar moral principles that Walzer cannot readily dismiss as the flat assertions of discovery or invention. The core normative principles Pogge relies on are: that political systems should be judged by how they treat the worst-off under them; and that it is a gross injustice to inflict serious harm on the undeserving when it can be avoided. These beliefs are both present and powerful in our existing moral commitments; indeed, Walzer's humane-treatment principle seems based on the former and his just war principle of non-combatant immunity is rooted in the latter. It remains an open question whether Walzer can still hold on to his current understanding of international justice in light of these more recent contributions.

Reforming the state system

Before one can pronounce definitively on that issue, one needs to see the full picture as Walzer himself paints it. We have seen that he is neither a fan of far-reaching global governance nor of the unreformed status quo. He suggests that what we want from international relations is respect for human rights as well as space for communal difference. Walzer believes that both are possible and together form a coherent and attractive world-view. What is needed to achieve these twin goals, he suggests, is the 'completion and then complication of the state system'.[27] The goal of international reform, for him, should not be to transcend or discard the state system but rather to let it run its course to completion. Following that, the state system should be complicated by allowing for a myriad of freely chosen social arrangements which best express diverse political commitments, *provided* they all meet the requirements of moral minimalism.

This minimalism, on the global scale, refers to respect for the human rights of individuals and respect for the self-determination of other political communities, provided they reciprocate on both fronts. Subject to this thin yet purportedly intense constraint, people *'ought to be allowed to govern themselves'*, which he elsewhere enunciates as 'this critical principle, *for every nation its own state* [both italics his]'. '[I]nsofar as nations can decently do that', Walzer asserts that our socially constructed idealism commits us to respecting it:

We act immorally when we deny to other people ... the right to act autonomously and the right to form attachments in accordance with a particular understanding of the good life. Or, immorality is commonly expressed in a refusal to recognize the moral agency and the creative powers that we claim for ourselves.

In other words, moral and political consistency commit us to allowing every nation to establish its own state mechanism, subject to the minimal injunctions on rights-protection inherent in the thin universalism Walzer finds present at the core of every thick moral code.[28] Walzer concedes that his proposal for nation-state proliferation, followed by international toleration, is fraught with grave difficulties. For example, there is only so much land to go around, and many nations have competing and often compelling claims to the same land. We might say that religious tolerance is one thing, since we all have our own consciences, but this kind of international tolerance seems quite another, for we do not all have our own territory, much less our own government, and it is not clear that we all could have our own. The complex reality, of course, is that nations now reside within other nations, which in turn reside within other nations. Is Walzer opening up a Pandora's box of territorial claims, and counter-claims, permitting an infinite regression into political chaos, a free-for-all over territorial control? Or does he believe that some nations are not entitled to their own land and state, on grounds that 'one nation's freedom is, often, another nation's oppression'?[29]

While recognizing the considerable dangers involved, Walzer asserts that they 'need not' be realized, and that the achievement of international tolerance will allow for an international peace similar to the domestic peace which obtained in Western societies following the spread of religious toleration. 'Good fences', after all, 'make good neighbours.' But this is true only when, among other things, there is agreement on where the fences should go. How are we to 'disentangle the tribes' in a manner which is fair and which can ensure respect for the moral minimum to which we are all, supposedly, committed?[30] Walzer's first principle is that 'the land should follow the people'. Given that a nation has forged a common life on a piece of territory, their communal claims to secure possession of that land outweigh any rival claims to it based on such technicalities as the provisions of a dated treaty or the result of some ancient battle. It is the current realities which are the most important and authoritative. Walzer believes that respect for this basic principle could go some way towards meeting the territorial needs of genuine nations, who have forged a vibrant and continuing communal existence which its members find meaningful and worth preserving.[31]

'Going some way' towards meeting territorial needs, though, is not the same thing as fully satisfying them. Even if we let the land follow the people, some people are going to be left with more land than they need, while others may not be left with any, or at least nowhere near enough. What are we to do then? Walzer suggests that the thin, shared principle of mutual aid can provide a plausible answer: if some peoples have more than they need, then some accommodation or redistribution of land may be in order. Walzer's specific example is of sparsely populated Australia, surrounded by a sea of south-eastern Asian nations bursting at the seams. He suggests that, in light of the mutual aid principle, a political community like Australia faces one of two choices: either to retain its cultural identity but shrink in territorial size, or to keep its size but allow for greater pluralism and diversity in its culture. There is, Walzer asserts, a moral need to let in truly necessitous strangers where they can be absorbed at reasonable cost (and, one presumes, where such strangers can gain no satisfaction back home). But the exact method of permitting such entrance must be left up to the nation-state in question: a nation can never be forced to give up its right to autonomy within its own borders. For 'to give up the state is to give up any effective self-determination.' The political community may decide to adjust its borders to retain its Burkeian 'community of character', the shared way of life its members have created. Alternatively, the community may decide – as 'immigrant societies' like America and Canada have done – to keep its borders and run the risk of changing the existing culture in exchange for greater diversity.[32]

So, then, Walzer makes what for him is a crucial distinction between physical access to territory and membership access to a political community. Physical access to territory is a vital human need, giving rise to a 'Hobbesian right to survival'. We all have to live somewhere; we all need secure access to some material resources if we are going to live at all, much less live well and meaningfully. Thus, it is a matter of thin morality that we all have a human right to 'a place where we can make a life'. This human right roots the claims of physical access to territory by genuinely needy strangers from wildly overpopulated lands.[33] But this right to access does not entail a right to become a fully-fledged citizen member of the political community currently occupying the land in question. That community may choose to shrink, ceding some territory so that the necessitous strangers can settle on it and forge a new state. While I am not sure that has actually happened historically, Walzer insists that there would be nothing unjust about such shrinkage: if a community wants to protect its existing culture, it may shrink and exclude the strangers from membership even as it cedes to them adjoining territory to survive on. No political community is required, as a matter of justice, to throw open both its doors and its arms to greet enthusiastically all who want to come in. Membership is a choice that a political community has complete control over, a Burkeian or even Hegelian choice about belonging and recognition which 'is not pervasively subject to the constraints of justice'. 'We', Walzer says, 'who are already members do the choosing in accord with our understanding of what membership means in our community, and of what sort of community we want to have.' 'Admission and exclusion', with regard to membership,

> are at the core of communal independence. They suggest the deepest meaning of self-determination. Without them, there could not be communities of character, historically stable, ongoing associations of men and women with some special commitment to one another and some special sense of their common life.[34]

So, then, territorial concessions ought to be offered, by those who have more land than they need, to the truly needy who do not have stable claims to enough land back home. The offer does not have to be accepted, of course, since the group may press for accommodation in the old country. But if the needy group does take up the territorial concession, the community making the concession does not have to welcome them into its culture as members. It may decide to cede land to them, in exchange for keeping its culture as it is. But if it keeps all the land to itself, and still lets the needy group in, it must over time allow members of that group full membership, at least in the sense of naturalized citizenship rights equal to those of all other citizens. For Walzer, it is axiomatic of membership that a member is a member is a member. A community's decision to welcome people into its land, into its home under its governance, is a decision eventually to welcome such people into fully-fledged membership. A community may not, on pain of hypocrisy, welcome new people as *de facto* members, embedding them in a shared way of life, and yet, at the same time, deny them full membership rights *de jure*. That is at odds with the very meaning of membership. Walzer is thus critical of such countries as Germany and Japan, which have welcomed into their political space Turks and Koreans respectively: groups who have now lived there for generations without even the potential to become full members with equal citizenship rights. While Walzer is frustratingly silent as to the details of a just naturalization process, he insists that, as a matter of justice, a community faces one of two choices here: keep your culture and make room for a new neighbouring state; or keep your land and make room for new members who may modify your culture.[35]

The previous options, however, still do not resolve the manifold difficulties of the principle that every nation should have its own state. The most obvious case is when two or more peoples have settled on the same territory, creating close yet separate communal lives, under a variety of changing political arrangements. What would Walzer's principle have us do in these familiar cases? Walzer stresses, firstly, the need for complex accommodations, tightly tailored to the actual case: 'What has been called "the national question", doesn't have a single correct answer, as if there were only one way of "being" a nation, one version of national history, one model of relationships among nations.' Walzer stresses that there are many options here: '[s]ecession, border revisions, federation, regional or functional autonomy, cultural pluralism: there are many designs for a room of one's own.'[36]

In a case of a country where there are many nations under control of a single political authority, one option is a neutral political structure, which is maximally inclusive of all the nations under its authority. Such neutrality would imply a very minimal conception of citizenship in that country, focused on individual human rights. Walzer suggests that this kind of arrangement is likely to succeed only in immigrant societies, like America, where most of the people have been 'voluntarily transplanted, cut off from homeland and history'. In most other cases, owing to thick particularities and close ties to particular pieces of land, such neutrality cannot for long be sustained. A relevant example might be the former communist states in central and eastern Europe, especially Yugoslavia. Tito tried to construct a neutral Yugoslav state, and enjoyed some success for one or two generations. But then, starting in the 1980s, the arrangement unravelled and particularist identities with territorial attachments resurfaced with a dark vengeance.[37]

Walzer stresses the importance of two sets of distinctions: whether the nations within the state in question are territorially dispersed or not; and the degree of difference there is between the nations. Dispersed and largely assimilated national groupings, for instance, have very weak *communal* claims on the political structure of the country they inhabit. Walzer insists that such groups, contrary to some recent high-profile claims, do not enjoy a right of cultural – as opposed to physical – survival. This seems at first quite curious for Walzer to claim, since he makes so much of community, particularist identities and shared ways of life. But his point is that the dispersal and assimilation in question have eroded the communal rights of these people over time, whereas such rights remain intact for peoples who have maintained their separateness and their connection to a particular piece of land. People who hardly differ from most other members of their society – perhaps, say, only in terms of their mother tongue – do not enjoy a right to claim special cultural protections for that minor difference from the state in question, unless of course such protections were universalized to all other relevant groups. In that event, though, Walzer believes that they would be unlikely to have the protective effects sought after. Walzer, of course, permits voluntary and private measures on behalf of preserving the linguistic difference; his contention focuses on state sanction and funding. He is inclined to believe, perhaps surprisingly, that no minority group in a multinational state enjoys a group right to cultural survival. Perhaps this is owing to what Walzer believes rights are truly designed to protect: vital human needs and such fundamental values as life and liberty, political self-rule and secure access to land and resources. Cultural claims presumably rank further down his scale of value and thus are not entitled to the same degree of protection as the genuine objects of rights claims, whether individual or communal.[38]

Another reason Walzer might offer for denying cultural rights to minority groups in multinational states is this: the very fact that the group in question has failed to retain its distinctiveness has resulted in the forfeiture of its cultural rights. Why this is the case Walzer does not exactly say, though one suspects the general idea is that the fact that the group has lost its distinctiveness means that it was not very valuable to its members, and thus they have consented to assimilation. They have, so to speak, contracted out of their culture. This is an interesting and provocative claim but we recall here Walzer's previous disclaimers about radical coercion. Are there cases of a minority offering genuine consent to assimilation into the majority, or is the norm rather that the majority over time exerts such control over salient aspects of life that minorities have little choice but to blend in? Is Walzer's view here elevating, in true conservative fashion, the status quo on to the plane of political principle? The fact that your attempt at cultural protection failed means that now it must fail, on principle? Walzer may believe that the American experience, where a number of incoming groups arguably did consent to assimilate into the majority culture, is more universal than it really is. Given the importance of shared ways of life to him, why does he not make it mandatory that the government in a multinational state afford various cultural protections to minorities, assuming those will not violate basic human rights? Presumably, he would not object if the state in question decides of its own accord to do so, as Canada, for example, has done with a public policy of multiculturalism, providing state funding and tax benefits to minority cultures. The reason why, it seems, making such policies mandatory is out of the question for Walzer is that he suspects it may threaten the overall cohesion of the broader community in the state. It would be at odds with the development of a truly common and broadly shared way of life. But is that a sufficient reason for leaving minority cultures either to sink or to swim?

Nations territorially concentrated and substantially different from the other nations in the country in question face a number of different, and stronger, options, ranging from secession and subsequent statehood to provincial autonomy in a federative structure within the existing state. The precise answer, Walzer emphasizes, depends on the precise case in question. But a few general principles are discernible. First, their right to full nationhood and a separate state depends not only upon the reality of the communal life they enjoy but equally upon their recognition of the rights of 'the nation-which-comes-next', which is to say their making reasonable accommodation for any other nations remaining in their midst after they separate. Walzer is especially critical of nations which refuse to recognize for others the rights vindicated by their own drive for independence and state rights: these display the kind of hypocrisy Walzer denounces as the most obvious betrayal of core principles.[39] Second, their right to nationhood depends upon general agreement on where the border should go and, most interestingly, on questions of sufficient access to resources for all affected groups after the fact. Walzer says we should be suspicious of a wealthy national group in a resource-rich part of its country which wants to separate from the rest of the country to enhance its own standard of living. One is reminded of the political party in north-western Italy striving to secede and establish its own state in order to stop the burden of subsidizing the poorer southern regions, especially Sicily. Walzer suggests that the apparent greediness of such a separation does not necessarily undermine the entitlement of that wealthy nation to secede but it may well require 'the international equivalent of alimony and child support'. Though he is frustratingly short on specifics here, Walzer tries to justify this by stressing that the details cannot be defined in abstraction from the details of the case. The general idea, though, seems to share surprising affinities with some of the redistributive ideals, and concern for the poor, featured in Pogge's work.[40]

'The goal' of these complex Walzerian accommodations, in favour of national proliferation and subsequent toleration, 'is a world of states within relatively secure borders, from which no sizable group of people is excluded.' It is a world maximally inclusive of communal difference, subject to thin constraints of human rights protection. Does Walzer therefore rule out alliances between states, or condemn the apparent trend towards greater globalization in international institutions? Not at all. If nation-states, *after being liberated*, freely choose to enter into alliances, or even 'federal or confederal' arrangements with other nation-states, then there ought to be nothing barring the way for them.[41] Such arrangements promise escape from the limits of sovereignty, and offer 'more resources, more power, a stronger and safer position in international affairs'. Walzer is often tempted to portray his problem with globalism as an issue not with supranational association *per se* but rather with the move to impose such association coercively on nation-states who may not want to join. This disagreement still separates him from neo-Kantians like Pogge, who insist that all who *can* affect each other *must* enter into relations of justice, but it also separates Walzer from accusations that his is a narrow defence of nineteenth-century nationalism, a reactionary refusal to consider the world outside his borders. Indeed, in a shocking concession to globalist and even Kantian rhetoric, Walzer refers at one point to the general desirability of 'a pacific union . . . of satisfied nations'. He even nods towards the European Community, a favoured citation of globalists.[42]

Walzer's insistence, though, is that states be allowed to discern their own interests with regard to joining such supranational associations, and that they must not be coerced into joining them. He even offers the success of international arrangements like the European Union as reason in favour of allowing his programme of national proliferation to run its course, since '[m]any of them won't go all that far'. We should 'allow the tribes first to separate and then to negotiate their own voluntary and gradual, even if only partial, incorporation in a community of interest' in peace, security, commerce and rights-protection. Adopting a more tolerant and permissive attitude towards the quest for national independence can pave the way for this world of free and diverse arrangements. Success in this process would allow for 'a kind of peace-in-pieces'. By channelling sovereignty 'downwards and outwards', we can 'steady the state system, as extra wheels steady a bicycle for an unsure rider'. The most pressing task, as he sees it, is thus to develop and secure a global consensus in favour of international toleration.[43]

Walzer's proposals seem feasible, if only because they are already so widely realized in the contemporary world. One wonders, following Pogge, whether they amount to more than a justification for the current context, in which an increasing number of nations have been receiving either autonomy or statehood, even as others move towards effective supra-state associations. One is confronted here, if nowhere else, by the conservatism of Walzer's conventionalist methodology. His most interesting and provocative contentions – like those involving land transfers, international alimony payments and pacific unions – are only briefly mentioned, and then quickly set aside. The bulk of his work on the general structure of international society is neither revelatory nor as reformist as Walzer would have us believe. It essentially describes and endorses the fundamental lineaments of the current world order. Much as we might prefer otherwise, it is clear that the structure of global society is not Walzer's main interest. One must reluctantly look elsewhere, at least for now, for a more searching theory about how international society ought to be structured.

One interesting candidate for status as a more searching theory of a just international ordering is the most recent work offered by none other than John Rawls. Rawls, one of Walzer's favourite foils, has just come out with a major work entitled *The Law of Peoples*.[44]

Though its newness unfortunately prevents detailed commentary at this point, some general observations suggest themselves. Rawls believes that his famous method of liberal contractarianism – described in chapter 1 – can be applied to international affairs. Just as we should, within a nation, follow the principles of justice that self-interested rational agents would agree to in a free and fair social contract negotiation, so too should nations abide by those principles which representatives of nations would consent to in a free and fair contractual agreement amongst the world's peoples. While Walzer would, of course, echo his prior criticism of Rawls's abstract methodology of invention, he might be surprised at the degree of overlap between his view and Rawls's latest offering. For example, Rawls now makes much out of tolerating international differences, at least amongst 'well-ordered', decent and non-aggressive societies. Rawls also highlights the role of human rights in global justice. Moreover, Rawls acknowledges a prominent place for the nation-state within a just international ordering. At the same time, he has a more supportive attitude towards international institutions, especially the UN, than does Walzer. Rawls thus seems to split the difference between Walzer and Pogge on the question of global governance: no world state but no national insularity either, and perhaps even a presumption in favour of international co-operation within a shared institutional setting. Rawls feels completely comfortable talking about a 'Realistic Utopia' on the world stage, words that would no doubt make Walzer shudder.[45]

What principles of justice does Rawls understand as being authoritative for the international community? Very familiar ones, from Walzer's point of view: the equal sovereignty of peoples, including the freedom to contract with other peoples; non-intervention with other well-ordered, sovereign peoples; no resort to force internationally unless attacked by an aggressor; and if attacked, then resort only to a limited war of self-defence. By this last principle, we see that Rawls also endorses just war theory. But Rawls's just war theory is more sweeping and restrictive than Walzer's, and is more concerned with war prevention in comparison with Walzer's presumption in favour of an armed response to aggression. Rawls's international principles do go importantly beyond those endorsed by Walzer, and more in the direction of those endorsed by Pogge, in mandating a duty upon wealthy societies to assist less developed, 'burdened societies'. The difference between Rawls and Walzer over global distributive justice is only exacerbated by Rawls's more law-like understanding of the principles of international justice. Walzer is inclined, we have seen, to view international justice more as the product of a real-world political consensus between peoples than as the legislative mandate of public reason itself. International justice for Walzer is about adhering to rather standard principles of conduct we all just happen to agree on, and not about adhering to more invasive and demanding principles which reason itself (purportedly) demands we must agree on.[46]

Are Rawls's principles – more permissive of international institutions, more restrictive on war, more demanding in terms of sharing wealth – the outlines of a more satisfying theory of international justice than Walzer offers? Without a detailed analysis, one's conclusions can only be provisional, and yet I suggest that Rawls's principles may well hold out greater promise for us, at least in the absence of a fuller response from Walzer. Rawls acknowledges the import of the global distributive question, not only out of his keener concern for fairness for those worse-off, but also out of his acknowledgement that war itself often breaks out over the distribution of vital resources. Global justice must consider the adequacy of the global economy. Rawls also notes the fact that international co-operation is often unreliable without an institutional context, and so his more supportive attitude towards the current set of global institutions – fallible as they are – seems more plausible than Walzer's hostility. Though Rawls is, if anything, more abstract in his methodology than ever, his substantive conclusions seem to display a deeper regard for procedural fairness for all than do Walzer's. Rawls's universal guarantees for all seem an appropriate grounding for the more cosmopolitan world of the future, the land just over the horizon, where our destiny resides.

Summary

While Walzer does not ignore questions of international justice in general, it is clear that he does not devote much attention to them. Just war theory remains his overwhelming focus in international affairs. This is not, however, a mere difference in taste or relative expertise: it is rooted in his conviction that war remains the most significant interaction between states and so must be the main concern for theorists of international justice. Beitz and Pogge beg to differ about the extent and depth of interstate interaction, preferring to view war not as the crucial event between states but rather as a kind of symptom whose deeper cause is the very set-up of the international arena. Walzer does offer a response to these thinkers, but it is half-formed and lacking engagement with the most direct questions they pose. What is fair to say is that, when Walzer does turn his attention to international topics other than war, he does so from a standpoint suspicious of global governance and supportive of national self-determination. But his endorsement of communal difference is not unconstrained: national proliferation should occur but guided, as our own shared morality demands, by genuine concern for the lives and liberties of individual human beings. Free and diverse communities, populated and endorsed by free and diverse persons, would make for a better, more just world.

Conclusion

Walzer's renown as a contemporary political philosopher rests most heavily on his accomplishments in two fields: distributive justice and just war theory. The stark differences between the two topics has meant that each issue has generated its own critical discourse, with very few scholars broaching the question of how these two projects might be linked in a broader account of justice in general. That they are linked we now know to be the case. The link is at least twofold: formal, since Walzer's treatment of both topics demands we take a conventionalist, interpretative approach; and material, since Walzer's substantive principles in both topics are very similar, focusing on individuals and political communities having their own protected space for making free choices in accordance with their own conception of what is good and valuable in life.

Walzer's core commitment

The idea of protected space – more specifically, of self-determination within a protected space – is absolutely central to Walzer's political thinking. Violation of such space is, in his mind, the very height of injustice. This leads him to say, in his account of distributive justice, that if possession of one social good, like money, allows one to purchase disproportionate shares of another social good, like health care, without regard to the meaning of that latter good, then 'the autonomy of distributive spheres' has been violated. A kind of distributive aggression has occurred, a violation of the very meaning we place on who should get what good, how much of it, and in accordance with what principle. For Walzer, every social good should be distributed in accordance with its meaning in that culture. So, since the meaning of health care in most Western societies leads us to the idea that it ought to be distributed on the basis of medical need, it follows that a Western society which allows for money to determine the distribution of health care violates its own very meaning, permitting the violation of a sphere of activity whose autonomy it should protect. On the international level, Walzer favours protected spaces for all nations who have created, developed and nurtured a shared way of life through time, a way of life widely participated in and that is at least minimally just, in the sense of respecting individual human rights to life and liberty. For all nations, Walzer believes, there should be states, or at least reliable state protection worked out through complex accommodations. Hence the critical importance of borders between states, the violent crossing of which constitutes aggression, for him the only genuine crime which states can commit against each other. Walzer, most graphically, likens interstate aggression to an armed robber breaking into one's home, one of the clearest and most dangerous cases of violating self-determination within a protected space. Aggression is so serious that, for Walzer, it even justifies war, provided certain other conditions are also met.

It is interesting to reflect on the deepest reasons behind Walzer's core norm of there being protected spaces within which people are free to make their own choices, pursue their own conception of meaning in life. Some reasons might be linked to Walzer's own life experiences and political affiliations. In terms of his life experiences, Walzer's intellectual career has flourished as a result of his pursuing his own research interests under the protection of things like academic tenure, affording him both security and autonomy. In terms of his political affiliations, America has always thought of itself, going back to its Pilgrim founders in the early 1600s, as a City on a Hill, a separate, superior and shining exemplar for the rest of humanity. America defines itself as an oasis of freedom and moral rectitude, separated from the perceived corruptions and limitations of the Old World not only by miles of ocean but also by a different conception of political association, which itself places great value on individual self-determination. For very different reasons, Israel also embodies the value of self-determination within a protected space. For centuries spread out over Europe, the Middle East and the New World, the Jewish diaspora finally succeeded in establishing the state of Israel after the Second World War, convincing the victorious Western powers that one of the conclusions to be drawn from that brutal conflict was that they could not count on the protection of a state which was not their own. Thus the West aided in the founding of Israel in the late 1940s. For the past fifty years, Israelis have struggled mightily, and sometimes controversially, to carve out for themselves a protected space in this world wherein they are free to pursue their own vision of a meaningful life.

I would be remiss if I did not mention the religious overtones to the idea of a protected space, and if I failed to point out that, in his recent writings, Walzer has increasingly availed himself of religious references and language.[1] There is a clear consonance of imagery between the picture of a protected space in general and spaces of religious significance, like a church or synagogue: both are places of refuge from a rough-and-tumble world, oases of privacy that are vested with meaning and symbolic significance, sanctuaries of which one has a long memory. Both are institutions with traditional practices and rhythmic activities designed to settle and comfort, as well as to lift one's mind to a more resonant plane. They are places to pray individually as well as to worship in community with familiar, well-meaning faces. The allusion need not stop at religious institutions, for there is also a clear connection here to the central religious idea of a person's own soul, their ultimate private space and source of meaning and guidance in life. This soul, in religious terms the most precious thing about us, is the one space each of us must protect absolutely; and not only from 'invasion' by corrupting external influences but also from the internal temptation to betray one's own deepest commitments, whether out of contemptible weakness or out of a simple yet searing hypocrisy. The false self, the betrayed self, the corrupted soul: Walzer draws on a very rich tradition of imagery and motif referring to the need for a protected space of one's own, in which one can be true to oneself.

It is not mere autobiography, however, which drives Walzer's political theory. Substantive philosophical commitments are also present. There is, for example, obvious reliance on the value of autonomy in Walzer: both persons and peoples should be autonomous within their own proper spheres. *More specifically, it is the value of the equal right of all to enjoy autonomy that looms large as the most abiding of Walzer's principles.* One of his most moving comments about this value, this core commitment to universal self-determination within a protected space, runs as follows: 'We act immorally when we deny to other people ... the right to act autonomously and the right to form attachments in accordance with a particular understanding of the good life.'[2]

Classical sources of inspiration

Classical liberal philosophers – stalwart defenders of autonomy like Kant and Mill – also defended the value of there being protected spaces within which people could be free to make their own decisions in life, in accord with their own conception of meaning. For Kant, autonomy was justified as a necessary condition for having a good will, since only a will self-motivated to be moral could be considered good. Merely acting in accord with the moral law was for Kant insufficient: genuine goodness additionally required that the action be self-chosen, and appropriately motivated in terms of respect for the moral law within. A person displaying good will acted *from* her own motivation, *on* her own deepest principles as a rational agent. A good will, for Kant, was a thing of intrinsic value, a jewel shining by its own light. Less frequently noted, Kant also believed that a good will imbued not only our own lives, but the universe itself, with meaning and significance: 'Without man [and his potential for developing a morally good will] the whole of creation would be a mere wilderness, a thing in vain, and have no final end.' Since the autonomy of a rational being – this necessary condition for the development of good will – could be threatened externally by the force and fraud of others, Kant insisted that relations of justice had to be established between all those who could affect each other. The purpose of such a system of justice was to protect a maximally large space of personal freedom of action for each, consistent with the same space available for all. Autonomy stands out as the central political value for Kant, and we note that Walzer himself, in a footnote, refers approvingly to Nozick's citation of 'Kantian ideas' about human personality as the most appropriate grounding for human rights claims. Presumably, such 'Kantian ideas' include the intrinsic value of the human person, the associated inviolability and firmness of personal rights and the central importance of genuine consent to principles of morality and justice.[3]

Mill, for his part, grounded the value of autonomy very differently from Kant, suggesting that allowing people free space for making important choices in life contributed to the happiness and development not only of those people but also of society as a whole. Mankind are 'greater gainers' by respecting the value of autonomy than not: society breathes free; we get to experiment with different lifestyles, leading to progress; and the mind itself is free to create and explore new theories, increasing our chances of securing the truth. Crucially for Mill, a society in which autonomy was fostered was a society peopled by strong, self-reliant individuals, and thus liberated from the need to support constantly a burgeoning population through public finances. People would be free in the fullest sense of being out from under tutelage and dependence, whether with reference to God, or nature, or the state. Such people would be able to take care of themselves, think for themselves, make their own choices, live their own lives. The only reason to interfere with such autonomous goodness, as Mill famously remarked, would be the need to defend oneself or others from those tempted to abuse their freedom by attacking others. Many of these Millian motifs are echoed in Walzer, from the insistence that only aggression justifies war to his defence of 'the stern doctrine of self-help' with regard not only to when states may intervene in civil wars but also to whether minority groups should enjoy cultural protection from a multi-national state.[4]

The other classical liberal icon which Walzer draws on heavily is Hobbes. He shares with Hobbes a scepticism regarding claims to have discovered the objective moral truth, and so follows Hobbes in asserting that morality and justice result from conventional agreements, from a social contract. Walzer, like Hobbes, insists that each and every one of us must have reason to consent to any such contract: thus, bedrock protections of individual rights to life and liberty are essentials elements which a just society must enshrine and protect. Those reflecting on Walzer's many approving references to community and shared ways of life ought never to lose sight of the fact that he insists, as a matter of thin, universal morality, that just societies must also see to everyone's fundamental interests and vital human needs. The overwhelming obsession in Hobbes is on security, on protecting one's life and limb from grievous harm. This obsession with protection works its way into Walzer's conviction that 'the deepest purpose of the state . . . is defence'.[5]

Walzer's reference to defending an existing way of life, whether individual or collective, makes one mindful of more conservative aspects of his thought. The foremost exponent of conservatism in Western political philosophy, of course, is Burke, whom Walzer cites explicitly. Walzer employs Burkean intonation to suggest that the social contract is not merely a deliberate, hard-nosed deal amongst fearful and grasping rational agents. It is, rather, a social union deeper than self-interest, expressive also of a community's shared way of life over time. It is just as important to live in a Burkean 'community of character' as to live in a Hobbesian society of individual self-protection. We want, as we should, both personal protection and a sense of belonging, not just life but a way of life, not simply security but also meaning. Walzer finds meaningful the conservative emphasis on preserving one's cultural heritage and tending to the public good. Walzer follows conservatives in their attachment and loyalty to their own community, to their rootedness in a shared way of life and their patriotic pride in their nation. National membership is crucially important for Walzer, as is criticizing the universalizing ambitions of those global governance advocates who seek to suppress, or even supplant, it. Many commentators have noted how Walzer's very methodology in political philosophy smacks of conservatism: we are not to invent new theories for fresh commitment but, rather, to interpret existing shared commitments, and then remain faithful to them. Justice itself for Walzer is ultimately about loyalty: fidelity to the best interpretation of our already existing shared commitments. Who will offer us the best interpretation? Walzer's conservative answer: most probably a community of experts, a 'majority of sages'. While his conservatism does provide familiar starting-points, and respects our rootedness, it can also seem to elevate the status quo to the level of principle, and thus drag on progress, confirming institutions that may, by other lights, seem exclusionary or unfair, particularly with regard to the worst-off.[6]

Another classical thinker with conservative inclinations, with whom Walzer shares commonalities, is Hegel. Like Hegel, Walzer emphasizes the constitutive role of thought and meaning in people's lives, which translates into a deep concern for self-identity, recognition and belongingness in political life. This belongingness is central: following Hegel, Walzer stresses both the fact and the value of our rootedness in concrete communities, our membership in distinctive cultures, utterly contextualized within the flow of history. Of the major contemporary political philosophers, arguably none pays more respect to history – to how our ideals are embedded in the flow of real-world events – than does Walzer. This gives his theory palpable relevance and applicability: no one could accuse Walzer of indulging philosophical fantasies. Indeed, it is Walzer who makes substantive use of such criticism, levelling it repeatedly at 'the excessive abstraction' of Rawls's theory of justice. Apart from meaning and history, Walzer also shares with Hegel a very positive understanding of the role of the state in our lives. Not only should government protect our lives and express our communal distinctiveness, Walzer also believes it should play a powerful role in the distribution of social goods. The state should protect us from external attack, yet also serve as the internal provider of the necessities of social life. It ought to ensure distributive justice at home as well as to punish aggression abroad. For Walzer, the most plausible account of distributive justice, in Western societies, is that afforded by democratic socialism.

Walzer's democratic socialism is animated, above all, by criticism of both inequality and domination. In this respect, he makes us mindful of Rousseau, a famous fellow fan of the social contract. Like Rousseau, Walzer relishes in the role of social critic, taking particular aim at hypocrisy and privilege. Just as Rousseau loved to unmask the hypocrisies of the age of Enlightenment, Walzer draws our attention to how often we profess belief one way, then act another: i.e., to how often we betray our deepest and most natural commitments for the sake of some superficial, even artificial, social advantage. Walzer is also acutely sensitive to how the wealthy and powerful employ their advantages to enjoy disproportionate shares of social goods, in effect forming an ultra-privileged élite whose superior lifestyle grinds the faces of those less well-off. Walzer would have us resist such domination and inequality, and ideally institute in their place something much like Rousseau's republic of virtue: a series of smaller nations, which are each culturally distinct and in which all citizens are equal members and active participants in direct democratic governance. Social goods ideally should be distributed to different people in accord with their different meanings, thereby preventing any one group of people from gaining a monopoly and establishing an artificial, unnatural and unhealthy system of social domination. We ought to be free not only from unjust war and tyrannical government, but also from grinding socio-economic inequality.

One final classical comparison is in order, this one more off the beaten path.[7] Though Walzer almost never cites them, it is interesting to consider whether, as an American philosopher, he shares anything in common with the pragmatists. It seems that he does. Both Walzer and the pragmatists are sceptical about the discovery of objective truth, insisting that we stick with the beliefs we have and not subject them to contrived philosophical doubt if we do not actually doubt them in our everyday lives. Walzer, following the likes of Quine and Davidson, stresses the need to come up with coherent, powerful and persuasive interpretations of our existing 'webs of belief'. And, of course, both Walzer and the pragmatists are centrally concerned with how people are actually motivated to act in moral and political life. Drawing on these claims, pragmatists like Rorty, alongside Walzer, are convinced that we have no one else to turn to but ourselves – our own contingent beliefs, commitments and social arrangements – when it comes to seeking guidance in morality and politics. Ultimately, what matters most is what works best for us, what most fully realizes what we want out of life. A final abiding similarity between pragmatists and Walzer is the marked aversion to philosophical dualisms. John Dewey, in particular, dwelled at length upon the need to 'overcome dualisms', especially those traditionally drawn between belief and action, idea and sensation, mind and world, science and ethics. The goal is a unified approach to both thought and action. Walzer, we have seen, concurs on a number of fronts with this integrative yet applied approach. For instance, he sees a very close connection between facts and values. In the course of interpretation, description and prescription intermingle for him in an increasingly intimate fashion. Likewise, Walzer is most keen on overcoming one of the most pervasive dualisms in social thought, namely, that between persons and peoples, between the individual and the community. We have seen, throughout this work, that it is deeply mistaken to try and fit Walzer nicely and neatly into either an 'individualist' or a 'communitarian' slot. The complexity of his work resists such convenient conceptual categorization. He draws heavily on both aspects of the Western political tradition, running from Hobbes to Hegel, from Burke to Rousseau. Walzer sees no reason why we cannot keep our twin commitments to both personal freedom and social belongingness, to both human rights and cultural pluralism.[8]

Our desire to have our cake and eat it too can seem naïve and sometimes, no doubt, gets us into real trouble, especially in hard cases. But I believe Walzer is right to point out that we do, in fact, have such a desire, and thus must work out its implications for our shared political life. Though such a desire at times properly elicits critical questions, one cannot help but appreciate the limitations it reveals in the logic-chopping ways of the categorizers, of those who love – and live? – to label.

We should, then, strongly resist the temptation to slap a set of labels on Walzer. His thought is too complex and historically nuanced to deserve such treatment. He is not merely a 'liberal nationalist', any more than he is only a 'non-cosmopolitan democratic socialist'. He is equal parts Burkean conservative and Rousseauian revolutionary, as much a Hegelian communitarian as a Hobbesian contractarian. Liberal universalists, conservative patriots and leftist relativists can see themselves reflected in aspects of his work. Walzer draws in his own impressive, and utterly personal, way on the three major, mainstream traditions in Western political thought – conservatism, liberalism and socialism – and then combines the mixture with an interpretative method, an anchoring in history and a respect for our conventions, for who we are and who we most want to be.[9]

Summary of this book's argumentation

This book began with a discussion of Walzer's interpretative method, his very approach to sources of moral and political perplexity. This method stresses conventionalist appeal to our current set of beliefs. We should respect autonomy – and tolerate the pluralism resulting from it – because that is a foundational commitment that we all actually have, here and now. Walzer presupposes that it is always appropriate to remain faithful to those beliefs which have ordered one's life and one's community. Walzer is convinced that his is a more plausible and accessible method, since it does not purport to have discovered the objective truth or to have invented the ideal normative system. His approach, he would say, starts from the most plausible starting-point of all: from where we are right now. The difficult debate, though, centres around the possibility that there may not be a consensus as to where, exactly, we are right now. After all, it is by no means obvious that all of us are committed to respecting everyone's autonomy and to tolerating pluralism. We can easily imagine someone untouched by liberal sentiment retorting: a protected space for myself, sure; but for those I reject as malformed degenerates, forget it. Hence Walzer's efforts at defining what counts as 'the best interpretation' of our current commitments. While his criteria here are not trivial, the results he generates from applying them to questions of justice are by no means beyond dispute. He suggests that we are most deeply committed to respecting human rights, which correlate with duties not to murder and not to inflict gross cruelty. Commitment to these duties is universal and forms the thin core of all thick and particular social moralities. While this accords well with Western liberal sensibilities, serious questions remain about whether those of different acculturation make the same endorsement, whether at 'the deepest level' or no. The biting question Walzer fails to confront is this: even if there is universal condemnation of 'murder' and 'gross cruelty', does it follow that that condemnation is motivated by a globally shared understanding of what counts as 'murder' and 'gross cruelty'?

These doubts being expressed, I hasten to add that, for my money, Walzer makes the most plausible and sustained case in favour of conventionalism currently on offer in political theory. He has many more resources than his critics give him credit for, especially when it comes to answering the accusation that conventionalism is insufficiently critical. Furthermore, human rights really do seem to be the most plausible candidates for universal endorsement in the foundation of political morality. But is interpretation really different in kind from invention? Are the thin shared norms shared only in name but not content? Are they really 'more intensely held' than the thick norms which otherwise prevail?

Walzer asserts that, if we apply his method of interpretation to questions of justice, we shall come to see that we have commitments to both thin and thick kinds of morality. Thin morality is universally shared, and enshrines a set of human rights: rights to life and liberty, rights not to be subjected to things like murder, torture and tyranny. Thin morality is neither objective nor does it form the moral truth; it is simply that moral code we witness everyone endorsing. Thin morality is the minimal code shared by all the world's maximal codes. Just war theory is part of thin morality, and it regulates our conduct with all humanity. Distributive justice, by contrast, is part of maximal morality, which is culturally relative. Possible limitations to Walzer's theory of distributive justice revolve around questions of fairness: what is fair about distribution in accord with cultural meaning? What is the relationship between proceduralist concern with fair treatment for all and the substantive concern with retaining a meaningful shared way of life? Why can we not talk about distributive justice in terms of universal rights? Although we can agree with Walzer that domination and gross inequality ought to be resisted in distributions, what guarantees can he give us that his own privileging of the state's role in this process will not result in yet another kind of domination, just the latest version of the same old story?

We looked critically at Walzer's theory of distributive justice in considerable detail for two reasons: to discern the interaction between thick and thin morality more fully; and to understand Walzer's own political commitments. We know now that his commitments combine a respect for cultural difference worldwide with a preference for democratic socialism back home, and that they mix a concern with individual human rights everywhere with the maintenance of some degree of national pluralism and rootedness in history and political membership.

Walzer's just war theory, this work's main focus, features human rights protection at its foundations, and finds its ultimate justification in terms of our shared commitment to such protection. Just war theory rejects both realism and pacifism which, for different reasons, deny the claim that war can sometimes be morally justified. Walzer's criticisms of these two rival doctrines are acclaimed and effective, but too narrow in scope. Realism as a prescription for state behaviour in terms of self-regarding prudential choice, for example, is one formidable alternative to just war theory which Walzer fails to confront. And while pacifism does not offer much promise as an effective deterrent to, or punishment for, aggression, that need not be its only claim to normative fame. For pacifism's purely moral appeal is more resilient: that war cannot ever be fought justly and so resort to it will forever be stained not only in blood but in moral corruption. I sought, in chapter 3, to offer a strong response on Walzer's behalf but the question is, of course, hardly settled. The proposition that it is always wrong to perform an action which, regardless of its end and intent, will foreseeably result in the death of the innocent remains the most potent moral objection to just war theory.

Walzer's rights-based understanding of wartime justice competes for prominence, in a fierce internal struggle, with a utility-based understanding. While Walzer reserves some of his most ferocious criticisms for utilitarianism, he personally accommodates its manner of reasoning at multiple points in his theory. These points include the norms of last resort, probability of success and proportionality, as well as his doctrine of supreme emergency, which he dubs a 'utilitarianism of extremity'. As a result, he cannot at times distance himself from utilitarianism, or from the very criticisms he levels at it. Most serious here is the criticism that it permits human rights violations for the sake of a supposedly 'greater good', be it aggregate utility or communal independence. While his consequentialist concessions are animated by his conventionalism – he wants to stay true to those norms we really do appeal to, and cost–benefit analysis is clearly one of them – they end up causing him serious grief. They rest uneasily with a firm commitment to rights, resulting in sharp questions about consistency, especially during supreme emergency. While Walzer embraces the incoherence at that point, on his own terms he should not, for coherence is a necessary condition for 'the best interpretation' of our commitments, whether in war or peace.

Walzer's just war theory is split into three accounts, covering the three phases of wartime activity: the resort to war, conduct during war, and war's termination phase. One persistent query throughout this study has been whether such separation is carried too far by Walzer, treating the three phases of war as utterly distinct and discrete units of normative analysis. This superficially appealing strategy radically weakens when confronted by the power of Kant's insistence that the norms governing each phase must be not merely similar in principle but actually woven together into one consistent and forward-looking theory of wartime justice. Failure to do so leads Walzer into difficulties when excusing soldiers from guilt for aggression, when permitting methods which will result in civilian casualties, when allowing for supreme emergency exemptions and when sketching out the requirements of a just peace treaty.

Walzer is strongest when developing his account of *jus ad bellum*. A state must satisfy requirements of just cause, right intention, last resort, probability of success and proportionality of benefits to costs prior to unleashing armed force. To his detriment, Walzer fails to include the traditional rule of public declaration by a proper authority. The canonical just cause for launching a war for Walzer is to resist and punish aggression, defined as any violation of state rights to political sovereignty and territorial integrity. Contrary to some critics, Walzer does not by this advocate a 'statism without foundations',[10] since he grounds state legitimacy not only upon its protection of communal customs but also upon its protection of individual human rights. This is not to say that this Walzerian grounding is unambiguous or unproblematic: his exact conception of human rights is only gestured at, and certain of his thoughts, notably concerning foreign intervention and supreme emergency, only cloud over this relation.

Demonstrating that just war theory is not limited in application to interstate armed conflict, Walzer extends his account to cover anticipatory attack, civil wars and humanitarian interventions. This seems increasingly important, as Kalvi Holsti has determined that, in a very recent sample period of 1989–96, there were ninety-six armed conflicts, only five of which were classic cases of war between sovereign states.[11] Walzer offers a plausible perspective on anticipatory attack, revealing that his conception of aggression is more normative than descriptive in nature. Since aggression can, as a matter of exception, be committed without empirically launching the first military strike, it must be understood ultimately as a violation of rights. Aggression can be committed by posing a clear, severe and imminent threat to the sovereignty or integrity of a legitimate political community.

In contrast to his account of anticipatory attack, Walzer's justification for intervening forcibly in a civil war is so abstractly put as to be of little practical value. Urging that the goal can only be to offset the prior unjust intervention of another foreign power may be unobjectionable, but only because it lacks content as to how the intervenor can actually know whether it has merely counterbalanced the other intervening foreign power and not overextended itself in favour of the domestic party on whose behalf it is intervening. But his insistence that such counter-intervention is permissible only on behalf of a government (or would-be government) which is legitimate is both concrete and convincing.

An illegitimate government is one which does not 'fit' the people whom it governs. But for Walzer there are degrees of illegitimacy and he infuriates critics by permitting armed humanitarian intervention only against certain, but not all, kinds of illegitimate regime. A regime engaging in massacre and enslavement, for instance, is utterly illegitimate and may be on the receiving end of an armed humanitarian intervention. A recent, real-world example would be NATO's 1999 armed intervention in Serbia on behalf of ethnic Albanian Kosovars, rescuing them from the massacre and ethnic cleansing carried out by the government of Slobodan Milosevic. Walzer insists that only blatant and grievous rights violators, like Milosevic's Serbia, can be subjected to humanitarian attack. Lesser rights violators, so to speak, may only be dealt with forcibly by domestic groups exercising their right of revolution. Such lesser violators may be subject to non-violent humanitarian interference by foreign powers (such as pro-rights diplomacy) but not to violent intervention. Walzer does not specify the precise boundary between a lesser rights violator and a grievous one, and does not specify whether the levelling of economic sanctions, for example, would count as 'non-violent' interference. Moreover, it is not clear whether, according to his own minimalist conception of human rights (limited to security and freedom), he is logically at liberty to maintain that any kind of human rights violator is merely a 'lesser' one. Reading the bulk of his just war theory, one concludes that a rights violator is a rights violator: an aggressor, whether internal or external, deserving of repulsion and punishment, with force if need be and regardless of whether the source of the force is home-grown or imported. Walzer wavers, stressing the stern Millian virtue of self-help. He prefers to see revolution even when intervention could get the job done; he does so out of sincere affection for freely chosen shared ways of life and out of severe suspicion about the paternalism of foreign powers. The clearest principle he suggests is that only if local self-determination has no chance whatsoever to prevail in the victim's struggle with its unjust regime should a legitimate foreign power feel entitled to intervene.

Walzer's version of *jus in bello* incorporates three rules: discrimination and non-combatant immunity; proportionality; and a ban on methods or weapons which 'shock the moral conscience of mankind'. Walzer is most eloquent when pleading on behalf of non-combatant immunity, offering one of the most trenchant criticisms of indiscriminate targeting and total warfare, features often portrayed by commentators as the true face of modern war. Walzer argues movingly that, subject to the doctrine of double effect, civilians should not be made targets of armed force. They have, after all, done nothing deserving of such treatment; there is thus nothing right about subjecting them to it. His emphasis on non-combatant immunity does, however, detract from other aspects of his *jus in bello* theory: he all but ignores the question of prohibited weapons; his account of proportionality is muddied by his agnosticism about the causes for which soldiers fight; and his permission of reprisals and supreme emergency exemptions from the rules is ill-considered. In the name of being realistic and closely following shared conventions, he permits *jus in bello* violations if they either punish prior violations or defend a community from catastrophic loss of life and liberty. Though he wrings his hands and winces while doing so, he is not sufficiently troubled by the expected consequences of these permissions, or by the inconsistency of having them stand side-by-side with firm prohibitions on *jus in bello* violations. That he actually embraces the inconsistency is both rash and mistaken. Mistaken on his own terms, since consistency is required for a reading to count as 'the best interpretation' of wartime ethics; and mistaken on other terms, since the more plausible conclusion is that a genuine supreme emergency confronts the participants with moral tragedy. A nation confronted with a supreme emergency is confronted with a set of options all of which involve moral violation, but such violation may and ought to be excused on grounds of the most severe duress. Walzer also fails to discern how his supreme emergency doctrine commits him to a substantive link between *jus ad bellum* and *jus in bello* and to consider how dark situations like this may reveal that broader obligations exist in the international community than he is currently willing to recognize.

Jus post bellum is one of the most pressing and relevant considerations that just war theory has to offer the contemporary political scene. Terminating war properly has become one of the most prominent and convoluted problems facing soldiers and statesmen, as witnessed in the Persian Gulf and Bosnia. Walzer does set out a theoretical framework for dealing with some of these issues, but it is not fully developed. I sought to further that development in chapter 6, furnishing principles by which states ought to bring their wars to an end. Most interesting and important here are issues of ensuring rights vindication, punishing aggression by levying compensation requirements and by holding war crimes trials, and imposing some kind of pro-rights rehabilitation on the defeated aggressor. Further work on *jus post bellum* is a clear avenue for advancing the state of the art: the future of just war theory, in my view, will be as much concerned with these termination questions as with those of how to deal with non-traditional armed conflict, such as ethnic civil war.

Questions of international justice in general will themselves, no doubt, also become increasingly prominent. While there will always be conceptual and domestic political concerns which have not been exhaustively mined, it seems clear that an especially rich vein to be tapped in the millennial age concerns global justice. While Walzer does not ignore international justice, he fails to devote his full attention to it. Just war theory is his main international focus, since he persists in the (Hegelian) belief that war remains the most significant interaction between nation-states, themselves still the major actors on the global stage. More recently, theorists like Beitz and Pogge have contended that war is not the most significant international interaction: war is to the international arena as a crashing wave is to the deep blue sea. There are wide and deep structural connections between peoples which shape the outbreak and outcome of war, and which exert broader and more profound impacts on human beings. Pogge argues that it is these deeper socio-economic, and political, structures which ought to be the real focus of our attention, and not the surface skirmishes over which border goes where.

Walzer has at times commented on this perspective but, as a rule, does so very sparsely and from a viewpoint which is both sceptical about whether the deeper structures exist and hostile to claims about the need for global governance. The UN in particular bears the brunt of Walzer's contempt. For he is still committed to the nation-state, insisting that the rest of us also retain this commitment, as revealed by the increasing number of nations entering the community of states. Walzer urges us to tolerate, and perhaps even welcome, this process of national proliferation. We should not succumb to hysteria about a rising tide of tribalism, for we are tribal by nature – historically rooted in a culture – and communal attachment is not inconsistent with justice. As we defend the autonomy of persons, so too should we defend the autonomy of nations, owing to the value of participating in meaningful shared ways of life and to the fact that most shared ways of life require some form of state protection. Such communal toleration need not, Walzer claims, preclude such purportedly progressive interstate associations like the European Union, since toleration implies respect for the free choice of others, and some may prefer to join supra-state associations. There remain, however, crucial ambiguities with regard to some of the settlements Walzer recommends during this process of proliferation, especially regarding access to land, processes of naturalization, 'alimony' payments and cultural assurances. One comes away from his writings on these vital issues suspicious that he puts far too much weight on the claim that the results depend crucially on the details of the actual case being decided. A fuller fleshing out of general principles, it appears, would be both illuminating and useful.

Whatever the residual obscurities and insufficiencies, the bottom line for Walzer is this: for every nation there should be a legitimate state (or, at least, guaranteed state protection) and for every legitimate state there should be toleration for its political orientation, be it communitarian or cosmopolitan. Provided we all adhere to the elemental duty of non-harming, to which we are clearly committed as moral beings, we lack grounds for interfering in the central choices of persons and nations. We should do our duty, respect our rights, and enjoy not only our own lives and liberties but also the rich diversity implied by a world free of aggression and domination.

Notes

Introduction

1 M. Walzer, *Interpretation and Social Criticism* (Cambridge, MA: Harvard University Press, 1987); M. Walzer, 'Nation and Universe', in G. B. Peterson, ed., *The Tanner Lectures on Human Values* (Salt Lake City, UT: University of Utah Press, 1990), 507–57; M. Walzer, *Thick and Thin: Moral Argument at Home and Abroad* (Notre Dame, IN: Notre Dame University Press, 1994).

2 See, for example, D. Miller and M. Walzer, eds., *Pluralism, Justice and Equality* (Oxford: Oxford University Press, 1995). Other secondary sources on the topic will be cited in chapter 2. The primary source for the distributive theory is M. Walzer, *Spheres of Justice* (New York: Basic Books, 1983).

3 For these articles, see the citations in chapters 3–6.

4 For more on the promise at that time, see H. Williams, G. Matthews and D. Sullivan, *Francis Fukuyama and the End of History* (Cardiff: University of Wales Press, 1997).

5 H. Kissinger, *Diplomacy* (New York: Simon & Schuster, 1995); C. Reisman and C. Antoniou, eds., *The Laws of War* (New York: Vintage, 1994), 386ff; V. P. Nanda, 'The Establishment of a Permanent International Criminal Court: Challenges Ahead', *Human Rights Quarterly* (1998), 413–28.

6 M. Walzer, *Just and Unjust Wars* (New York: Basic Books, 1977; 2nd edition with added Preface, 1991). See p. xxviii for the self-description as a just war theorist. There is, of course, a just war tradition which predates Walzer's work and inspires it in many ways. See J. T. Johnson, *The Just War Tradition and the Restraint of War* (Princeton: Princeton University Press, 1981).

7 D. Luban, 'The Romance of the Nation-State', *Philosophy and Public Affairs* (1979/80), 392–7.

8 Walzer, *Wars*, 107.

9 B. Barry, *Theories of Justice* (Berkeley: University of California Press, 1989); C. Beitz, *Political Theory and International Relations* (Princeton: Princeton University Press, 1979); T. Pogge, *Realizing Rawls* (Ithaca: Cornell University Press, 1989); T. Pogge, 'Cosmopolitanism and Sovereignty', *Ethics* (1992), 48–75; Walzer, *Thick*, 63–84; M. Walzer, 'The Reform of the International System', in

O. Osterud, ed., *Studies of War and Peace* (Oslo: Norwegian University Press, 1986), 227–40; Walzer, *Spheres*, 60–2.

10 I. Kant, *The Metaphysics of Morals*, trans./ed. by M. Gregor (Cambridge: Cambridge University Press, 1995), 117–24.

1 Interpretation: The Method of Walzer's General Theory of Justice

1 Walzer, *Wars*, xxviii.

2 Walzer, *Wars*, 15; Walzer, *Spheres*, 5. An important note about noting: when, in a paragraph, there appears more than one quote, the citations listed in the notes will parallel the order of the quotes in the paragraph. Thus, this note provides first the citation for the first quote in the paragraph to which it refers, the second to the second. I have adopted this method so that the notes do not needlessly clutter up the text: rarely will there be more than one note per paragraph.

3 The first two quotes are at Walzer, *Wars*, xxix–xxx, the third at Walzer, *Social*, 23–4.

4 Walzer, *Spheres*, 8.

5 Walzer, *Social*, 5, 66.

6 Walzer, *Social*, 1–32.

7 Walzer, *Social*, 1–32; T. Nagel, *The View from Nowhere* (New York: Oxford University Press, 1986).

8 Walzer, *Social*, 13.

9 Rawls scholars will no doubt note that there seem to be two John Rawls: the Rawls of the first, landmark study, *A Theory of Justice* (Cambridge, MA: Harvard University Press, 1971); and the Rawls of the later work, *Political Liberalism* (New York: Columbia University Press, 1993). The Rawls which Walzer discusses, and is most serious about refuting, is the classical Rawls, author of the first edition of *A Theory of Justice*.

10 Rawls, *Theory, passim*.

11 Walzer, *Social*, 11, 14.

12 Walzer, *Social*, 14–17.

13 B. Barry, 'Spherical Justice and Global Injustice', in Miller and Walzer, eds., *Equality*, 67–81; B. Barry, 'Social Criticism and Political Philosophy', *Philosophy and Public Affairs* (1990), 360–73.

14 Walzer, *Social*, 20, 6, 26; T. Nagel, 'The Limits of Objectivity', *Tanner Lectures on Human Values*, 1 (Salt Lake City: University of Utah Press, 1980).

15 Walzer, *Social*, 17, 20–3.

16 There are interesting, unacknowledged similarities between this view

and American pragmatist Donald Davidson's 'On the Very Idea of a Conceptual Scheme', in his *Inquiries into Truth and Interpretation* (Oxford: Oxford University Press, 1984).

17 Walzer, *Social*, 27; Walzer, *Wars*, 20.

18 Walzer, *Social*, 23.

19 A very similar view is developed by American pragmatist Richard Rorty, in his *Contingency, Irony and Solidarity* (Cambridge: Cambridge University Press, 1989).

20 Walzer, *Social*, 21; M. Nussbaum, 'Human Functioning and Social Justice', *Political Theory* (1992), 202–46.

21 Walzer, *Thick*, 41–62; Walzer, *Social*, 33–66; R. Dworkin and M. Walzer, 'Spheres of Justice: An Exchange', *The New York Review of Books* (21 July 1983), 43–6; J. Cohen, review of Walzer's *Spheres*, *Journal of Philosophy* (1986), 457–68; G. Warnke, *Justice and Interpretation* (Oxford: Polity Press, 1992), 3–38.

22 Walzer, *Thick*, 41; Walzer, *Spheres, passim*.

23 Walzer, *Social*, 36–47; M. Walzer, *The Company of Critics* (New York: Basic Books, 1988).

24 Walzer, *Thick*, 39; Walzer, *Social*, 87; Walzer, *Wars*, xxix.

25 Warnke, *Interpretation*, 3–38.

26 Thus Walzer responds to Rorty's otherwise searching question: what if 'we' are an Orwellian police state? Rorty, *Irony, passim*.

27 Walzer, *Thick*, 27; Cohen, review of Walzer, 457–68. At *Social*, 64, Walzer even suggests that appealing to objectivity in moral debate can itself seem like 'an external intervention, a coercive act, intellectual in form but pointing toward its physical counterpart'.

28 Walzer, *Social*, 25–6.

29 Walzer, *Wars*, 288; Walzer, *Social*, 25–35; Warnke, *Interpretation*, 3–38.

30 Barry, 'Spherical', 67–81.

31 Walzer, *Social*, 28–32.

32 Walzer, *Social*, 49; R. Dworkin, 'To Each His Own', *The New York Review of Books* (14 April 1983), 4–6.

33 Walzer, *Social*, 1–66; Walzer, *Wars*, 45.

2 Thick and Thin: The Content of Walzer's General Theory of Justice

1 Walzer, *Thick*, xi. The ultimate source of the original form of the quotation is usually attributed to Cyril Connolly.

2 Walzer, *Social*, 23–5, 29, 93; Walzer, *Thick*, x, 10, 42–52, 60; Walzer, *Spheres*, xv, 65, 70; Walzer, *Wars*, xxx.

3   Walzer, *Thick*, 5, 7, 15.
4   Walzer, *Thick*, 21–2.
5   Walzer, *Spheres, passim*; Walzer, *Thick*, 18, 26–40.
6   Walzer, *Thick*, xi, 3, 18.
7   Walzer, *Thick*, 5; Walzer, *Social*, 29.
8   Walzer, *Wars*, 3.
9   See, for example, Walzer, *Wars*, 43, where he cites ancient Indian
    and Hebrew sources. He also cites ancient Greek and medieval
    European sources. Indeed, all of *Wars* contains numerous cross-
    cultural examples. See also his 'War and Peace in the Jewish
    Tradition', in T. Nardin, ed., *The Ethics of War and Peace: Religious
    and Secular Perspectives* (Princeton: Princeton University Press,
    1996), 95–114. Other examples of cross-cultural agreement on the
    moral vocabulary of war, which Walzer does not cite, might be the
    Islamic tradition of *jihad*, and Chinese sage Sun Tzu's ancient yet
    much-cited tome, *The Art of War* (New York: HarperCollins, 1987).
    On *jihad*, see the above Nardin collection as well as J. Kelsay, *Islam
    and Just War: A Study in Comparative Ethics* (Louisville, KY: John
    Knox Press, 1992).
10 Walzer, *Wars*, 16. This reference to a thing's being 'true enough'
    (presumably to be useful and/or believable) has a flavour similar to that
    of certain expressions of American pragmatism. For more on Walzer
    and pragmatism, see the notes for the last chapter, as well as for the
    Conclusion.
11 Walzer, *Wars*, 19.
12 Walzer, *Wars*, 47, 15.
13 Walzer, *Wars*, 12.
14 Walzer, *Wars*, xxix–xxx.
15 Walzer, *Thick*, 22; Walzer, *Spheres*, 28, 313.
16 Walzer, *Spheres*, 68–75, 84–6; Walzer, *Thick*, 28.
17 Walzer, *Thick*, 28–30.
18 Walzer, *Spheres*, 86–91; Walzer, *Thick*, 30–2.
19 Walzer, *Spheres*, 9; Walzer, *Thick*, 26–40.
20 Walzer, *Spheres*, 318.
21 Walzer, *Spheres*, 167.
22 Warnke, *Interpretation*, 3–38.
23 R. Dworkin and M. Walzer, '*Spheres of Justice*: An Exchange', *New
    York Review of Books* (21 July 1983), 43–6.
24 Ibid.
25 Walzer, *Spheres*, 3–30.
26 Ibid.
27 Walzer, *Spheres, passim*; Walzer, *Thick*, 26–40.
28 Walzer, *Thick*, 31–3; Walzer, *Spheres, passim*.

29 Walzer, *Spheres*, 95–128; M. Ignatieff, 'Review', *Political Quarterly* 56 (1985), 91–3.
30 Walzer, *Thick*, 33–8.
31 Walzer, *Thick*, 81–101.
32 Walzer, *Spheres*, 250–80; Walzer, *Thick*, 32, 81–104.
33 Walzer, *Thick*, 81–101; M. Walzer, *On Toleration* (New Haven, CT: Yale University Press, 1997).
34 Walzer, *Spheres*, 3–30, 56–90, quotations at 65, 82.
35 Walzer, *Spheres*, 316–21; Walzer, *Thick*, 37.
36 Walzer, *Spheres*, 129–64 and 281–321.
37 J.-J. Rousseau, *Basic Political Writings*, trans./ed. by D. Cress (Indianapolis: Hackett, 1987).
38 Walzer, *Spheres*, 312–13.
39 Walzer, *Spheres*, 26–8 and 313.
40 Warnke, *Interpretation*, 3–38.
41 Rawls, *Theory*, *passim*.
42 Walzer, *Spheres*, xvii and R. Nozick, *Anarchy, State and Utopia* (New York: Basic Books, 1974). Of course, Nozick's work was written in response to Rawls's.
43 Walzer, *Thick*, 25–33.
44 Walzer, *Thick*, 21, 60; Walzer, *Spheres*, 33–40.
45 G. W. F. Hegel, *Philosophy of History*, trans. by L. Rauch (Indianapolis: Hackett, 1988); G. W. F. Hegel, *Philosophy of Right*, trans. by H. Nisbet, ed. by A. Wood (Cambridge: Cambridge University Press, 1991).
46 C. Taylor, *Hegel and Modern Society* (Cambridge: Cambridge University Press, 1979); C. Taylor, *The Politics of Recognition* (Princeton: Princeton University Press, 1996).
47 Walzer, *Spheres*, 6–8 and 320.
48 Walzer, *Thick*, x.
49 Walzer, *Thick*, 26.
50 Walzer, *Spheres*, 50–64.

3 Walzer on Alternatives to Just War Theory

1 D. Lackey, 'A Modern Theory of Just War', *Ethics* (April 1982), 546.
2 Walzer, *Wars*, 3.
3 Notable realist tracts include Morgenthau's *Politics among Nations* (New York: Knopf, 1973), Kennan's *Realities of American Foreign Policy* (Princeton: Princeton University Press, 1954) and Waltz's *Man, The State and War* (Princeton: Princeton University Press, 1978). See also R. Keohane, ed., *Neorealism and its Critics* (New York: Columbia

University Press, 1986); D. Boucher, *Political Theories of International Relations* (Oxford: Oxford University Press, 1998); and S. Forde, 'Classical Realism', 62–84, and J. Donnelly, 'Twentieth Century Realism', 85–11, both in T. Nardin and D. Mapel, eds., *Traditions in International Ethics* (Cambridge: Cambridge University Press, 1992).

4   Walzer, *Wars*, 3–4, 117.
5   Walzer, *Wars*, 5.
6   Walzer, *Wars*, 5–10, 15.
7   Walzer, 'Nation', 537–40; Walzer, *Wars*, 78.
8   Walzer, *Wars*, 20.
9   Walzer, *Wars*, 12, 4, 117.
10 Walzer, *Wars*, 19, 20, 110.
11 Walzer, *Wars*, 110, 117.
12 Walzer, *Wars*, 13–16.
13 Walzer, *Wars*, 110. See also D. Welch, *Justice and the Genesis of War* (Cambridge: Cambridge University Press, 1988) for further reflection on this contention.
14 Walzer, *Wars*, 122.
15 For more on characterizing the complex options within contemporary realism, see chapter 5 of my *War and International Justice: A Kantian Perspective* (Waterloo, Ont.: Wilfrid Laurier University Press, 2000) and my forthcoming 'A Just War Critique of Realism and Pacifism', *Journal of Philosophical Research*.
16 T. Pogge, *Realizing Rawls* (Ithaca, NY: Cornell University Press, 1989), 211–81.
17 Lackey, 'Modern', 533–48 and G. Mavrodes, 'Conventions and the Morality of War', *Philosophy and Public Affairs* (1974/5), 117–31.
18 Walzer, *Wars*, 329.
19 J. Teichman, *Pacifism and the Just War* (Oxford: Basil Blackwell, 1986); R. Holmes, *On War and Morality* (Princeton: Princeton University Press, 1988); R. Norman, *Ethics, Killing and War* (Cambridge: Cambridge University Press, 1995); J. Narveson, 'Pacifism: A Philosophical Analysis', 41–61, and G. E. M. Anscombe, 'War and Murder', 20–40, both in R. Wasserstrom, ed., *War and Morality* (Belmont, CA: Wadsworth, 1970).
20 Walzer, *Wars*, 252.
21 Walzer, *Wars*, xvi. The reference, of course, is to Iraq's aggressive invasion of Kuwait in August 1990.
22 Walzer, *Wars*, 329–36; Holmes, *War*, 260–96; Norman, *Ethics*, 210–15.
23 Rawls, *Theory*, 370–82; Walzer, *Wars*, 329–36.
24 Walzer, *Wars*, xxii, 330–5.
25 Holmes, *War, passim*. It should be noted that the CP/DP distinction is

only intended as one of degree and not necessarily one in kind. There are many well-known problems with regard to distinguishing between consequentialism and deontology.

26 Norman, *Ethics*, 290–3; Narveson, 'Pacifism', 62–77. For more on refuting CP, see my forthcoming 'Evaluating Pacifism', *Dialogue: Canadian Philosophical Reviews*.

27 In my *International*, chapter 5.

28 Ibid.

29 Holmes, *War*, 146–213.

30 Walzer, *Wars*, 138.

31 Walzer, *Wars*, 152.

32 Walzer, *Wars*, 152–9, 257, 277–83 and 317–21; Norman, *Killing*, 73–118 and 159–200.

33 Of course, these are not the only two options. G. Davis, in *Warcraft and the Fragility of Virtue* (Lincoln: University of Nebraska Press, 1992), develops a neo-Aristotelian, or 'virtue ethics', version of wartime justice. I lack space here to call this conception into doubt but note that Walzer himself overlooks it, focusing entirely on the canonical clash between rights and utility.

34 Walzer, *Wars*, xxix–xxx.

35 Walzer, *Wars*, 133–4; C. MacKinnon, 'Crimes of War, Crimes of Peace', in S. Shute and S. Hurley, eds., *On Human Rights* (New York: Basic Books, 1993), 83–110.

36 Walzer, *Wars*, 228, 268 and 230. See also M. Walzer, 'The Moral Standing of States: A Response to Four Critics', *Philosophy and Public Affairs* (1979/80), 222, n. 24: 'Nozick goes on to argue, on Kantian grounds, that rights must be understood as constraints on action rather than as goals of a maximizing politics. Though I don't share his views as to the substance of a rights theory, the same conception of its structure underlies my own position in *Just and Unjust Wars*.'

37 J. Narveson, *Morality and Utility* (Baltimore: Johns Hopkins University Press, 1969); J. Waldron, *Nonsense upon Stilts* (London: Methuen, 1990); J. Glover, ed., *Utilitarianism and Its Critics* (London: Macmillan, 1990).

38 Walzer, at pp. 330–1 in his untitled contribution to *Dissent*'s Summer 1995 symposium on the fiftieth anniversary of Hiroshima.

39 Walzer, *Wars*, 262–8, and 210; Walzer, 'Untitled', 330–1. See also T. Nagel, 'War and Massacre', *Philosophy and Public Affairs* (1971/2), 126.

40 Walzer, *Wars*, 67–77 and I. Kant, 'Perpetual Peace', in H. Reiss, ed., and H. Nisbet, trans., *Kant: Political Writings* (Cambridge: Cambridge University Press, 1995), 116.

41 Walzer, *Wars*, 132, 242–68.

[42] Walzer, 'Standing', 226.

[43] Narveson, *Utility*; J. S. Mill, *On Liberty* (Harmondsworth: Penguin, 1992); A. Sen and B. Williams, eds., *Utilitarianism and Beyond* (Cambridge: Cambridge University Press, 1982); J. W. Bailey, *Utilitarianism, Institutions and Justice* (Oxford: Oxford University Press, 1997).

[44] The concession should here be made that Walzer's supreme emergency override for the human rights he otherwise staunchly defends during wartime seems to have certain affinities with rule-utilitarianism. It may well suffer from related problems, as will be considered in chapter 5 on Walzer's theory of *jus in bello*.

[45] R. B. Brandt, 'Utilitarianism and the Rules of War', *Philosophy and Public Affairs* (1971/2), 146–55.

[46] R. Regan, *Just War: Principles and Cases* (Washington, DC: Catholic University of America Press, 1996), 192–211; D. Reiff, *Slaughterhouse: Bosnia and the Failure of the West* (New York: Simon & Schuster, 1995); Human Rights Watch, *Slaughter among Neighbours* (New Haven: Yale University Press, 1995); and my 'Crisis in Kosovo: A Just Use of Force?', *Politics* (1999), 125–30.

[47] Brandt, 'Rules', 154–7. Walzer's only actual response to Brandt makes for puzzling reading in his unusual article, 'Political Action: The Problem of Dirty Hands', *Philosophy and Public Affairs* (1972/3), 160–80.

[48] Brandt, 'Rules', 157.

[49] Brandt, 'Rules', 158.

[50] Brandt, 'Rules', 159.

4 Aggression and Defence: Walzer's Theory of *Jus ad Bellum*

[1] Walzer, *Wars*, 51.

[2] Walzer, *Wars*, 44, 288–301

[3] On the law, see W. Reisman and C. Antoniou, eds., *The Laws of War: A Comprehensive Collection of Primary Documents Governing Armed Conflict* (New York: Vintage, 1994), 317–405. For more on traditional just war theory, see: J. B. Elshtain, ed., *Just War Theory* (Oxford: Blackwell, 1992); R. Wasserstrom, ed., *War and Morality* (Belmont, CA: Wadsworth, 1970); W. V. O'Brien, *The Conduct of Just and Limited War* (New York: Praeger, 1981); R. Phillips, *Can Modern War Be Just?* (New Haven: Yale University Press, 1984); and P. Ramsey, *The Just War: Force and Political Responsibility* (New York: Scribner, 1968). The best historical studies of this corpus are J. T. Johnson,

Ideology, Reason and the Limitation of War: Religious and Secular Concepts, 1200–1740 (Princeton: Princeton University Press, 1981) and J. T. Johnson, *Just War Tradition and the Restraint of War: A Moral and Historical Inquiry* (Princeton: Princeton University Press, 1981). For the primary documents themselves, see St Augustine, *Basic Writings* (New York: Random House, 1948); St T. Aquinas, *Summa Theologica* (San Francisco: Washbourne, 1912–22), II, Q. 40, A. 1; Q. 64, AA. 6, 7; and the following from J. B. Scott, ed., *Classics of International Law* (Oxford: Clarendon, 1925): H. Grotius, *De Jure Belli ac Pacis Libri Tres*; E. Vattel, *The Law of Nations*; F. Vitoria, *De Indis et De Jure Belli Reflectiones*; and F. Suarez, *De Triplici Virtute Theologica (De Caritate, Disputatio 13).*

4   Walzer, *Wars, 62.*

5   Walzer, *Wars, 52.*

6   Walzer, *Wars, 55–62.*

7   Walzer, *Wars,* 89. Though what constitutes a purely 'domestic' policy is, of course, not always clear: domestic in intent? In effect? Neither Walzer nor I deal with these perplexities. Some political scientists have even begun to argue that the old left–right continuum in policy debates is being replaced by a new domestic–international spectrum.

8   Walzer, *Wars, 53.*

9   Walzer, *Wars,* 51; and D. Luban, 'The Romance of the Nation-State', 392–7, and G. Doppelt, 'Statism without Foundations', 398–403, both in *Philosophy and Public Affairs* (1980).

10 Walzer, *Wars, 53–4.*

11 Walzer, *Wars,* 54 and xxx.

12 For contrasting, high-profile views as to the nature of human rights – in particular, for extending their scope beyond that of life and liberty – see H. Shue, *Basic Rights: Subsistence, Affluence and U.S. Foreign Policy* (Princeton: Princeton University Press, 1980); and J. Nickel, *Making Sense of Human Rights* (Berkeley, CA: University of California Press, 1987).

13 Walzer, *Wars, 58.*

14 Walzer, *Wars, 54.*

15 Walzer, *Spheres,* 65 and 82.

16 M. Walzer, 'The Moral Standing of States', *Philosophy and Public Affairs* 3 (1979/80), 211; Walzer, *Spheres,* 31.

17 Walzer, *Wars,* 54, 86–106; Walzer, 'Standing', 211; Walzer, *Spheres,* 62.

18 Walzer, *Wars,* 62, 292.

19 Walzer, *Wars,* 51, 67–72 and 233–8.

20 Reisman and Antoniou, eds., *Laws,* 8.

[21] P. Christopher, *The Ethics of War and Peace* (Englewood Cliffs, NJ: Prentice-Hall, 1994), 102–5.

[22] Walzer, *Wars*, xix.

[23] Walzer, *Wars*, xix–xx. For more on the Gulf War, see: D. Decosse, ed., *But was it Just? Reflections on the Morality of the Persian Gulf War* (New York: Doubleday, 1992). Note Walzer's own opening essay, 'Justice and Injustice in the Gulf War'.

[24] For more on this posited addition to right intention, see my 'Kant on International Law and Armed Conflict', *Canadian Journal of Law and Jurisprudence* (July 1998), 329–81, and my 'Kant's Just War Theory', *The Journal of the History of Philosophy* (April 1999), 323–52.

[25] For more on the Bosnian civil war of 1992–5, see Regan, *Just*, 192–212; Reiff, *Slaughterhouse*, and Human Rights Watch, *Neighbors*.

[26] Walzer, *Wars*, 58; H. Suganami, *The Domestic Analogy and World Order Proposals* (Cambridge: Cambridge University Press, 1989).

[27] See Regan, *Cases*, 20–47 for more on legitimate authority, especially as applied to the United States. Also relevant is L. Fisher, *Presidential War Power* (Lawrence, KS: University of Kansas Press, 1995) and Reisman and Antoniou, eds., *Laws*, 40–1.

[28] Walzer, *Wars*, 34–40 and 138–43 and M. Walzer, *Obligations: Essays on Citizenship, War and Disobedience* (Cambridge, MA: Harvard University Press, 1970).

[29] Walzer, *Wars*, 84, xiv.

[30] Walzer, *Wars*, xiii–xiv. See also L. Freedman and E. Karsh, eds., *The Gulf Conflict (1990–91): Diplomacy and War in the New World Order* (Princeton, NJ: Princeton University Press, 1993); W. Danspeckgruber and C. Tripp, eds., *The Iraqi Aggression against Kuwait* (Boulder, CO: Westview, 1996); US News and World Report, *Triumph without Victory* (New York: Random House, 1992); James Turner Johnson and G. Weigel, eds., *Just War and Gulf War* (Washington, DC: University Press of America, 1991); and A. Beyer and B. Green, eds., *Lines in the Sand: Justice and the Gulf War* (Louisville, KY: John Knox Press, 1992).

[31] Walzer, *Wars*, xxv–xxxii; A. Pierce, 'Just War Principles and Economic Sanctions', *Ethics and International Affairs* (1996), 99–113; L. F. Damrosch, 'The Collective Enforcement of International Norms through Economic Sanctions', *Ethics and International Affairs* (1994), 60–80; and D. Cortright and G. Lopez, *Economic Sanctions: Panacea or Peacebuilding in a Post-Cold War World?* (Boulder, CO: Westview, 1995). For *jus in bello*, see next chapter.

[32] Article 2(4) of the UN Charter seems evidence of our deep commitment to such a presumption. It reads: 'All Members shall refrain in their international relations from the threat or use of force against the terri-

torial integrity or political independence of any state.' See Regan, *Cases*, 214; Reisman and Antoniou, eds., *Laws*, 5–9.

33 Walzer, *Wars*, 107.

34 Walzer, *Wars*, 67–74.

35 Walzer, *Wars*, xv–xxi.

36 Walzer, *Wars*, xv–xxi.

37 M. Walzer, 'World War II: Why Was This War Different?', *Philosophy and Public Affairs* (1971/2), 3–21; Walzer, *Wars*, 233–68; and A. J. P. Taylor, *Origins of the Second World War* (London: Hamish Hamilton, 1961).

38 On Somalia and Bosnia, see Regan, *Cases*, 179–212. On Rwanda, see G. Prunier, *The Rwanda Crisis: History of a Genocide* (New York: Columbia University Press, 1995). On Kosovo, see my 'Crisis', 125–30.

39 Walzer, *Wars*, 74–80.

40 Walzer, *Wars*, 74–85.

41 Ibid.

42 Walzer, *Wars*, 96–100, 186–96, 296–303 and 309–15. Walzer cites the Vietnam War as the event which first triggered his interest in just war theory.

43 Walzer, *Wars*, 87–8.

44 Walzer, *Wars*, 86–95.

45 Walzer, *Wars*, 96–100; Walzer, 'Standing', 210–25.

46 Something it pledged to do in the 1954 Geneva Agreement, which was a peace treaty ending the first phase of the Vietnam War, between the communist north and the French-sponsored south. See Regan, *Cases*, 136–50.

47 Walzer, *Wars*, 99.

48 Walzer, *Wars*, 103–8.

49 I say 'in principle' because both Beitz and Doppelt agree that such intervention might be ruled out on grounds that it fails the proportionality test. See Luban, 'Romance', 392–98, Doppelt, 'Statism', 398–403, and C. Beitz, 'Nonintervention and Communal Integrity', *Philosophy and Public Affairs* (1980), 385–91.

50 Walzer, 'Standing', 211.

51 Walzer, *Wars*, 103–8.

52 Walzer, *Wars*, 102–8; M. Walzer, 'Kosovo', *Dissent* (Summer 1999), 5–7.

53 He steps gingerly around this topic at 'Standing', 223 in n. 26. See also Beitz, 'Communal', 389.

54 Walzer, *Wars*, 87.

5 Innocence and Emergency: Walzer's Theory of *Jus in Bello*

1   M. Walzer, *Just and Unjust Wars* (New York: Basic Books, 2nd edn
    1991; 1st edn 1977), 158, 210.
2   Walzer, *Wars*, 34–5.
3   Walzer, *Wars*, 34–49, 127–224.
4   Walzer, *Wars*, 42–3, 135.
5   Walzer, *Wars*, 37, 40, 136. James Dubik seems the first to note and
    explain this murkiness, in his 'Human Rights, Command Respon-
    sibility and Walzer's Just War Theory', *Philosophy and Public Affairs*
    (1982), 354–71. See also Lackey, 'Theory', 540–2.
6   Walzer, *Wars*, 135.
7   Thomas Pogge, Philosophy, Columbia University in New York City.
    Walzer himself notes the British prosecutor's arguments in his *Wars*,
    38.
8   Walzer, *Wars*, 127, 39.
9   Walzer, *Wars*, 39.
10 Walzer, *Wars*, 128.
11 Walzer, *Wars*, 40, 138.
12 Walzer, *Wars*, 299–300 in the note.
13 See Dubik, 'Command', 359–61, for an excellent analysis of Walzer's
    difficulties in this regard. See also Walzer, *Wars*, 138–60.
14 Walzer, *Wars*, 142.
15 Walzer, *Wars*, 142, 46. Both the Hague and Geneva Conventions
    enshrine these claims. See Reisman and Antoniou, eds., *Laws*,
    149–231.
16 Walzer, *Wars*, 146–51.
17 Lackey, 'Modern', 540–2; T. Nagel, 'War and Massacre', *Philosophy
    and Public Affairs* (1971/2), 123–44; and R. K. Fullinwider, 'War and
    Innocence', *Philosophy and Public Affairs* (1976), 90–7.
18 Walzer, *Wars*, 151. For the conventions, see Reisman and Antoniou,
    eds., *Laws*, 47–132. See also G. Best, *War and Law since 1945*
    (Oxford: Clarendon, 1994).
19 Walzer, *Wars*, 146, 219; Nagel, 'Massacre', 133–41.
20 Walzer, *Wars*, xx.
21 Walzer, *Wars*, 153–4.
22 Walzer, 'Jewish', 106.
23 Walzer, *Wars*, 151, 157.
24 Walzer, *Wars*, 152 and 156, in the note. See also Walzer's comments,
    discussed in chapter 3, about the need to reject utilitarian thinking
    during wartime.
25 See my 'Kant's Just War Theory', *Journal of the History of Philosophy*

(April 1999), 323–52 and my 'Kant on International Law and Armed Conflict', *Canadian Journal of Law and Jurisprudence* (July 1998), 329–81. The most relevant primary source is I. Kant, *The Metaphysics of Morals*, trans. by Mary Gregor (Cambridge: Cambridge University Press, 1995), especially 114–24.

26 Walzer, *Wars*, 129, xxi.

27 Walzer, *Wars*, 42 and 215; Reisman and Antoniou, eds., *Laws*, 35–132.

28 Regan, *Cases*, 87–99, 136–50.

29 Walzer, *Wars*, 282. While there have been two UN General Assembly resolutions, in 1961 and 1972, banning the use of nuclear weapons (see Reisman and Antoniou, eds., *Laws*, 66–7), these do not carry the binding force of a ratified international treaty. Obviously, the fact that the world's most powerful countries are also nuclear powers inhibits the passing of such a treaty.

30 Walzer, *Wars*, 129–37; MacKinnon, 'Crimes of War', 83–110.

31 Reisman and Antoniou, eds., *Laws*, 84–94; Walzer, *Wars*, 257, 323.

32 Walzer, *Wars*, 207–22; Regan, *Cases*, 172–8.

33 Walzer, *Wars*, 207.

34 This seems the eerie equivalent of Walzer's earlier refusal, discussed in chapter 2, to afford baseline distributive protections to the poorest of the poor. Walzer's attitudes towards the worst-off, both in society generally and in the military in particular, can at times seem rather callous and unconcerned, which I have pointed out seems somewhat ironic for a socialist.

35 Walzer, *Wars*, 47.

36 Walzer, *Wars*, 131. It should be noted that, in most of the laws themselves, the appeal to military necessity is explicitly ruled out as grounds for violation. See Reisman and Antoniou, eds., *Laws*, xvii–xxxii.

37 Walzer, *Wars*, 195, 228.

38 Churchill quoted in Walzer, *Wars*, 245.

39 Walzer, *Wars*, 241, 251–4, 257.

40 Walzer, *Wars*, 253; and Walzer, 'World War II', 3–21.

41 Walzer, *Wars*, 325 and 323.

42 Walzer, *Wars*, 258–63.

43 Walzer, *Wars*, 254.

44 Ibid.

45 Walzer, *Wars*, 325–8, 251–68; Walzer, 'Political Action', 160–80.

46 Walzer, *Wars*, 231, 259.

47 I concur with Walzer's notion that 'let justice be done though the heavens fall' is a rather hard doctrine for people to accept during a supreme emergency, since here it really means what it says. Walzer, *Wars*, 230.

48 I believe this is the deepest meaning of the article which Walzer mistakenly cites in favour of his own paradoxical reading of supreme emergency: Nagel's 'Massacre', 123–44. The DDE, it should be noted, cannot justify actions which violate *jus in bello* during a supreme emergency. And this for at least two reasons. First, the DDE stipulates that the action which produces both good and bad effects must be otherwise permissible. But actions which violate *jus in bello*, like murder, are not otherwise permissible. Furthermore, the DDE stipulates that the bad effects cannot be the means whereby the good effects are to be achieved. But in a supreme emergency, the bad effects (like massive civilian casualties) are intended to bring about the good effects (to make the aggressor cease and desist).

49 For other views on Walzer's supreme emergency escape clause, see: Lackey, 'Modern', 540–2; and T. Nardin, *Law, Morality and the Relations of States* (Princeton: Princeton University Press, 1983). A revised version of this chapter will appear as an article in a future edition of *Law and Philosophy*.

6 Terms of Peace: Walzer's Theory of *Jus post Bellum*

1 Walzer, *Wars*, 288.

2 Recent contributions include: chapter 7 of Walzer, *Wars*, 109–23; S. Albert and E. Luck, eds., *On the Endings of Wars* (London: Kennikat Press, 1980), 157–71; N. Oren, ed., *Termination of War: Processes, Procedures and Aftermaths* (Jerusalem: Hebrew University Press, 1982); A. J. P. Taylor, *How Wars End* (London: Hamish Hamilton, 1985); and F. O. Hampson, *Nurturing Peace: Why Peace Settlements Succeed or Fail* (Washington, DC: US Institute of Peace, 1996). See also my 'Terminating Wars and Establishing Global Governance', *Canadian Journal of Law and Jurisprudence* (July 1999), 253–96.

3 Walzer writes two chapters on war crimes trials, filling over forty pages. See *Wars*, 287–328.

4 Walzer, *Wars*, xvii, 121.

5 When it looks as though a just state is about to lose a war to an aggressor, the core recommendation to the just state, as Frances Kamm of New York University points out, is to cut its losses. A just and rational state will, where possible, attempt to spare its people from the full wrath of the aggressor nation by offering it enough to satisfy its unjust desires and make it desist from its criminal activity. But, obviously, if the aggressor desires something like total conquest, then the recommendation would be to fight on, clearly while imploring the international community to intervene on its behalf and turn the tide

against the aggressor. Indeed, it might be argued that a state on the verge of such a defeat to an aggressor has a fully-fledged right *to claim* such international intervention.

6   I. Kant, *The Metaphysics of Morals*, trans. by M. Gregor (Cambridge: Cambridge University Press, 1995), 114–24.

7   Walzer, *Wars*, 119, xx.

8   Walzer, *Wars*, 110, 117, 123; J. Rawls, 'The Law of Peoples', in S. Shute and S. Hurley, eds., *On Human Rights* (New York: Basic Books, 1993), 40–80.

9   'General view' because of his supreme emergency exemption clause discussed in the last chapter. Perhaps no one has stressed the notion that a just war is a limited war more than W. V. O'Brien, *The Conduct of Just and Limited War* (New York: Praeger, 1981).

10   Churchill, quoted in Walzer, *Wars*, 112; Walzer, *Wars*, 113, 263–8.

11   Walzer, *Wars*, 118.

12   This image of just war as radical surgery, and just settlement as the subsequent therapy, came to mind while reading N. Oren, 'Prudence in Victory', in Oren, ed., *Termination*, 147–64.

13   Nickel, *Human Rights*, passim.

14   Walzer, *Wars*, 297.

15   Walzer, *Wars*, 113, 119, 267–8.

16   Walzer, *Wars*, 113, 119.

17   Walzer, *Wars*, xvii–xx.

18   On Bosnia, see Reiff, *Slaughterhouse* and the text of the Dayton Accord itself, which ended the war in November 1995. See also the text of the Ahtìsaari Accord, Serbia's initial agreement in May 1999 to NATO's terms on ending its armed intervention in favour of the Kosovars.

19   Walzer, 'Untitled', 330.

20   Walzer, *Wars*, 288.

21   Walzer, *Wars*, 292–301. See also: Reisman and Antoniou, eds., *Laws*, 317–405; R. Wasserstrom, ed., *War and Morality* (Belmont, CA: Wadsworth, 1970), 102–34; S. L. Paulson, 'Classical Legal Positivism at Nuremberg', *Philosophy and Public Affairs* (1974/5), 132–58; P. Christopher, *The Ethics of War and Peace* (Englewood Cliffs, NJ: Prentice-Hall, 1994), 139–64; R. Wasserstrom, 'The Relevance of Nuremberg', *Philosophy and Public Affairs* (1971/2), 22–46; S. Levinson, 'Responsibility for Crimes of War', *Philosophy and Public Affairs* (1972/3), 244–73; and D. A. Peppers, 'War Crimes and Induction: A Case for Selective Nonconscientious Objection', *Philosophy and Public Affairs* (1973/4), 129–66.

22   Walzer, *Wars*, 123.

23   For brief summaries of both of these conflicts, and for more detailed sources about them, see Regan, *Cases*, 172–212.

24 For more on (positive international law regarding) war crimes trials, especially those at Nuremberg, see Reisman and Antoniou, eds., *Laws*, 317–405. Also relevant is the citation of the Nuremberg decision at 102–14 in Wasserstrom, ed., *Morality*; and S. L. Paulson, 'Classical Legal Positivism at Nuremberg', *Philosophy and Public Affairs* (1974–5), 132. All these sources contain references to further sources.

25 Walzer, *Wars*, 290–1, 298.

26 Refreshingly, Walzer does not succumb to the delusion that modern democracies are incapable of waging aggressive war, a popular academic distortion of Michael Doyle's influential scholarship – modelled after Kant's – regarding the importantly different claim that liberal democracies do not wage war *against other liberal democracies*. See M. Doyle, 'Kant, Liberal Legacies and Foreign Affairs', *Philosophy and Public Affairs* (1984), 204–35 and 323–53; and I. Kant, 'Perpetual Peace', trans. by H. Nisbet in H. Reiss, ed., *Kant: Political Writings* (Cambridge: Cambridge University Press, 1991), 93–130.

27 Walzer, *Wars*, 299–301.

28 Walzer, *Wars*, 301.

29 Walzer, *Wars*, 301–3.

30 Christopher, *Ethics*, 139–64; and Walzer, *Wars*, 304–28. See also G. Lewy, 'Superior Orders, Nuclear Warfare and the Dictates of Conscience', in Wasserstrom, ed., *Morality*, 115–34; R. Wasserstrom, 'The Relevance of Nuremberg', *Philosophy and Public Affairs* (1971–2), 22; S. Levinson, 'Responsibility', 244–73; and D. A. Peppers, 'Induction', 129–66.

31 Nanda, 'Establishment', 413–28.

32 Walzer, *Wars*, 305–16.

33 Walzer, *Wars*, 323–8.

7 Considering Globalism, Proposing Pluralism: Walzer on International Justice in General

1 Walzer, 'Standing', 227–8.

2 T. Pogge, 'An Egalitarian Law of Peoples', *Philosophy and Public Affairs* (1994), 224.

3 Walzer, *Wars*, xxvi.

4 Walzer, *Wars*, xxii–xxvi, 107; Walzer, 'Reform', 239–40.

5 Walzer, 'Reform', 238; Walzer, *Wars*, xxii.

6 Walzer, 'Nation and Universe', 555; Walzer, *Wars*, xxii; Walzer, *Spheres*, 48.

7 Walzer, 'Reform', 229; Walzer, *Thick*, 68–9.

8 Walzer, 'Standing', 226–9; Walzer, 'Reform', 227–9.

9 C. Beitz, *Political Theory and International Relations* (Princeton:

Princeton University Press, 1979); T. Pogge, *Realizing Rawls* (Ithaca, NY: Cornell University Press, 1989); I. Kant, *Political Writings*, trans. by H. Nisbet and ed. by H. Reiss (Cambridge: Cambridge University Press, 1995).

10 Beitz, *Political Theory*, *passim*.

11 Walzer, *Toleration*, 19–20; Walzer, *Wars*, 61–6.

12 Walzer, 'Standing', 227.

13 Ibid.

14 Articles on globalism fill the recent issues of the academic journals, especially those on international affairs and foreign policy. See also: T. Spybey, *Globalization and World Society* (Cambridge: Polity Press, 1996); J. Mittelman, ed., *Globalization: Critical Reflections* (Boulder, CO: Lynne Rienner, 1996); K. Booth and S. Smith, eds., *International Relations Theory Today* (Cambridge: Polity Press, 1995).

15 Walzer, 'Standing', 227.

16 These pressures are often now summarized under the heading 'glocalization'. The term refers to pressure from two directions: one, the 'upward' pressure from global institutions and practices, notably competition within the global economy; and the other, the 'downward' pressure from regional, state or provincial levels of governance and public service. Nation-states are sometimes seen as being pulled in both directions, and thus under serious pressure in the post-Cold War world.

17 Walzer, 'Standing', 227.

18 M. Walzer, 'Response', in Miller and Walzer, eds., *Pluralism*, 281–98.

19 Ibid.

20 T. Pogge, 'A Global Resources Dividend', in D. Crocker and T. Linden, eds., *Ethics of Consumption* (Boston: Rowman Littlefield, 1998), 501; T. Pogge, 'How Should Human Rights Be Conceived?', *Jahrbuch für Recht und Ethik* (1995), 103–20.

21 T. Pogge, 'Cosmopolitanism and Sovereignty', *Ethics* (1992), 48–75; Rawls, *Theory*, *passim*; J. Rawls, 'The Basic Structure as Subject', in A. Goldman and J. Kim, eds., *Values and Morals* (Dordrecht: Reidel, 1978). Note, however, that Rawls only talks about the basic structure of a national society, and not of the international arena. Pogge is the one who extends it globally. More on Rawls's own recent thoughts on this issue below.

22 Pogge, *Realizing*, 15–62.

23 Ibid.; Pogge, 'Dividend', 505.

24 Pogge, *Realizing*, 15–62, 211–80.

25 Pogge, 'Dividend', 504.

26 Pogge, *Rawls*, 273ff. See Pogge, 'Dividend', 501–36, for one proposal for institutional reform that would help shape an alternative global basic structure which would not give rise to such stark depravities.

27 Walzer, 'Reform', 240.
28 Walzer, *Thick*, 63–70; Walzer, 'Reform', 229; Walzer, 'Nation', 535.
    He explicitly refers to the need for international toleration at 19–22 in
    his *On Toleration* (New Haven, CT: Yale University Press, 1997).
29 Walzer, 'Reform', 230–1; Walzer, *Thick*, 66–70.
30 Walzer, *Thick*, 66.
31 Walzer, *Wars*, 53–8; Walzer, *Spheres*, 42–52.
32 Walzer, *Spheres*, 44–62.
33 Walzer, *Spheres*, 42–3.
34 Walzer, *Spheres*, 32, 62.
35 Walzer, *Spheres*, 45–62.
36 Walzer, *Thick*, 80.
37 Walzer, *Thick*, 70; Regan, *Cases*, 192–212.
38 Walzer, *Thick*, 71–2. This argument is formulated explicitly in opposi-
    tion to Will Kymlicka, *Liberalism, Community and Culture* (Oxford:
    Clarendon, 1991).
39 Walzer, *Thick*, 79–83.
40 Walzer, *Thick*, 76. See also the note at *Wars*, 93.
41 Walzer, *Thick*, 231.
42 Walzer, 'Reform', 231–3.
43 Walzer, *Thick*, 77–9; Walzer, 'Reform', 227–40.
44 J. Rawls, *The Law of Peoples* (Cambridge, MA: Harvard University
    Press, 1999). This new book expands upon two earlier pieces of work,
    cited in previous chapters: his essay of the same name in Shue and
    Hurley, eds., *On Human Rights*, 41–82; and his untitled *Dissent*
    contribution (Summer 1995).
45 Rawls, *Law*, 59–62 and 11–23.
46 Rawls, *Law*, *passim*.

Conclusion

1 Walzer, *Interpretation*, 67–94; Walzer, 'Jewish', 95–114; and the dedi-
   cation in Walzer, *Thick*, quoting to his wife from the Book of Judges in
   Hebrew.
2 Walzer, 'Nation', 535.
3 I. Kant, 'The End of All Things', trans. by T. Humphrey in his edn,
   Perpetual Peace and Other Essays (Indianapolis, IN: Hackett, 1983),
   96. See also I. Kant, *Political Writings*, ed. by H. Reiss/trans. by H.
   Nisbet (Cambridge: Cambridge University Press, 1991). Walzer quotation at 'Standing', 222, n. 24.
4 J. S. Mill, *On Liberty* (Harmondsworth: Penguin, 1987); Walzer,
   Wars, 40–73, 87–91.

5 Walzer, *Spheres*, 62.
6 Walzer, *Spheres*, 58–64; Walzer, *Social*, 28–32.
7 I am indebted to Howard Williams for encouraging me to explore it.
8 For more on pragmatism, see: C. West, *Pragmatism and the American Evasion of Philosophy* (Ithaca, NY: Cornell University Press, 1989); and J. P. Murphy, *Pragmatism: From Pierce to Davidson* (Boulder, CO: Westview, 1990). Also, see the notes to chapter 1.
9 M. Walzer, 'The Communitarian Critique of Liberalism', *Political Theory* (1990), 6–23. I am grateful to Peter Nicholson for noting how Walzer's drawing on each of the major Western political traditions is a logical consequence of his conventionalist methodology: since current beliefs have been shaped by conservatism, liberalism and socialism, it follows that an interpretative account of contemporary justice must itself draw on each of them.
10 Doppelt, 'Statism', 398–403.
11 K. Holsti, *The State, War and the State of War* (Cambridge: Cambridge University Press, 1996).

Bibliography

Barry, B. 'Social Criticism and Political Philosophy', *Philosophy and Public Affairs* (1990), 360–73.

Beitz, C. *Political Theory and International Relations.* Princeton, NJ: Princeton University Press, 1979.

—— 'Nonintervention and Communal Integrity', *Philosophy and Public Affairs* (1979/80), 385–91.

—— 'Cosmopolitan Ideals and National Sentiment', *The Journal of Philosophy* (1983), 591–600.

—— et al, eds. *International Ethics.* Princeton, NJ: Princeton University Press, 1985.

Best, G. *War and Law since 1945.* Oxford: Clarendon, 1994.

Brandt, R. B. 'Utilitarianism and the Rules of War', *Philosophy and Public Affairs* (1971/2), 145–65.

Brown, P. and H. Shue, eds. *Boundaries: National Autonomy and Its Limits.* Totowa, NJ: Rowman Littlefield, 1981.

Clausewitz, Carl von. *On War,* trans. by A. Rapoport. Harmondsworth: Penguin, 1995.

Cohen, J. Review of Walzer's *Spheres of Justice, Journal of Philosophy* (1986), 457–63.

Davis, G. S. *Warcraft and the Fragility of Virtue.* Lincoln, NB: University of Nebraska Press, 1992.

Davis, G. S. *Religion and Justice in the War over Bosnia.* New York: Routledge, 1996.

Dinstein, Y. *War, Aggression and Self-Defence.* Cambridge: Cambridge University Press, 1995.

Doppelt, G. 'Walzer's Theory of Morality in International Relations', *Philosophy and Public Affairs* (1978/9), 3–26.

—— 'Statism without Foundations', *Philosophy and Public Affairs* (1979–80), 398–403.

Dubik, J. 'Human Rights, Command Responsibility and Walzer's Just War Theory', *Philosophy and Public Affairs* (1982), 354–71.

Elshtain, J. B., ed. *Just War Theory.* Oxford: Basil Blackwell, 1992.

Elshtain, J. B., et al. *But was it Just? Reflections on the Morality of the Persian Gulf War,* ed. by D. DeCosse. New York: Doubleday, 1992.

Fullinwinder, R. 'War and Innocence', *Philosophy and Public Affairs* (1975), 90–7.

Gallie, W. B. *Understanding War.* London: Routledge, 1991.

Gelven, M. *War and Existence*. Philadelphia, PA: Pennsylvania State University Press, 1994.

Glossop, R. J. *World Federation? A Critical Analysis of Federal World Government*. London: McFarland, 1993.

—— *Confronting War: An Examination of Humanity's Most Pressing Problem*. London: McFarland, 3rd edn, 1994.

Hampson, F. O. *Nurturing Peace: Why Peace Settlements Succeed or Fail*. Washington, DC: United States Institute for Peace, 1996.

Hare, R. M. 'Rules of War and Moral Reasoning', *Philosophy and Public Affairs* (1971/2), 166–81.

Held, V., S. Morgenbesser and T. Nagel, eds. *Philosophy, Morality and International Affairs*. New York: Oxford University Press, 1974.

Hoffman, S. *Duties beyond Borders*. Syracuse, NY: Syracuse University Press, 1981.

—— *The Ethics and Politics of Humanitarian Intervention*. Notre Dame, IN: University of Notre Dame Press, 1996.

Holmes, R. *On War and Morality*. Princeton, NJ: Princeton University Press, 1989.

Holsti, K. *Peace and War: Armed Conflicts and International Order, 1648–1989*. Cambridge: Cambridge University Press, 1991.

—— *The State, War and the State of War*. Cambridge: Cambridge University Press, 1996.

Howard, M. *The Laws of War: Constraints on Warfare in the Western World*. New Haven, CT: Yale University Press, 1994.

Human Rights Watch. *Slaughter among Neighbours*. New Haven: Yale University Press, 1995.

Johnson, J. T. *Morality and Contemporary Warfare*. New Haven, CT: Yale University Press, 1999.

—— *The Just War Tradition and the Restraint of War*. Princeton, NJ: Princeton University Press, 1981.

Kant, I. *Political Writings*, trans. by H. Nisbet and ed. by H. Reiss. Cambridge: Cambridge University Press, 1970.

—— *The Metaphysics of Morals*, trans. by M. Gregor. Cambridge: Cambridge University Press, 1995.

Kennan, G. *Realities of American Foreign Policy*. Princeton, NJ: Princeton University Press, 1954.

Keohane, R., ed. *Neorealism and Its Critics*. New York: Columbia University Press, 1986.

Laberge, P. 'Humanitarian Intervention: Three Ethical Positions', *Ethics and International Affairs* 9 (1995), 15–35.

Lackey, D. 'A Modern Theory of Just War', *Ethics* (April 1982), 540–6.

Little, D. 'The "Just War" Doctrine and U.S. Policy in Vietnam', in S. Albert and E. Luck, eds., *On the Endings of Wars* (London: Kennikat Press, 1980), pp. 157–71.

Luban, D. 'Just War and Human Rights', *Philosophy and Public Affairs* (1979/80), 160–81.

—— 'The Romance of the Nation-State', *Philosophy and Public Affairs* (1979–80), 392–7.

Mavrodes, G. 'Conventions and the Laws of War', *Philosophy and Public Affairs* (1975), 117–31.

Mill, J. S. *On Liberty*. Harmondsworth: Penguin, 1988.

Morgenthau, H. *Politics among Nations*. New York: Knopf, 5th edn, 1973.

Nagel, T. 'War and Massacre'. *Philosophy and Public Affairs* (1971/2), 123–43.

—— 'Ruthlessness in Public Life', in his *Mortal Questions*. Cambridge: Cambridge University Press, 1979, pp. 75–90.

Nardin, T. *Law, Morality and the Relations of States*. Princeton, NJ: Princeton University Press, 1983.

Nardin, T., ed. *The Ethics of War and Peace: Religious and Secular Perspectives*. Princeton, NJ: Princeton University Press, 1996.

Nardin, T. and D. Mapel, eds. *Traditions of International Ethics*. Cambridge: Cambridge University Press, 1992.

Narveson, J. 'Violence and War' in T. Regan, ed., *Matters of Life and Death*. Philadelphia, PA: Temple University Press, 1980, pp. 109–47.

Nicholson, P. 'Philosophical Idealism and International Politics', *British Journal of International Studies* (1976), 76–83.

Nickel, J. *Making Sense of Human Rights*. Berkeley, CA: University of California Press, 1985.

Norman, R. *Ethics, Killing and War*. Cambridge: Cambridge University Press, 1995.

O'Brien, W. *The Conduct of Just and Limited War*. New York: Praeger, 1981.

Oren, N. *Termination of War: Processes, Procedures and Aftermaths*. Jerusalem: Hebrew University Press, 1982.

Orend, B. 'Armed Intervention: Principles and Cases', *Flinders Journal of History and Politics* (March 1998), 63–80.

—— 'Kant on International Law and Armed Conflict', *Canadian Journal of Law and Jurisprudence* (July 1998), 329–81.

—— 'Kant's Just War Theory', *Journal of the History of Philosophy* (April 1999), 323–55.

—— 'Terminating War and Establishing Global Governance', *Canadian Journal of Law and Jurisprudence* (July 1999), 253–95.

—— 'Crisis in Kosovo: A Just Use of Force?', *Politics* (September 1999), 125–30.

—— *War and International Justice: A Kantian Perspective*. Waterloo, Ont.: Wilfrid Laurier University Press, 2000.

Orend, B. 'Jus Post Bellum', Journal of Social Philosophy (Spring 2000), 117–37.

—— 'A Just War Critique of Realism and Pacifism', Journal of Philosophical Research (forthcoming, Winter 2000).

—— 'Evaluating Pacifism', Dialogue: Canadian Philosophical Reviews (forthcoming).

Pogge, T. Realizing Rawls. Ithaca, NY: Cornell University Press, 1989.

—— 'Cosmopolitanism and Sovereignty', Ethics (1992), 48–75.

—— 'An Institutional Approach to Humanitarian Intervention', Public Affairs Quarterly (1992), 89–103.

—— 'An Egalitarian Law of Peoples', Philosophy and Public Affairs (1994), 195–224.

—— 'Creating Supra-national Institutions Democratically', Journal of Political Philosophy (1997), 163–82.

—— 'The Bounds of Nationalism', in J. Couture et al., eds., Rethinking Nationalism, Calgary, Alta.: University of Calgary Press, 1998, pp. 463–504.

Porter, B. War and the Rise of the Modern State. New York: Macmillan, 1994.

Ramsbotham, O. and T. Woodhouse. Humanitarian Intervention in Contemporary Conflict. Cambridge: Polity Press, 1996.

Ramsey, P. The Just War: Force and Political Responsibility. New York: Charles Scribner's Sons, 1968.

Rawls, J. A Theory of Justice. Cambridge, MA: Harvard University Press, 1971.

—— 'The Law of Peoples', in Shute and Hurley, eds., On Human Rights, pp. 41–82.

—— Untitled, in Dissent's Summer 1995 symposium on the bombing of Hiroshima.

—— The Law of Peoples. Cambridge, MA: Harvard University Press, 1999.

Regan, R. Just War: Principles and Cases. Washington, DC: Catholic University of America Press, 1996.

Reiff, D. Slaughterhouse: Bosnia and the Failure of the West. New York: Simon & Schuster, 1995.

Reisman, M. and C. Antoniou, eds. The Laws of War. New York: Vintage, 1994.

Shue, H. Basic Rights: Subsistence, Affluence and U.S. Foreign Policy. Princeton, NJ: Princeton University Press, 2nd edn, 1996.

Shute, S. and S. Hurley, eds. On Human Rights. New York: Basic Books, 1993.

Suganami, H. The Domestic Analogy and World Order Proposals. Cambridge: Cambridge University Press, 1989.

Teichman, J. Pacifism and the Just War. Oxford: Basil Blackwell, 1986.

Waltz, K. *Man, the State and War*. Princeton, NJ: Princeton University Press, 1978.

Walzer, M. 'Moral Judgment in Time of War' in R. Wasserstrom, ed., *War and Morality*, pp. 54–62.

—— *Obligations: Citizenship, War and Disobedience*. Cambridge, MA: Harvard University Press, 1970.

—— 'World War II: Why Was This War Different?', *Philosophy and Public Affairs* (1971/2), 3–21.

—— 'Political Action: The Problem of Dirty Hands', *Philosophy and Public Affairs* (1972/3), 160–80.

—— 'The Moral Standing of States: A Response to Four Critics', *Philosophy and Public Affairs* (1979/80), 209–29.

—— *Radical Principles*. New York: Basic Books, 1980.

—— 'Philosophy and Democracy', *Political Theory* (1981), 379–99.

—— 'Response to Lackey', *Ethics* (April 1982), 547–8.

—— *Spheres of Justice: A Defense of Pluralism and Equality*. New York: Basic Books, 1983.

—— 'The Reform of the International System', in O. Osterud, ed., *Studies of War and Peace*. Oslo: Norwegian University Press, 1986, pp. 227–50.

—— *Interpretation and Social Criticism*. Cambridge, MA: Harvard University Press, 1987.

—— *The Company of Critics: Social Criticism and Political Commitment in the Twentieth Century*. New York: Basic Books, 1988.

—— 'The Communitarian Critique of Liberalism', *Political Theory* (1990), 6–23.

—— 'Nation and Universe' in G. B. Peterson, ed., *The Tanner Lecture on Human Values*. Salt Lake City, UT: Utah University Press, 1990, pp. 507–56.

—— *Just and Unjust Wars: A Moral Argument with Historical Illustrations*. New York: Basic Books, 2nd edn, 1992.

—— 'Justice and Injustice in the Gulf War', in J. B. Elshtain and D. DeCosse, eds., *Reflections*, pp. 2–25.

—— *What it Means to be an American*. New York: Marsillo, 1992.

—— *Thick and Thin: Moral Argument at Home and Abroad*. Notre Dame, IN: Notre Dame University Press, 1994.

—— 'A Conversation with Michael Walzer', *Conference* (Winter 1994–5), 3–13.

—— 'Response' in D. Miller and M. Walzer, eds., *Pluralism, Justice and Equality*. Oxford: Oxford University Press, 1995, pp. 281–98.

—— Untitled contribution to the summer symposium on the fiftieth anniversary of the bombing of Hiroshima, *Dissent* (1995), 330–1.

—— 'War and Peace in the Jewish Tradition', in T. Nardin, ed., *The Ethics of War and Peace: Religious and Secular Perspectives*. Princeton: Princeton

University Press, 1996, pp. 95–112.

—— *On Toleration.* New Haven, CT: Yale University Press, 1997.

—— 'Kosovo', *Dissent* (Summer 1999), 5–7.

Walzer, M. and R. Dworkin, '*Spheres of Justice:* An Exchange', *The New York Review of Books* (21 July 1983), 43–6.

Walzer, M. and D. Miller, eds. *Pluralism, Justice and Equality.* Oxford: Oxford University Press, 1995.

Warnke, G. *Justice and Interpretation.* Oxford: Polity Press, 1992.

Wasserstrom, R., ed. *War and Morality.* Belmont, CA: Wadsworth, 1970.

Williams, H. *International Relations in Political Theory.* Philadelphia, PA: Open University Press, 1992.

—— *International Relations and the Limits of Political Theory.* New York: St Martin's, 1996.

—— *Francis Fukuyama and the End of History.* Cardiff: University of Wales Press, 1997.

Index